Lives of the Three Mrs. Judsons

Arabella W. Stuart

Contents

PREFACE. 7
PART I. LIFE OF MRS. ANN H. JUDSON, ... 10
    FIRST WIFE OF REV. ADONIRAM JUDSON, D.D. 10
CHAPTER I. 10
CHAPTER II. 15
CHAPTER III. 19
CHAPTER IV. 24
CHAPTER V. 32
CHAPTER VI. 37
CHAPTER VII. 41
CHAPTER VIII. 46
CHAPTER IX. 51
CHAPTER X. 54
CHAPTER XI. 59
CHAPTER XII. 64
CHAPTER XIII. 68
CHAPTER XIV. 73
CHAPTER XV. 78
CHAPTER XVI. 83
CHAPTER XVII. 90
CHAPTER XVIII. 100

PART II. THE LIFE OF SARAH B. JUDSON. SECOND WIFE OF 109
    REV. ADONIRAM JUDSON, D.D. 109
CHAPTER I. 109
CHAPTER II. 117
CHAPTER III. 120
CHAPTER IV. 124
CHAPTER V. 135
CHAPTER VI. 140
CHAPTER VII. 146
CHAPTER VIII. 150
CHAPTER IX. 153
CHAPTER X. 160
CHAPTER XI. 164
CHAPTER XII. 176
CHAPTER XIII. 182
CHAPTER XIV. 187
CHAPTER XV. 191

PART III. BIOGRAPHICAL SKETCH OF MRS. EMILY C. JUDSON. ....
    THIRD WIFE OF REV. ADONIRAM JUDSON, D.D. 196
CHAPTER I 196
CHAPTER II 222

LIVES OF THE THREE MRS. JUDSONS

BY
Arabella W. Stuart

PREFACE.

Among the many benefits which modern missions have conferred on the world, not the least, perhaps, is the field they have afforded for the development of the highest excellence of female character. The limited range of avocations allotted to woman, and her consequent inability to gain an elevated rank in the higher walks of life, has been a theme of complaint with many modern reformers, especially with the party who are loud in their advocacy of woman's rights. That few of the sex have risen to eminence in any path but that of literature, is too well known to admit of denial, and might be proved by the scantiness of *female* biography. How few of the memoirs and biographical sketches which load the shelves of our libraries, record the lives of women!

The missionary enterprise opens to woman a sphere of activity, usefulness and distinction, not, under the present constitution of society, to be found elsewhere. Here she may exhibit whatever she possesses of skill in the mastery of unknown and difficult dialects; of tact in dealing with the varieties of human character; of ardor and perseverance in the pursuit of a noble end under the most trying discouragements; and of exalted Christian heroism and fortitude, that braves appalling dangers, and even death in its most dreadful forms, in its affectionate devotion to earthly friends, and the service of a Heavenly Master. Compared with the true independence, the noble energy, the almost superhuman intrepidity of the Mrs. Judsons, how weak and despicable seem the struggles of many misguided women in our day, who seek to gain a reluctant acknowledgment of equality with the other sex, by a noisy assertion of their rights, and in some instances, by an imitation of their attire! Who would not turn from a female advocate at the bar, or judge upon the bench, surrounded by the usual scenes of a court-house, even if she filled these offices with ability and talent, to render honor rather to her, who laying on the altar of sacrifice whatever of genius, or acquirement, or loveliness she may possess, goes forth to cheer and to share the labors and cares of the husband of her youth, in his errand of love to the heathen?

And it seems peculiarly appropriate that woman, who doubtless owes to Christianity most of the domestic consideration and social advantages, which in enlightened countries she regards as her birthright, should be the bearer of these blessings to her less favored sisters in heathen lands. If the Christian religion was a Gospel to the ***poor***, it was no less emphatically so to woman, whom it redeemed from social inferiority and degradation, the fruit for ages of that transgression which "brought death into the world, and all our wo." Never until on the morning of the resurrection "she came early unto the sepulchre," was she made one in Christ Jesus (in whom "there is neither in male nor female") with him who had hitherto been her superior and her master. Nor does she seem ***then*** to have misunderstood her high mission, or to have been wanting to it. The 'sisters' in the infant churches rivalled the brethren in attachment and fidelity to the cause, and to their "ministry" the new religion was indebted in no small degree for its unparalleled success.

Perhaps an apology may be deemed necessary for ***another*** memoir of the distinguished females whose names adorn our title-page. With regard to the ***first*** Mrs. Judson, it has been thought that a simple narrative of her life, unencumbered with details of the history of the mission, would be more attractive to youthful readers than the excellent biography by Mr. Knowles. Of the ***second***, though we cannot hope or wish to rival the graceful and spirited sketch by Fanny Forrester, still it is believed that a plain, unembellished story of a life which was in itself so exceedingly interesting, may also find favor with the public.

As to the last of these three Christian heroines who has so lately departed from among us, as full a sketch as practicable is given, from a wish to embalm in one urn--perhaps a fragile one--the memories of ***all*** those whose virtues and affections have contributed so largely to the happiness and usefulness of one of the noblest and most successful of modern missionaries--the Rev. Adoniram Judson.

The approval of several of the friends of the subjects of these memoirs, has encouraged us in our undertaking, and it is our sincere desire that the manner of its execution may be found acceptable, not only to them, but to the friends of missions in general. And should the work gain favor with our youthful readers, especially with female members of Sunday-schools and Bible-classes, and prompt them to a noble emulation of so illustrious examples, the author's fondest hopes will be more than realized.

PART I.
LIFE OF MRS. ANN H. JUDSON,
FIRST WIFE OF REV. ADONIRAM JUDSON, D.D.

CHAPTER I.
MRS. JUDSON'S BIRTH, EDUCATION AND CONVERSION.

When an individual attains a position of eminence which commands the admiration of the world, we naturally seek to learn his early history, to ascertain what indications were given in childhood of qualities destined to shine with such resplendent lustre, and to discover the kind of discipline which has developed powers so extraordinary. But in no researches are we more apt to be baffled than in these. Few children are so remarkable as to make it worth while, even to a parent, to chronicle their little sayings and doings; and of infant prodigies--though there is a superstitious belief that most of them die early, which is expressed in the adage--

"Whom the Gods love, die young,"

those that live commonly disappoint the hopes of partial friends, who watched their infancy with wonder and expectation.

There are certain qualities, however, which we shall rarely miss even in the childhood of those who attain eminence by a wise employment of their talents and acquirements. These are: firmness of purpose, industry and application, and an ardent, and sometimes enthusiastic temperament. These qualities were possessed in no common degree by Ann Hasseltine, the subject of this memoir. She was born in

Bradford, Massachusetts, on the 22d of December, 1789. In a sketch which she has given of her life, between twelve and seventeen years of age, we find evidence of an active, ardent, and social disposition, gay and buoyant spirits, persevering industry, and great decision of character.

Whatever engaged her attention, whether study or amusement, was pursued with an ardor that excited the sympathy and love both of her teachers and school-fellows. Though little of her writing at this period is preserved, and the generation that knew her personally is mostly passed away, yet her whole subsequent career gives evidence of an intellect of a very high order, carefully cultivated by study and reflection.

She seems scarcely to have been the subject of serious impressions before her seventeenth year. Until that time she enjoyed the pleasures of the world with few misgivings and with a keenness of relish which led her to think herself, as she says, "the happiest creature on earth." She adds, "I so far surpassed my friends in gayety and mirth, that some of them were apprehensive I had but a short time to continue in my career of folly, and should be suddenly cut off. Thus passed the last winter of my gay life."

During the spring of 1806, she began regularly to attend a series of conference meetings in Bradford, her native town. She soon felt that the Spirit of God was operating on her mind. Amusements lost their relish; she felt that she must have a new heart or perish forever; and she often sought solitude, that she might, unseen by others, weep over her deplorable state. Soon, however, her fears that her distress might be noticed by her companions, were merged in her greater terrors of conscience, and she "was willing the whole universe should know that she felt herself to be a lost and perishing sinner." Her distress increased as she became more and more sensible of the depravity of her heart, and the holiness and sovereignty of God. Her mind rose in rebellion against a Being, who after all her prayers and tears and self-denial, still withheld from her the blessing of pardon and peace. She says, "In this state I longed for annihilation, and if I could have destroyed the existence of my soul with as much ease as that of my body, I should quickly have done it. But that glorious Being who is kinder to his creatures than they are to themselves, did not leave me to remain in this distressing state." The plan of salvation through a crucified Redeemer, gradually unfolded itself before her; she began to take delight in those attributes of God which before had filled her with abhorrence; and although she did not at first imagine that this was the new heart for which she had sought so earnestly, yet she was constrained to commit all her interests for time and eternity unreservedly to that Saviour, who now seemed infinitely worthy of the service of her whole existence[1].

The change in her from extreme worldliness to a life of piety and prayer was deep and permanent. Hers was no half-way character. While she was of the world, she pursued its follies with entire devotion of heart; and when she once renounced it as unsatisfying, and unworthy of her immortal aspirations, she renounced it solemnly and finally. Her ardor for learning did not abate, but instead of being inspired, as formerly by a thirst for human applause and distinction, it was now prompted by her sense of responsibility to God for the cultivation of the talents he had given her, and her desire to make herself increasingly useful. In the sketch referred to she remarks, "I attended my studies in school with far different feelings and different motives from what I had ever done before. I felt my obligation to improve all I had to the glory of God; and since he in his providence had favored me with advantages for improving my mind, I felt that I should be like the slothful servant if I neglected them. I therefore diligently employed all my hours in school in acquiring useful knowledge, and spent my evenings and part of the night in spiritual enjoyments." "Such was my thirst for religious knowledge, that I frequently spent a great part of the night in reading religious books." A friend says of her: "She thirsted for the knowledge of gospel truth in all its relations and dependencies. Besides the daily study of the scripture with Guise, Orton, and Scott before her, she perused with deep interest the works of Edwards, Hopkins, Belamy, Doddridge, &c. With

---

1   She thus describes more particularly the exercises of her mind, in an entry in her Journal a year later.
"July 6. It is just a year this day since I entertained a hope in Christ. About this time in the evening, when reflecting on the words of the lepers, '*If we enter into the city, then the famine is in the city and we shall die there, and if we sit still here we die also,*'--I felt that if I returned to the world, I should surely perish; if I stayed where I then was I should perish; and I could but perish if I threw myself on the mercy of Christ. Then came light, and relief, and comfort, such as I never knew before."

Edwards on Redemption, she was instructed, quickened, strengthened. Well do I remember the elevated smile that beamed on her countenance when she first spoke to me of its precious contents. When reading scripture, sermons, or other works, if she met with anything dark or intricate, she would mark the passage, and beg the first clergyman who called at her father's to elucidate and explain it."

How evidently to us, though unconsciously to herself, was her Heavenly Father thus fitting her for the work he was preparing for her. Had she known that she was to spend her days in instructing bigoted and captious idolaters in religious knowledge, she could not have trained herself for the task more wisely than she was thus led to do.

While, under the guidance of the Spirit of truth, she was thus cultivating her intellect, that same Spirit was also sanctifying and purifying her heart. She loathed sin both in herself and others, and strove to avoid it, not from the fear of hell, but from fear of displeasing her Father in heaven.

In one place she writes: "Were it left to myself whether to follow the vanities of the world, and go to heaven at last, or to live a religious life, have trials with sin and temptation, and sometimes enjoy the light of God's reconciled countenance, I should not hesitate a moment in choosing the latter, for there is no real satisfaction in the enjoyments of time and sense."

On the fourteenth of August, 1806, she made a public profession of religion, and united with the Congregational church at Bradford, being in her seventeenth year.

Very early in her religious life she became sensible that if unusual advantages for acquiring knowledge had fallen to her lot, she was the more bound to use her talents and acquirements for the benefit of others less favored than herself. Actuated by such motives, she opened a small school in her native place, and subsequently taught in several neighboring villages. Her example in this respect is surely worthy of imitation. Perhaps no person is more admirable than a young lady fitted like Miss Hasseltine by a cultivated mind and engaging manners to shine in society, who having the choice between a life of ease and one of personal exertion, chooses voluntarily, or only in obedience to the dictates of conscience, the weary and self-denying path of the teacher. And probably such a course would oftener be chosen, were young persons aware of the unquestionable fact, that the school in which we make the most solid and rapid improvement, is that in which we teach others.

An extract from her journal will sustain what we have said of her conscientiousness and purity of motive in endeavoring to instruct the young:

"***May 12, 1809.*** --Have taken charge of a few scholars. Ever since I have had a comfortable hope in Christ, I have desired to devote myself to him in such a way as to be useful to my fellow-creatures. As Providence has placed me in a situation in life where I have an opportunity of getting as good an education as I desire, I feel it would be highly criminal in me not to improve it. I feel, also, that it would be equally criminal to desire to be well educated and accomplished, from selfish motives, with a view merely to gratify my taste and relish for improvement, or my pride in being qualified to shine. I therefore resolved last winter to attend the academy from no other motive than to improve the talents bestowed by God, so as to be more extensively devoted to his glory, and the benefit of my fellow-creatures. On being lately requested to take a small school for a few months, I felt very unqualified to have the charge of little immortals; but the hope of doing them good by endeavoring to impress their young and tender minds with divine truth, and the obligation I feel ***to try to be useful***, have induced me to comply. I was enabled to open the school with prayer. Though the cross was very great, I felt constrained by a sense of duty to take it up. O may I have grace to be faithful in instructing these children in such a way as shall be pleasing to my heavenly Father."

Such being the principles by which she was actuated in commencing the work of instruction, we cannot doubt that her efforts ***to be useful*** were blessed not only by the temporal, but the spiritual advancement of her pupils, some of whom may appear, with children from distant Burmah, as crowns of her rejoicing in the last great day.

CHAPTER II.
HER MARRIAGE, AND VOYAGE TO INDIA.

In 1810, the calm current of Miss Hasseltine's life was disturbed by circumstances which were to change all her prospects, and color her whole future destiny. From the quiet and seclusion of her New England home, she was called to go to the ends of the earth, on a mission of mercy to the dark browed and darker minded heathen.

It is perhaps impossible for us to realize now what was then the magnitude of such an enterprise. Our wonderful facilities for intercourse with the most distant nations, and the consequent vast amount of travel, were entirely unknown forty years ago. A journey of two hundred miles then involved greater perplexity and required nearly as much preparation, and was certainly attended with more fatigue than a voyage to England at the present day. The subject of evangelizing the heathen in foreign countries had scarcely received any attention in Europe, and in this country there was not even a Missionary Society. That a female should renounce the refinements of her enlightened and Christian home, and go thousands of miles across unknown oceans

"to the farthest verge   Of the green earth, to distant barbarous climes,"

to spend her life in an unhealthy climate, among a race whose language was strange to her ear, whose customs were revolting to her delicacy, and who might moreover make her a speedy victim to her zeal in their behalf,--a thing so common now as to excite no surprise and little interest--was then hardly deemed possible, if indeed, the idea of it entered the imagination. To decide the question of such an undertaking as this, as well as another question affecting her individual happiness through life, was Miss Hasseltine now summoned.

* * * * *

Mr. Judson, a graduate of Brown University, "an ardent and aspiring scholar," was one of four or five young men in the then newly founded Theological Seminary at Andover, whose minds had become deeply impressed with the wants of the heathen, and a desire to go and labor among them. By their earnestness and perseverance, they so far awakened an interest in their project, that a Board of Commissioners for Foreign Missions was appointed, and the young men were set apart as missionaries. During the two years in which Mr. Judson and his associates were employed in efforts to accomplish this result, he had formed an acquaintance with Miss Hasseltine, and made her an offer of his hand. That he had no wish to blind her to the extent of the sacrifices she would make in accepting him, his manly and eloquent letter to her father, asking his daughter in marriage, abundantly proves. He says:

"I have now to ask whether you can consent to part with your daughter early next spring, to see her no more in this world; whether you can consent to her departure for a heathen land, and her subjection to the hardships and sufferings of a missionary life; whether you can consent to her exposure to the dangers of the ocean; to the fatal influence of the southern climate of India; to every kind of want and distress; to degradation, insult, persecution, and perhaps a violent death? Can you consent to all this for the sake of Him who left his heavenly home, and died for her and for you; for the sake of perishing immortal souls; for the sake of Zion and the glory of God? Can you consent to all this in hope of soon meeting your daughter in the world of glory, with a crown of righteousness, brightened by the acclamations of praise which shall redound to her Saviour from heathens saved, through her means, from eternal woe and despair?"

The writer of this letter, who, after nearly forty years of missionary labor in which he endured all and more than all he has thus almost prophetically described, has just gone to join "the noble army of martyrs" and "those who came out of great tribulation," in his final home,--as he looks back on the hour when he thus gave up his life and what was more precious than life to the service of those souls, dear as he believed to the Redeemer, though perishing for lack of vision,--with what deep and serene joy must he contemplate the sacrifice! And she--

"Not lost, but gone before,"

who was there to meet and welcome him to

"happier bowers than Eden knew,"

where they rest from their labors, does she now regret that to his solemn appeal, she answered, "I will go?"

Mr. and Mrs. Judson were married at Bradford on the fifth of February, 1812, and on the nineteenth of the same month embarked on the brig Caravan, bound for Calcutta. Mr. and Mrs. Newell, also missionaries sailed in the same vessel. We will here give some extracts from letters written by Mrs. Judson to her friends at home, dated "at sea."

To her sister she writes, "I find Mr. Judson one of the kindest, most faithful and affectionate of husbands. His conversation frequently dissipates the gloomy clouds of spiritual darkness which hang over my mind and brightens my hope of a happy eternity. I hope God will make us instrumental of preparing each other for usefulness in this world, and greater happiness in a future world."

"*June 16*.--Day before yesterday, we came in sight of land, after having been out only one hundred and twelve days. We could distinguish nothing but the lowering mountains of Golconda. Yesterday we were nearer land ... and the scene was truly delightful, reminding me of the descriptions I have read of the fertile shores of India--the groves of orange and palm trees. Yesterday we saw two vessels.... You have no idea how interesting the sight--a vessel at the side of us, so near we could hear the captain speak--for he was the first person we have heard speak since we sailed, except what belong to our ship.

"*Tuesday*.--Last night was the most dangerous, and to me, by far the most unpleasant we have had.... To-day the scene is truly delightful. We are sailing up the river Hoogly, a branch of the Ganges, and so near the land that we can distinctly discover objects. On one side of us are the Sunderbunds, (islands at the mouth of the Ganges.) The smell which proceeds from them is fragrant beyond description.

"*Wednesday*.--On each side of the Hoogly are the Hindoo cottages, as thick together as the houses in our seaports. They are very small, and in the form of hay-stacks, without either chimneys or windows. They are situated in the midst of trees which hang over them and appear truly romantic. The grass and fields of rice are perfectly green, and herds of cattle are everywhere feeding on the banks of the river, and the natives are scattered about, ... some fishing, some driving the team, and some sitting indolently on the bank of the river. The pagodas we have passed are much handsomer and larger than the houses. There are many English seats near the shore.... Oh, what reason we have to be thankful for so pleasant and prosperous a voyage....

"Well, sister, we are safe in Calcutta harbor, and almost stunned with the noise of the natives. Mr. Judson has gone on shore to find a place for us to go. The city is by far the most elegant of any I have ever seen. Many ships are lying at anchor, and hundreds of natives all around. They are dressed very curiously--their white garments hanging loosely over their shoulders. But I have not time to describe anything at present.

"*Thursday*.--Harriet and I are yet on board the vessel, and have not been on land. Mr. Judson has not yet gained permission for us to live in the country. He and Mr. Newell are gone again to-day, and what will be their success I know not. The East India Company are violently opposed to missions, and have barely given permission to their own countrymen to settle here as preachers. We have nothing to expect from man, and everything from God.... If God has anything for us to do here, he will doubtless open a door for our entrance, ***if not he will send us to some other place***."

CHAPTER III.
HER ARRIVAL AT CALCUTTA.--DIFFICULTIES WITH THE BENGAL GOVERNMENT.--VOYAGE TO THE ISLE OF FRANCE.--DEATH OF MRS. NEWELL.--CHANGE OF SENTIMENTS.--VOYAGE TO RANGOON.

Mr. and Mrs. Judson landed at Calcutta on the 18th of June, 1812, and were hospitably received by the venerable Dr. Carey, who immediately conducted them to his home in Serampore. There they found a delightful mission family, consisting of Messrs. Carey Marshman and Ward, with their wives and children who welcomed them most cordially, and invited them to remain until the arrival of their brother missionaries. Of the arrangements in this truly Christian family--the schools, the religious exercises, the cultivation of the gardens belonging to the establishment, and the instruction communicated to the natives, they express themselves in the highest terms of eulogy.

Hitherto the course of our missionaries in their enterprise had indeed run smooth, and they had begun to flatter themselves that they had over-estimated the trials and dangers of the life they had chosen; but sad reverses awaited them. They had been in Serampore but ten days, when Messrs. Judson and Newell were summoned to Calcutta, where an order from government was read to them, commanding them immediately to leave the country, and return to America. The British East India Company were at that time unfriendly to missions, and especially intolerant to missionaries from America. The idea of returning, without effecting the object for which they had left their native land, was too painful to be endured by the missionaries, and they immediately attempted to gain permission to go to some country not under the company's jurisdiction.--Burmah, the field to which they had been assigned by their brethren at home, seemed, for various reasons, utterly inaccessible; but they finally got leave to take passage in a ship bound for the Isle of France. The vessel would, however, accommodate but two passengers, and the health of Mrs. Newell requiring that she should be in a place of quiet, it was agreed that she and her husband should embark in it. For three months the rest of their company remained in Calcutta, watched with jealousy by the British Government, but unable to find a vessel to convey them away. At length they had peremptory orders to embark in a vessel bound to England. All hope of escape seemed now cut off, when Mr. Judson accidentally learned that a ship was about sailing for the Isle of France. They applied for a passport to go on board of her, but were refused. They informed the captain of the vessel of their circumstances, and were allowed to go on board without a pass. They had got but a few miles down the river, however, when a government despatch overtook them, commanding the pilot to conduct the ship no further, as there were persons on board who had been ordered to England.

By advice of the captain, the missionaries left the ship, and went on shore, while the pilot wrote a certificate that no such persons were on board. The captain being angry at the detention of his vessel, ordered them to take their baggage from it immediately, but at length consented to let it remain on board until he should reach a tavern sixteen miles further down the river. Mrs. Judson also remained in the ship until it came opposite the tavern, "where," she says, "the pilot kindly lent me his boat and a servant to go on shore. I immediately procured a large boat to send to the ship for our baggage. I entered the tavern *a stranger*, a *female* and *unprotected*. I called for a room and sat down to reflect on my disconsolate situation. I had nothing with me but a few rupees. I did not know that the boat which I had sent after the vessel would overtake it, and if it did, whether it would ever return with our baggage; neither did I know where Mr. Judson was, or when he would come, or with what treatment I should meet at the tavern. I thought of *home* and said to myself, *These are some of the trials attendant upon a missionary life, and which I have anticipated.* In a few hours Mr. J. arrived, and toward night our baggage."

After two or three days of great perplexity and distress, and when they had given up all hope of being able to proceed to the Isle of France, they unexpectedly received from an unknown friend a magistrate's *pass* to go on board the Creole, the vessel they had left. Their only difficulty now was that she had probably got out to sea, as it was three days since they had left her. However they hastened down the river seventy miles, to Saugur, where, among many ships at anchor, they had the inexpressible happiness to find the Creole, on which they embarked for the Isle of France, their first destination.

Their dangers on the passage to the Isle of France were great, the vessel being old and leaky; and when they reached there, they found little encouragement to remain. While on the island, Mrs. J. had a severe attack of illness, as well as much depression of spirits from the uncertainties of their situation. After much deliberation they determined to establish themselves on an island near Malacca, to reach which they must first go to Madras, and they accordingly sailed for that place. War having broken out between England and America, the hostility of the East India Directors to American missionaries was of course much increased, so that it would be impossible for them to make any stop at all in Madras, without incurring the danger of being sent back to America. What, then, was their distress on their arrival there, to find no ship bound for the island they wished to visit! Their way seemed entirely hedged up, for the only vessel in Madras harbor ready for sea, was destined to Burmah, a country pronounced by all their friends in India, utterly inaccessible.

In her journal, at this time, Mrs. J. writes: "Oh, our heavenly Father, direct us aught! Where wilt thou have us to go? What wilt thou have us to do? Our only hope is in thee, and to thee only do we look for protection. Oh, let this mission live before thee!" "To-morrow," she adds, at a somewhat later date, "we expect to embark for Rangoon, (in Burmah.) Adieu to polished, refined, Christian society. Our lot is not cast among you, but among pagans, among barbarians, whose tender mercies are cruel. Indeed, we voluntarily forsake you, and for Jesus' sake choose the latter for our associates. O may we be prepared for the pure and polished society of heaven, composed of the followers of the Lamb, whose robes have been washed in his blood!"

Everything combined to render the passage to Rangoon unpleasant and perilous;--sickness, threatened shipwreck, and the want of all comforts;--but at length on the 14th of July, 1813, about eighteen months from the time they left Salem, in Massachusetts, they set their 'weary, wandering feet' on that shore which was to be their future home.

Among the depressing circumstances that had occurred in this gloomy period, not the least painful was the death of Mrs. Judson's early friend, and companion in her eastern voyage, Mrs. Harriet Newell. Of less mental and physical vigor than Mrs. Judson, this amiable and ardent Christian had gladly relinquished all other objects in life, for that of sharing the privations and soothing the cares of a husband to whom she was tenderly attached, in his labors among the heathen. But this privilege was denied her; she was not even permitted to reach a scene of missionary labor. Her heart-broken husband was compelled to bury her in a far distant isle of the ocean, and finish his short earthly course alone. But he lived to see the grave of that young martyr missionary visited by many pilgrim feet, and her name embalmed in many admiring hearts.

How keenly Mrs. Judson felt her loss, may be learned from a letter written from the Isle of France, whither she and her husband went on being driven from Calcutta:--"Have at last arrived in port; but oh, what news, what distressing news! Harriet is dead. Harriet, my dear friend, my earliest associate in the mission, is no more. Oh death, could not this wide world afford thee victims enough, but thou must enter the family of a solitary few whose comfort and happiness depended so much on the society of each other? Could not this infant mission be shielded from thy shafts!" "But be still, my heart, and know that God has done it. Just and true are thy ways, oh thou King of saints!"

Another heavy trial, was the separation of herself and husband from the church in which they were both educated, from the missionary association on which they depended for support, and from the sympathies of those Christians in their native land who had hitherto given them the most cordial encouragement in their enterprise. This separation was in consequence of a change in their sentiments in regard to baptism. So liberal has the church become at this day, that all now look upon this change as having decidedly advanced the cause of missions by enlisting a large and respectable body of Christians in this country, not hitherto engaged in it. But in 1813, a step like this on the part of beneficiaries of the Board, could not but be regarded with much disfavor and prejudice, render those who had taken it highly unpopular, and even subject their motives to unworthy imputations. Whatever may be thought of the soundness of their new views, therefore, there is not the shadow of a reason to doubt their conscientiousness in adopting them. That they did it in the face of every worldly motive, their letters and journals abundantly prove. Mrs. Judson writes: "It is extremely trying to reflect on the consequences of our becoming Baptists. We must make some very painful sacrifices." "We must be separated from our dear missionary associates, and labor alone in some isolated spot. We must expect to be treated with contempt, and to be cast off by many of our American friends--forfeit the character we have in our native land, and probably have to labor for our own support wherever we are stationed." "These things are very trying to us, and cause our hearts to bleed for anguish--we feel that we have no home in this world, and no friend but each other." "A renunciation of our former sentiments has caused us more pain than anything which ever happened to us through our lives."

Thus "perplexed but not in despair, cast down but not destroyed," they reached Rangoon, then the capital of the Burman Empire, and established themselves in what they regarded as their future home. Here, "remote, unfriended" and solitary--"reft of every stay but Heaven"--they were destined to pass nearly two years, before their hearts could be cheered by the intelligence from America, of the general interest awakened for them there in the denomination with which they had connected themselves; and the formation of a Baptist Board of Missions, which had appointed them its Missionaries. Of one thing, however, they must have felt sure, that they were conducted there by the special providence of God. The honor of commencing the Burman Mission, says Prof. Gammell, "is to be ascribed rather to the Divine Head of the Church, than to any leading movement or agency of the Baptist denomination. The way was prepared and the field was opened by God alone, and it only remained for true-hearted laborers to enter in and prosecute the noble work to which they had been summoned."

CHAPTER IV.

DESCRIPTION OF BURMAH.--ITS BOUNDARIES, RIVERS, CLIMATE, SOIL, FRUITS AND FLOWERS.--BURMAN PEOPLE.--THEIR DRESS, HOUSES, FOOD, GOVERNMENT AND RELIGION.

The Burman Empire being thus the place to which the feet of the first "bringers of good tidings" from America were so signally directed, and having been now, for nearly forty years, missionary ground of the most interesting character, it is proper to pause here and give something more than a passing glance at its natural features, its government and religion, and the character of its population. For information on these points we are indebted chiefly to the researches of the Rev. Howard Malcom.

Burmah, or the Burman Empire, lies between the Salwen river on the east, and the Burrampooter on the northwest and north, while its western and southern shores are washed by the great bay of Bengal, which separates it from the peninsula of Hindustan. Besides the noble rivers which form its eastern and north-western boundaries, its entire length from north to south is traversed by the Irrawaddy, which after a course of 1200 miles, empties by many mouths into the Bay of Bengal. Its territory is generally so much elevated above the level of the sea, that it enjoys, though in the torrid zone, a comparatively salubrious and temperate climate. The heat is rarely excessive; while winter in our sense of the word, is unknown.

"The general features of a country so extensive are, of course, widely diversified. It may be said of it as a whole, in the language of Dr. Hamilton, that in fertility, beauty and grandeur of scenery, and in the variety, value, and elegance of its natural productions, it is equalled by few on earth."

In the parts of the country lying near the sea there are two seasons, the wet and the dry. About the 10th of May showers commence, and increase in frequency, until, in the latter part of June, it begins to rain almost daily, and this continues until the middle of September. Heavy rains then cease, but showers continue, diminishing in frequency until the middle of October, when "the air is cool, the country verdant, fruits innumerable, and everything in nature gives delight." Even in the rainy season, the sun shines out a part of the day, so that the rankest vegetation covers everything; even walls and buildings, unless smoothly coated with plaster, are not exempt from grass and weeds. Of the climate during the warmest portion of the year, Dr. Malcom thus writes: "I have now passed the ordeal of the entire hot season, and of nothing am I more convinced, both from experience and observation, than that the climate is as salubrious and pleasant as any other in the world. I have suffered much more from heat in Italy, and even in Philadelphia, than I have ever done here; and have never found a moment when I could not be perfectly comfortable by sitting still. To go abroad at mid-day, is, however, for any but natives, eminently hazardous."

The soil, in the maritime provinces, is represented as unsurpassed in fertility, and under the imperfect cultivation of the natives, yields from eighty to a hundred fold, and sometimes more.

The heights are crowned with forests, while the low lands are jungle, that is, "a region of many trees, but scattered; with much undergrowth;" and the haunt of tigers and other wild animals.

The fruit-trees are numerous, and of names and kinds unknown in America. There is found the mangosteen, with a fruit said by travellers to be the most delicious in the world; the noble mango, growing to the height of one hundred feet, and of vast diameter, and bearing as great a variety of delicious fruit as the apple-tree does with us; the cocoa-nut, whose fruit we are acquainted with, and whose husk is formed into excellent cordage; the plantain, that invaluable blessing to the natives of the torrid zone, as it supplies them bread without much labor; a circumstance of importance in countries where hard labor is oppressive by reason of heat; the splendid tamarind, with wide-spreading limbs, and a dense foliage of vivid green, among which appear clusters of beautiful yellow flowers, delicately veined with red, and the long shining pods which contain the fruit; the custard-apple, with its pulpy fruit contained in a husk resembling the pineapple in shape; and the curious palmyra, whose leaves furnish the natives with paper, while its trunk yields a liquor much prized by them as drink, and capable of being boiled down into sugar, like the juice of our maple.

Hundreds of other trees might be named, many valuable for their fruit, others for their timber, and some for both. Most of the trees are evergreen, that is, few of them shed their leaves annually and at once; but a constant succession of leaves makes the forest always verdant.

Besides the fruits which grow upon trees, there is a variety of others such as berries, tomatoes, pineapples, &c.; and among roots are found the ginger, licorice, arrow-root, sweet-potatoe, Irish potatoe, asparagus, ground-nut, &c. The country abounds in flowers of most splendid colors, but generally deficient in fragrance; though some have a fine perfume.

The favorite food of the country being rice, this is, of course, the grain most extensively cultivated. There are no *farms* as with us; cultivators of the soil always reside in villages, for mutual protection against wild beasts and robbers. Each family cultivates a patch of the neighboring jungle, and brings the produce into the village, where the cattle are also brought for security. Besides rice, they cultivate wheat, Indian-corn, sugar-cane, millet and indigo; but generally in a slovenly and unskilful manner. In the dry season, the land is watered by artificial means, some of which are quite ingenious.

Of animals there is, of course, a vast variety, one of the most useful of which is the buffalo, which is used to draw their carriages, as well as to perform the labor that the ox does with us. Elephants are the property of the king, but great men are allowed to keep them.

The birds in Burmah, though of gay plumage, have little melody in their song; splendid as they are, we would scarce exchange for them our cheerful robin and merry bobolink.

Reptiles and insects, though numerous, are not so troublesome or so venomous as in many parts of the torrid zone. The white ant is perhaps as destructive as any other insect, and the greatest precaution hardly preserves one from its intrusion.

The Burmans are, as a race, superior to the Hindoos, being more athletic and vigorous, and more lively and industrious. They are less tall than Americans, their complexions dark, their noses flat, and their lips thick and full. The hair is very abundant, black and glossy, but generally rather coarse. "Men tie it in a knot on the ***top*** of the head, and intertwine it with the turban. Women turn it all back, and without a comb, form it into a graceful knot ***behind***, frequently adding chaplets of fragrant natural flowers strung on a thread. Both sexes take great pains with their hair, frequently washing it with a substance which has the properties of soap, and keeping it anointed with sweet oil."

The custom of blacking the teeth is almost universal. When asked the reason of this custom, the answer is, "What! should we have white teeth like a dog or a monkey?"

Smoking and chewing are also universal. Malcom says, "I have seen little creatures of two or three years, stark naked, tottering about with a lighted cigar in their mouth." Tobacco is not used alone for these purposes, but mixed with several other substances.

The dress of the men is a cotton cloth about four and a half yards long, covering, when the man is not at work, nearly the whole body in a graceful manner. A jacket, with sleeves generally of white muslin but often of broadcloth or velvet, is sometimes added, especially among the higher classes. On the feet, when dressed, are worn sandals of wood or cowhide, covered with cloth, and held on by straps, one of which passes over the instep, the other over the great toe. On entering a house, these are always left at the door.

Women wear a ***temine***, or petticoat, of cotton or silk, lined with muslin, extending from the arm-pits to the ankles. Over this is sometimes worn a jacket, open in front with close, long sleeves. Both sexes wear ornaments in the ears. Men wear mustachios, but pluck out the beard with tweezers. Women, in order to render their complexions more fair, rub over the face a delicate yellow powder; and they occasionally stain the nails of the fingers and toes with a scarlet pigment. All ranks are exceedingly fond of flowers, and display great taste in arranging them.

The houses are made of timbers, or bamboos, set in the earth, with lighter pieces fastened transversely. The sides are covered, some with mats, more or less substantial and costly, others with thatch, fastened with split ratans. The roof is very ingeniously made and fastened on, and is a perfect security against wind and rain. The floor is of split cane, elevated a few feet from the earth, which secures ventilation and cleanliness. The windows and doors are of mat, strengthened with a frame of bamboo, and strongly fastened at the top. When open they are propped up with a bamboo, and form a shade. Of course, there are no chimneys. Cooking is done on a shallow box a yard square, filled with earth.

We must not judge of the architectural skill of the people by their private houses. A Burman conceals his wealth with as much care as we exhibit ours, for a display of it only subjects him to extortion from the officers of government. Malcom describes some of their zayats, pagodas and bridges, especially in and near Ava, as truly noble.

Rice may be said to be the universal food. It is generally eaten with a nice curry, and sauces of various vegetables are added. Wheat is not made into bread by the natives, but boiled like rice. Its name in Burmah is "foreigner's rice," which shows it is not native to the country.

* * * * *

The natural good traits of the Burman character are almost rendered nugatory by their religion, and the oppressive nature of their government. The latter is an absolute despotism. The king has a nominal council with whom he may advise, but whose advice he may, if he chooses, treat with utter contempt. It is not, however, the direct oppression of the monarch that causes most suffering among his subjects. It is rather that of the inferior officers of government whose rapacity and extortion renders property, liberty, and life itself insecure. Deceit, fraud and lying are the natural, if not necessary consequences of a system which leaves the people entirely at the mercy of those who bear rule over them.

The religion is Buddhism, one of the most ancient and wide-spread superstitions existing on the face of the earth. Its sacred Divinity, or Buddh, is Gaudama, who has passed into a state of eternal and unconscious repose, which they consider the summit of felicity; but which seems to us to differ little from annihilation. Images of this god are the chief objects of worship. These are found in every house, and are enshrined in pagodas and temples, and in sacred caves which appear to have been used from time immemorial for religious purposes. The wealth and labor bestowed on the latter show how great the population must have been in former ages. Dr. Malcom describes one cave on the Salwen, which is wholly filled with images of every size, while the whole face of the mountain for ninety feet above the cave is incrusted with them. "On every jutting crag stands some marble image covered with gold, and spreading its uncouth proportions to the setting sun. Every recess is converted into shrines for others. But imposing as is this spectacle, it shrinks into insignificance compared with the scene presented on entering the cavern itself. It is of vast size, and needs no human art to render it sublime. The eye is confused and the heart appalled at the prodigious exhibition of infatuation and folly. Everywhere--on the floor, over head and on every jutting point, are crowded together images of Gaudama--the offerings of successive ages. A ship of five hundred tons could not carry away the half of them."

Pagodas are innumerable. In the inhabited parts there is scarcely a peak, bank, or swelling hill, uncrowned by one of these structures. In general, they are almost solid, without door or window, and contain some supposed relic of Gaudama.

The religious system of the Burmans contains many excellent moral precepts and maxims, which, however being without sanction or example, are utterly powerless to mould the character of the people to wisdom or virtue.

A curious feature of Buddhism is, that one of the highest motives it presents to its followers is the "obtaining of merit." Merit is obtained by avoiding sins, such as theft, lying, intoxication, and the like; and by practising virtues and doing good works. The most meritorious of all good works is to make an idol; the next to build a pagoda. It confers high merit, also, to build a zayat, to transcribe the sacred books, to erect any useful public edifice, to dig public wells, or to plant shade or fruit-trees by the wayside. If they give alms, or treat animals kindly, or repeat prayers, or do any other good deed, they do it entirely with this mercenary view of obtaining merit. This "merit" is not so much to procure them happiness in another world, as to secure them from suffering in their future transmigrations in this; for they believe that the soul of one who dies without having laid up any merit, will have to pass into the body of some mean reptile or insect, and from that to another, through hundreds of changes, perhaps, before it will be allowed again to take the form of man.

This reliance on 'merit,' and certainty of obtaining it through prescribed methods, fosters their conceit, so that ignorant and debased as they are, "there is scarcely a nation more offensively proud." It also renders them entirely incapable of doing or appreciating a disinterested action, or of feeling such a sentiment as gratitude. If you do them a favor, they suppose you do it to obtain merit for yourself, and of course feel no obligation to you; the simple phrase, "I thank you," is unknown in their language.

Like the ancient Romans, the Burmans believe in dreams, omens, and unlucky days; observe the flight and feeding of fowls, the howl of dogs, and the aspect of the stars; they regard the lines in the hand, the knots in trees, and a thousand other fortuitous circumstances, and by these allow their actions to be governed.

The priesthood in Burmah is arranged into a regular hierarchy. The highest functionary is a kind of archbishop, who presides over all the other priests in the empire, and appoints the presidents of the monasteries. He resides at the imperial court, where he has a high rank, and is considered one of the greatest men in the kingdom. Below him are various ranks of priests, each having his appointed sphere and appropriate duties, and all supported by the so-called ***voluntary*** contributions of the people. The number of priests is exceedingly great, and their sway over the minds of the people almost unlimited.

"But great and potent as the priests of Buddh are," says a writer in the Foreign Quarterly Review, "there is a kind of sacred personage still greater than the highest of them, and next in rank to the sovereign; this is no other than that diseased animal, the White Elephant, far more highly venerated here than in Siam. The creature is supposed by the Burmans to lodge within its carcass a blessed soul of some human being, which has arrived at the last stage of the many millions of transmigrations it was doomed to undergo, and which, when it escapes, will be absorbed into the essence of the Deity." This most sacred personage has a regular cabinet composed of a prime minister, secretary of state, transmitter of intelligence, &c., possesses estates in various parts of the country, and receives handsome presents from foreign ambassadors. His residence is contiguous to the royal palace, and connected with it by a long open gallery, at the further end of which a curtain of black velvet embossed with gold, conceals his august person from vulgar eyes. His dwelling is a lofty hall splendidly gilded, and supported by sixty-four pillars, to four of which he is chained with massive silver chains. His bed is a thick mattress, covered with blue cloth, over which is a softer one of crimson silk. His trappings are magnificent, being gold, studded with diamonds, sapphires, rubies, and other precious stones; his betel-box, *spittoon*, and the vessel out of which he feeds, are of gold inlaid with precious stones. His attendants, according to Hamilton, from whom we take a part of this description, amount to over a thousand persons.

"Buddhism in its moral precepts is perhaps the best religion ever invented by man. The difficulty is, its entire basis is false. It is a religion of Atheism. Instead of a Heavenly Father forgiving sin, and filial service from a pure heart, as the effect of love--it presents nothing to love, for its Deity is dead; nothing as the ultimate object of action but self; and nothing for man's highest and holiest ambition but annihilation."

"Their doctrine of merit, leaves no place for holiness, and destroys gratitude either to God or man." It also ministers to the grossest pride, for the very fact of his being *now a man*, assures the Buddhist that in numberless former unremembered transmigrations, he must have acquired incalculable merit, or he would not now occupy so distinguished a rank in the scale of being.

Their system of balancing evil with good, reduces all sin to a thing of little importance. "If any man sin" in Burmah, his religion tells him of no "advocate with the Father" on whose altar he may lay the tribute of a believing, penitent, obedient and grateful heart; but instead, it tells him he may repeat a form of words, he may feed a priest, he may build a pagoda, he may carve an idol, and thus balance his iniquity with merit. If any man suffer in Burmah, his religion points him to no place where "the wicked cease from troubling, and the weary are at rest," and where "God himself will wipe away all tears from all faces;" but it dictates a proud submission to unalterable fate, and flatters him that his sufferings here may purchase immunity from torment in some unknown future existence; and finally if any man die, in Burmah, his religion tells him of no Saviour who has "passed through the grave and blessed the bed," and "swallowed up death in victory;" but it threatens degradation, perhaps into a soulless brute; or at best, a place of expiatory misery;--in short, "living or dying," the Burman may be said emphatically to be "without hope, and without God in the world."

Such was the stupendous system of superstition and ignorance, which two feeble missionaries armed like David when he met the Philistine with "trust in the Lord his God," ventured to attack, and hoped to subdue.

CHAPTER V.

RANGOON; LETTERS FROM MRS. JUDSON.

Rangoon, one of the chief seaports of the Burman Empire, situated on one of the numerous mouths of the Irrawaddy, and having a splendid harbor, is yet one of the meanest, and most uninteresting cities that can well be imagined. It is situated in a flat, marshy plain, and is merely a vast collection of bamboo huts, with narrow streets, and here and there an ugly building of brick or wood, and would give a stranger a most unfavorable impression of the noble country to which it is the entrance.

On their arrival at this city, Mr. and Mrs. Judson took up their abode in a deserted mission-house just outside the wall, which had formerly been occupied by some Baptist missionaries from Serampore. The house was large and not unsuited to the climate, but unfinished and comfortless. However, it had a garden full of flowers and fruit-trees, and the scenery around it was rural and pleasant. Here they found one Christian female, the only person remaining of the former mission family, and she was a native of the country. Mrs. Judson's peculiar trials and encouragements at this time will be best learned by extracts from her letters and journal.

July 30, 1813, she writes: "We felt very gloomy and dejected the first night we arrived, in view of our prospects; but we were enabled to lean on God, and to feel that he was able to support us under the most discouraging circumstances.

"The next morning I prepared to go on shore, but hardly knew how I should get to Mr. Carey's house; it was, however, concluded that I should be carried in an arm-chair; consequently, when I landed one was provided, through which were put two bamboos, and four of the natives took me on their shoulders. When they had carried me a little way into the town, they set me down under a shade, when great numbers of the natives gathered round, having seldom seen an English female. Being sick and weak, I held my head down, which induced many of the native females to come very near, and look under my bonnet. At this I looked up and smiled, on which they set up a loud laugh. They again took me up to carry, and the multitude of natives gave a shout which much diverted us. They next carried me to a place they call the custom-house. It was a small open shed, in which were seated on mats, several natives, who were the custom-house officers. After searching Mr. Judson very closely, they asked liberty for a native female to search me, to which I readily consented. I was then brought to the mission-house, where I have nearly recovered my health."

"*July 22.* --It is now a week since we arrived here. My health is quite restored, and I feel much more contented and happy than I ever expected to be in such a situation. I think I enjoy the promises of God in a higher degree than ever before, and have attained more true peace of mind and trust in the Saviour. When I look back to my late situation in that wretched old vessel, without any accommodations--scarcely the necessaries of life--no physician--no female attendants--so weak that I could not move--I hope I am deeply sensible of the kind care of my heavenly Father in carrying me safely through the peculiar dangers of the voyage, and giving me once more a resting-place on land.

"Still, were it not for the support we derive from the gospel of Jesus, we should be ready to sink down in despondency in view of the dark and gloomy scenes around us. But when we recollect that Jesus has commanded his disciples to carry the gospel to the heathen, and promised to be with them to the end of the world; that God has promised to give the heathen to his Son for an inheritance, we are encouraged to make a beginning, though in the midst of discouragement, and leave it to Him to grant success in his own time and way."

"I find here no female friends with whom I can unite in social prayer, nor even one with whom I can converse. I have, indeed, no society at all except that of Mr. Judson, yet I feel happy in thinking that I gave up this source of pleasure, as well as most others, for the sake of the poor heathen."

In her journal we find the following sentiment: "Though we find ourselves almost destitute of all those sources of enjoyment to which we have been accustomed, and are in the midst of a people who are at present almost destitute on account of the scarcity of provisions[2]; though we are exposed to robbers by night and invaders by day, yet we both unite in saying that we never were happier, never more contented in any situation than the present. We feel that this is the post to which God hath appointed us; that we are in the path of duty; and though surrounded with danger and death, we feel that God can with infinite ease, preserve and support us under the most heavy sufferings.

"Oh, if it may please the dear Redeemer to make me instrumental of leading some of the females of Burmah to a saving acquaintance with Him, my great object will be accomplished, my highest desires gratified, I shall rejoice to have relinquished my comforts, my country and my home." "Oh Lord, here I am; thou hast brought me to this heathen land, and given me desires to labor for thee. Do with me what pleaseth thee. Make me useful or not as seemeth good in thy sight. But oh, let my soul live before thee; let me serve none but thee; let me have no object in life but the promotion of thy glory."

"*Aug. 15.* --I have begun to study the language. Find it very hard and difficult, having none of the usual helps in acquiring a language, except a small part of a grammar, and six chapters of St. Matthew's Gospel by Mr. Carey, now at Ava."

"*Aug. 28.* --Have been writing letters this week to my dear friends in America. Found that a recollection of former enjoyments in my own native country, made my situation here appear less tolerable. The thought that I had parents, sisters, and beloved friends still in existence, and at such a distance that it was impossible to obtain one look or exchange a word, was truly painful. While they are still in possession of the comforts I once enjoyed, I am an exile from my country and my father's house, deprived of all society and every friend but one, and with scarcely the necessaries of life. ***These privations would not be endured with patience in any other cause but that in which we are engaged.*** But since it is thy cause, blessed Jesus, we rejoice that thou didst give us so many enjoyments to sacrifice, and madest it so plainly our duty to forsake all in order to bring thy truth to the benighted heathen. We would not resign our work, but live contented with our lot, and live to Thee."

"*Sept. 5.* --Yes, I do feel thankful that God has brought me to this heathen land, and placed me in a situation peculiarly calculated to make me feel my dependence on him and my constant need of the influences of the Holy Spirit. I enjoy more in

---

2 The war had almost produced a famine.

reading the Scriptures, and in secret prayer than for years before; and the prosperity of this mission, and the conversion of this people, lie with weight on my mind, and draw forth my heart in constant intercession. ***And I do confidently believe that God will visit this land with Gospel light, that these idol temples will be demolished***, and temples for the worship of the living God be erected in their stead."

Let us here pause for a moment and contemplate the picture brought by these words before our imagination. Let us survey the scene in which the lonely missionary penned this prediction. A vast country not waste and uninhabited, but enriched by the partial sun with every natural gift to cheer the sense and gratify the taste of man; swarming with human beings endowed with capacities for advancement in knowledge, and virtue, and temporal enjoyment, as well as for immortal happiness; yet who, having said in their heart there is no God 'that minds the affairs of men,' have built up for themselves a fabric of absurd superstitions, and unmeaning rites, and senseless formalities, to which they cling with a stubbornness that nothing but the power of God can subdue; on such a shore are cast by the providence of God two 'pilgrim strangers,' not endowed with apostolic gifts; not able to control disease, or raise the dead, or even to speak in a foreign tongue without long and patient and assiduous study to acquire it; and yet with a simple and sublime faith in the clear and sure word of their master, "Go--preach my Gospel--lo, I am with you," these pilgrim strangers can CONFIDENTLY BELIEVE that God will visit this land with gospel light, and that those gilded fanes which now glisten in the morning and evening sun, on every hill-top, will fall, and those poor idolaters will say, "What have we to do any more with idols?" "our trust is in the name of the Lord that made heaven and earth."

In one of the last paragraphs of her private journal which has been preserved, dated Oct. 8th of the same year, she says: "To-day I have been into the town, and I was surprised at the multitude of people with which the streets are filled. Their countenances are intelligent; and they appear to be capable under the influence of the Gospel, of becoming a valuable and respectable people. But at present their situation is truly deplorable, for they are given to every sin. Lying is so universal among them that they say, 'we cannot live without telling lies.' They believe the most absurd notions imaginable. My teacher told me the other day, that when he died he would go to my country; I shook my head, and told him he would not; but he laughed, and said he would. I did not understand the language sufficiently to tell him where he would go, or how he could be saved. Oh thou Light of the world, dissipate the thick darkness that covers Burmah. Display thy grace and power among the Burmans--subdue them to thyself, and make them thy chosen people."

CHAPTER VI.

LEARNING THE LANGUAGE.--MRS. JUDSON VISITS THE WIFE OF THE VICEROY.--HER SICKNESS.--HER VOYAGE TO MADRAS.--HER RETURN TO RANGOON.--BIRTH OF A SON.

Those who have acquired a modern European language with the aid of grammars, dictionaries, and other suitable books, can scarcely estimate the labor of learning without such aids, such a language as the Burman. In fact Mr. Judson thinks more progress can be made in the *French* in a few months, than in the Burman in two years. Mrs. Judson took the whole management of family affairs on herself, in order to leave her husband at liberty to prosecute his studies and the consequence was, that being obliged constantly to use all the Burman she knew, in her intercourse with servants, traders, and others, her progress was more rapid than his.

One cause of difficulty in learning their language was that their books were made of palm-leaves, marked or engraved with an iron style or pen, **without ink**. We who are accustomed to clear characters on paper can hardly imagine the difficulty of tracing out these obscure scratches on the dried palm-leaves. Another was that in writing, "their words are not fairly divided like ours by breaks, and points, and capitals, but run together in a long continuous line, a sentence or paragraph seeming like one long word." Another difficulty was, that in their idiom, a great variety of verbs must be used to express one action, either as performed by persons of different rank, or as done under different circumstances. Thus there are three or four ways to speak of eating rice, sleeping, dying, &c. one of which is always used of the king, another of priests, another of rulers, and another of common persons, and it would be an insult to use a phrase lower than one is entitled to. Again, for our term to *wash*, for instance, there are many words; one is used for to *wash the face*, another, the hands, another, linen, another, dishes, &c. They have in their language eleven vowels and thirty-three consonants, but of these there are so many combinations, that about one thousand characters must be used in printing. Printing, however, was unknown to the Burmans until our missionaries introduced it.

As no progress at all could be made in their missionary labors until the language was mastered, they applied themselves cheerfully and diligently to its acquisition.

An interesting incident is related by Mrs. Judson under date of Dec. 11th, 1813, her first visit to the wife of a man in power. "To-day for the first time I have visited the wife of the Viceroy. I was introduced to her by a French lady who has frequently visited her. When we first arrived at the government house, she was not up, consequently we had to wait some time. But the inferior wives of the Viceroy diverted us much by their curiosity, in minutely examining everything we had on, and by trying on our gloves, bonnets, &c. At last her Highness made her appearance, richly dressed in the Burman fashion, with a long silver pipe in her mouth, smoking. At her appearance all the other wives took their seats at a respectful distance, and sat in a crouching posture without speaking. She received me very politely, took me by the hand, seated me upon a mat and herself by me. One of the women brought her a bunch of flowers, of which she took several and ornamented my cap. She was very inquisitive whether I had a husband and children, whether I was my husband's first wife,--meaning by this whether I was the highest among them, supposing that Mr. Judson, like the Burmans, had many wives; and whether I intended tarrying long in the country.

"When the Viceroy came in I really trembled, for I never before beheld such a savage-looking creature. His long robe and enormous spear not a little increased my dread. He spoke to me, however, very condescendingly, and asked whether I would drink some rum or wine. When I arose to go, her highness took my hand again, told me she was happy to see me, and that I must come to see her every day. She led me to the door, I made my *salam* and departed.

"My object in visiting her was, that if we should go into any difficulty with the Burmans, I could have access to her, when perhaps it would not be possible for Mr. Judson to have an audience with the Viceroy."

In pursuing his study of the language, Mr. Judson had fortunately secured as a teacher a Burman of more than ordinary intelligence, and who had a perfect knowledge of the grammatical construction of the Burman dialect, and also of the *Pali*, or language of the sacred books. Day after day he sat with his teacher in the open verandah which surrounded their dwelling, reading, writing, and talking, joined by Mrs. Judson in every interval she could spare from family cares, and thus were they fitting themselves to teach to the poor idolaters the new religion. Nor did they neglect such opportunities of doing good as presented themselves even then; but every effort to inculcate their sentiments was met with the objection, "Your religion is good for you, ours for us." "You will be rewarded for your good deeds in your way, we in our way." They found they had to deal with one of the proudest and most conceited races on earth. Their very religion, as we have before said, encourages this conceit, by leading them constantly to make "a merit" of their good actions, or what they suppose such; while it inculcates neither contrition nor penitence. The peculiar doctrines of Christianity, its justification through the merits of another, its humility and charity, were in the last degree opposed to the character of the Burman race. The missionaries were made daily more sensible that the Spirit of God must come "with power," before the truth could ever enter those darkened understandings. Prayer was therefore their only reliance, as it was their only comfort.

But even this enjoyment, as far as it was social, was soon broken in upon by the increasing illness of Mrs. Judson, which obliged her to try the effect of a change of scene and climate. She could not think of taking Mr. Judson from his labors, and therefore embarked alone in January, 1815, for Madras. We may imagine the joy experienced by the missionary, thus left behind, on receiving during her absence letters from this country, containing an account of the general movement in America in favor of the Mission, and the formation of the Baptist General Convention. His heart overflowed with gratitude, and the thought that though he had no friend near him, there were yet hundreds in his native land praying and laboring in the same cause, inspired him with new zeal in his beloved enterprise.

Mrs. Judson's journey, though solitary, was prosperous and successful. Friends appeared for her where she least expected them. The influence of her engaging person and winning manners is observable in one obliging attention she received even from strangers. The Viceroy appointed a woman to accompany her free of expense; the captain refused money for her passage; and the physician at Madras, from whom she had received visits for six weeks, returned the fee which she sent him, saying he was happy if he had been of service to her. Her health being perfectly restored she returned to Rangoon after an absence of three months, and "on the 11th of September, was made the happy mother of a little son." She soon resumed her studies, and though she saw little other result of her labors, was cheered by noticing that she and her husband were gradually gaining the confidence of the natives, who, as she says, would say to each other "that they need not be afraid to trust us, for we do not tell falsehoods as the Burmans do." The indolent and deceitful Burmans saw with surprise that these two Christians always kept themselves busily employed, and paid every debt they contracted with strict punctuality. Thus was laid the foundation of respect for the new religion.

CHAPTER VII.

DIFFICULTY OF INCULCATING THE GOSPEL.--DEATH OF HER SON.--FAILURE OF MR. JUDSON'S HEALTH.--ARRIVAL OF MR. AND MRS. HOUGH AT RANGOON.

In a letter which Mrs. Judson wrote to her sisters in December, 1815, she says: "Doubtless you expect by this time that some of the Burmans have embraced the Christian religion, or at least are seriously inquiring respecting it." "But you cannot imagine how very difficult it is to give them any idea of the true God and the way of salvation by Christ, since their present ideas of Deity are so very low." "They have not the least idea of a Divinity who is eternal, without beginning or end. All their deities have been through the several grades of creatures, from a fowl to a God...." "They know of no other atonement for sin, than offerings to their priests or their pagodas."

She goes on to mention some instances of serious inquiry among the people, which from time to time had raised their hopes, only to dash them again by the relapse of the inquirers into indifference; but adds "These things do not discourage us. It is God alone who can effectually impress the mind with divine truths; and though seed may lie buried long in the dust, yet at some future period it may spring up and bear fruit to the glory of God."

In this letter she gives an account of the recall of the Viceroy from Rangoon to Ava, the imperial residence, and the consequent confusion of the people, ten thousand of whom accompanied him to Ava. She regretted his departure, as both he and his lady had ever treated her with civility and kindness. The newly appointed Viceroy was a stranger, and might not be equally kind to them.

She says, "Oh how I long to visit Bradford; to spend a few evenings by your firesides, in telling you what I have seen and heard. Alas! *we* have no fireside, no social circle. We are still alone in this miserable country, surrounded by thousands ignorant of the true God." ... "But we still feel happy in our employment, and have reason to thank God that he has brought us here. We do hope to live to see the Scriptures translated into the Burman language, and a church formed from among these idolaters."

Her next letter details "with all the pathos of a mother's sorrow," a new trial to which they were called by Him, who though "clouds and darkness are about him" yet "doeth all things well."

"*May 7th, 1816.* --My dear Parents,--Little did I think when I wrote you last, that my next letter would be filled with the melancholy subject upon which I must now write. Death, regardless of our lonely situation has entered our dwelling, and made one of the happiest of families wretched. Our little Roger Williams, our only little darling boy, was three days ago laid in the silent grave. Eight months we enjoyed the precious little gift, in which time he had so completely entwined himself around his parents' hearts that his existence seemed necessary to their own. But God has taught us by affliction, what we would not learn by mercies--that our hearts are his exclusive property, and whatever rival intrudes, he will tear it away."

"He was a remarkably pleasant child--never cried except when in pain, and what we often observed to each other was the most singular, he never during his little existence manifested the least anger or resentment at anything. This was not owing to the want of intellect, for his tender feelings of sensibility were very conspicuous. Whenever I or his father, passed his cradle without taking him, he would follow us with his eyes to the door, when they would fill with tears, his countenance so expressive of grief, though perfectly silent, that it would force us back to him, which would cause his little heart to be as joyful as it had before been sorrowful. He would lie hours on a mat by his papa's study-table, or by the side of his chair on the floor, if he could only see his face. When we had finished study or the business of the day, it was our exercise and amusement to carry him round the house or garden, and though we were alone, we felt not our solitude when he was with us." ...

Her account of his last sickness and death follows, and she adds: "Thus died our little Roger:

'Short pain, short grief, dear babe, was thine--   Now joys eternal and divine.'

We buried him in the afternoon of the same day, in a little enclosure, the other side of the garden. Forty or fifty Burmans and Portuguese followed with his afflicted parents the last remains to the silent grave. All the Burmans who were acquainted with us, tried to sympathize with us and console us under our loss." ... "We do not feel a disposition to murmur, or inquire of our Sovereign why he has done this. We wish rather to sit down submissively under the rod and bear the smart, till the end for which the affliction was sent shall be accomplished. Our hearts were bound up in this child; we felt he was our earthly all, our only source of innocent recreation in this heathen land. But God saw it was necessary to remind us of our error and strip us of our little all. Oh may it not be in vain that he has done it. May we so improve it that he will stay his hand and say, 'It is enough.'" A while after this she writes: "Since worship I have stolen away to a much loved spot, where I love to sit and pay the tribute of affection to my lost, darling child. It is a little enclosure of mango-trees, in the centre of which is erected a small bamboo house, on a rising spot of ground, which looks down on the new-made grave of our infant boy. Here I now sit, and though all nature around wears a most delightful, and romantic appearance, yet my heart is sad, and my tears frequently stop my pen. You, my dear Mrs. L. who are a mother, may imagine my sensations, but if you have never lost a first born, an only son, you can never know my pain. Had you even buried your little boy, you are in a Christian country, surrounded by friends and relatives, who could soothe your anguish and direct your attention to other objects. But behold us, solitary and alone, with this one source of recreation! Yet this is denied us, this must be removed, to show us that we need no other source of enjoyment but God himself.

"Do not think though I write thus, that I repine at the dealings of Providence. No! though he slay me yet will I trust in him!... Though I say with the Prophet, Behold and see if there be any sorrow like unto my sorrow, yet I would also say, It is of the Lord's mercies that we are not consumed because his compassions fail not. God is the same when he afflicts, as when he is merciful, just as worthy of our entire trust and confidence now, as when he entrusted us with the precious little gift. There is a bright side even to this heavy affliction."

The following tender and beautiful effusion was written by the Rev. J. Lawson of the Serampore Mission and presented to Mrs. Judson on this occasion. As it has not been published in former notices of Mrs. J. we take pleasure in inserting it here.

"Hush'd be the murmuring thought! Thy will be done
O Arbiter of life and death. I bow   To thy command--I yield the precious gift   So late bestowed; and to the silent grave   Move sorrowing, yet submissive. O sweet babe!   I lay thee down to rest--the cold, cold earth   A pillow for thy little head. Sleep on,   Serene in death. No care shall trouble thee.   All undisturbed thou slumberest; far more still   Than when I lulled thee in my lap, and sooth'd Thy little sorrows till they ceased....   Then felt thy mother peace; her heart was light   As the sweet sigh that 'scaped thy placid lips,   And joyous as the dimpled smile that played   Across thy countenance.--O I must weep   To think of thee, dear infant, on my knees   Untroubled sleeping. Bending o'er thy form,   I watch'd with eager hope to catch the laugh   First waking from thy sparkling eye, a beam Lovely to me as the blue light of heaven.   Dimm'd in death's agony, it beams no more!

Oh yet once more I kiss thy marble lips,   Sweet babe I and press with mine thy whitened cheeks.   Farewell, a long farewell!--Yet visit me   In dreams, my darling; though the visioned joy   Wake bitter pangs, still be thou in my thoughts And I will cherish the dear dream, and think   I still possess thee. Peace, my bursting heart!   O I submit. Again I lay thee down,   Dear relic of a mother's hope. Thy spirit,   Now mingled with cherubic hosts, adores   That grace that ransomed it, and lodg'd it safe   Above the stormy scene."

She then gives an interesting account of a visit paid them by the wife of the Viceroy, who on hearing of the death of the 'little white child' as she called him, came to condole with his parents. She was attended by about two hundred of her officers of state and members of her household, expressed great sympathy in Mrs. Judson's affliction, and reproached her for not having sent her word that she might have come to the funeral. Mrs. Judson says, "I regaled her with tea, sweetmeats, and cakes, with which she seemed much pleased." She adds, "I sometimes have good opportunities of communicating religious truths to the women in the government-house, and hope I shall have an opportunity of conversing with the wife of the Viceroy herself." ... "Oh that she might become a real disciple of Jesus!"

In the same melancholy letter she relates another affliction--Mr. Judson, who had frequently been asked by the natives, 'Where are your religious books?' had been diligently employed in preparing a Tract in the Burman language called 'A Summary of Christian Truth;' when his nervous system, and especially his head became so afflicted, that he was obliged to lay aside all study, and seriously think of a voyage to Calcutta as his only means of restoration. But he was prevented from executing his design by the joyful news that two additional missionaries were about to join them. Mr. and Mrs. Hough, from America, arrived in Rangoon in October, 1816; and brought with them as a present from the Mission at Serampore, a printing press, with a fount of types in the Burman character than which nothing could have been more acceptable.

Can we wonder that after laboring in loneliness and sorrow three years, such an event as this should fill their hearts with joy and consolation?

The Burmans are very generally taught to read, though having little that is attractive in their own literature, and books being scarce and dear, they could not at the time of which we write, be said to be a reading people. Still the fact that numbers were able to read, was a strong encouragement to print tracts and books for them. On the occasion of printing the tract above-mentioned, and a catechism, Mr. Hough writes thus:

"These two little tracts are the first printing ever done in Burmah; and it is a fact grateful to every Christian feeling, that God has reserved the introduction of this art here, for his own use."

CHAPTER VIII.

MISSIONARY LABORS.--FEMALE INTELLECT IN BURMAH.--DESCRIPTION OF A PAGODA, OF BURMAN WORSHIP AND OFFERINGS.

A circumstance still more cheering to the hearts of the missionaries than even the arrival of companions from their beloved native land, was a visit of a Burman who having read the "two little books" from the press of Mr. Hough, came to inquire further into the new religion. When Mr. Judson first heard from the lips of an idolater the confession that "God is a Being without beginning or end, not subject to old age or death, but who always is,"--his feelings were indescribable and overpowering. Here at length was a germination of that seed they had so long been sowing in tears! For if one heathen heart could be thus led by the Spirit to investigate the truth, why not more.--Why not many? and why might not the same Spirit lead them to him who is not only the truth, but the way,--the way to Heaven?

They soon received visits from other Burmans who had seen the tracts issued by them; and who seemed desirous of learning the truth, but still very fearful of being known as inquirers. It became necessary therefore to seek the patronage of the government, and Mr. Judson determined, so soon as he should have finished his dictionary of the language, to proceed to Ava, the residence of the emperor.

Mrs. Judson met every Sabbath a society of fifteen or twenty females, to whom she read the Scriptures, and talked about God. They were attentive, and willing to ask and answer questions, but for a long time experienced no abiding convictions of sin or of duty. Some were willing to serve Christ if they could do it without renouncing dependence on their own merits. Others would serve God, if they might serve Gaudama also.

As there is a tendency in enlightened minds to feel a contempt for the intellect of barbarians; and as some have even felt that time spent as Mrs. Judson's was with those native females, was thrown away, we will here record her testimony to the intelligence of the Burmese women. "The females of this country are lively, inquisitive, strong and energetic, susceptible of friendship and the warmest attachment, and possess minds capable of rising to the highest state of cultivation and refinement.... This is evident from their mode of conversing," and may be illustrated by some particulars in the experience of one of them, named May-Meulah.

Previous to the arrival of the missionaries in her country, her active mind was led to inquire the origin of all things. Who created all that her eyes beheld? She inquired of all she met, and visited priests and teachers in vain; and such was her anxiety, that her friends feared for her reason. She resolved to learn to read, that she might consult the sacred books. Her husband, willing to gratify her curiosity, taught her to read himself. In their sacred literature she found nothing satisfactory. For ten years she prosecuted her inquiries, when God in his providence brought to her notice a tract written by Mr. Judson in the Burmese language, which so far solved her difficulties, that she was led to seek out its author. From him she learned the truths of the gospel, and by the Holy Spirit those truths were made the means of her conversion. "She became an ornament to her profession, and her daily walk and conversation would shame many professors in Christian countries."

Christians in America, was Mrs. Judson's time thrown away, when she was leading Burmese females to the knowledge of the truth as it is in Jesus?

One of the most splendid buildings in the empire is a pagoda at Rangoon, in which is enshrined a relic of Gaudama. At this pagoda, a yearly feast is celebrated which lasts three days, and draws people together from all parts of the country.

Mrs. Judson says--"If Dr. Young could have seen the devotion of this people to their idolatry, he might well have exclaimed, 'O for a heathen zeal in Christian hearts!' Even while I am writing my ears are stunned with the noise and confusion of preparation for an approaching festival. Could you, my dear sir, but once witness this annual feast, could you behold the enthusiasm of their devotions, you would readily admit that nothing short of an Almighty arm could break down these strong barriers, and cause the introduction of the gospel."

The pagoda itself is thus described by Dr. Malcom.

"Two miles from Rangoon stands the celebrated pagoda called Shooda-gon. It stands upon a small hill surmounted by many smaller pagodas, and many noble trees. The hill has been graduated into successive terraces, sustained by brick walls; and the summit, which is completely leveled, contains about two acres.

"The two principal approaches from the city are lined on each side, for a mile, with fine pagodas, some almost vieing for size with Shoodagon itself. Passing these, on your way from the city, you come to a flight of time-worn steps, covered by a curious arcade of little houses of various forms and sizes, some in partial decay, others truly beautiful. After crossing some terraces, covered in the same manner, you reach the top and passing a great gate, enter at once this sad but imposing theatre of Gaudama's glory. One's first impressions are, what **terrible** grandeur; what **sickening** magnificence; what absurd imagery; what extravagant expenditure; what long successions of devotees to procure this throng of buildings of such various dates; what a poor religion which makes such labors its chief meritoriousness! Before you, stands the huge Shoodagon, its top among the clouds, and its golden sides blazing in the glories of an eastern sun. Around are pompous zayats, noble pavements, Gothic mausoleums, uncouth colossal lions, curious stone umbrellas, graceful cylindrical banners of gold-embroidered muslin hanging from lofty pillars, enormous stone jars in rows to receive offerings, tapers burning before the images, exquisite flowers displayed on every side filling the air with fragrance, and a multitude of carved figures of idols, griffins, guardians, &c.

"Always in the morning, men and women are seen in every direction kneeling behind their gift, and with uplifted hands reciting their devotions, often with a string of beads counting over each repetition; aged persons sweep out every place, or pick out the grass from the crevices; dogs and crows struggle around the altars, and devour the recent offerings; the great bells utter their frequent tones; and the mutter of praying voices makes a hum like the buzzing of an exchange.

"Every worshipper brings a present, often a bunch of flowers or a few green twigs plucked on the way; but generally the nicest eatables ready cooked, beautiful bunches of flowers, articles of raiment, &c. The amount of offerings here is very great. Stone vases, some of which will hold fifty or sixty gallons, stand round the pagoda, into which the devotees carefully lay their leafy plates of rice, plantain, cakes, &c. As these are successively filled, appointed persons empty them into their

vessels, carefully assorting the various kinds. The beautiful flowers remain all night and are swept out in the morning. No one ever objected however to my gathering them at pleasure. A gift once deposited is no more regarded by the worshipper."
"I could not but feel as I gazed upon the rich landscape and bright heavens, and marked the joy of the young men and maidens as they passed on, that he who has so long forborne with them, will in his abundant mercy, give them pastors after his own heart, who shall feed them with knowledge and understanding."

After reading this description, who can wonder at the difficulty of turning this semi-barbarous people from a religion of such a gorgeous and imposing ceremonial, and of such perfect congeniality with the unhumbled heart, to the spiritual, self-denying, pride-abasing doctrines of the cross?

Mrs. Judson in a letter to a friend, mentions the splendor and costliness of some of the religious offerings, one of which cost three thousand tickals, or twelve hundred dollars. After a description of the pagoda and its worshippers, she says: "The ground on which the pagoda is situated, commands a view of the surrounding country, which presents one of the most beautiful landscapes in nature. The polished spires of the pagodas, glistening among the trees at a distance, appear like the steeples of meeting-houses in our American seaports. The verdant appearance of the country, the hills and valleys, ponds and rivers, the banks of which are covered with cattle and fields of rice; each in turn attract the eye, and cause the beholder to exclaim, "Was this delightful country made to be the residence of idolaters?" ... Oh my friend, scenes like these, productive of feelings so various and so opposite, do notwithstanding, fire the soul with an unconquerable desire to rescue this people from destruction, and lead them to the Rock that is higher than they."

* * * * *

Under date of January 18, 1818, Mrs. Judson writes that they still live quietly, unmolested by government, and that they receive much respect and affection from the Viceroy and his family. She had some opportunities of private religious conversation with the Vicereine, to whom she presented a translation of Matthew's Gospel and a catechism. Still the heart of the lady appeared unaffected, though she ordered her daughters to be instructed in the new catechism. The inquirer who was mentioned as having afforded Mr. Judson such lively satisfaction, had been appointed to a government in a distant province, so that they saw little of him, but were gratified to learn that his interest in religious books still continued.

CHAPTER IX.

DISTRESSING EVENTS.--MR. JUDSON'S ABSENCE FROM RANGOON.--PERSECUTION OF MR. HOUGH.--HIS DEPARTURE FOR BENGAL.--MRS. JUDSON'S HEROIC FORTITUDE.--MR. JUDSON'S RETURN.

We have now to relate some distressing events connected with the mission, which for a time threatened its very existence. Mr. Judson having decided to commence a course of public preaching to the natives, thought best to secure the assistance of a native convert from the province of Arracan, who spoke the Burman language, to assist him in his first public efforts. He therefore embarked for that province, leaving Mrs. Judson to continue her efforts with the females under her instruction; while Mr. and Mrs. Hough were to prosecute the study of the language. He intended to be gone but three months, but at the end of that period, when his return was daily expected, a vessel from Chittagong, the port to which he had sailed, arrived at Rangoon, bringing the distressing tidings, that neither he, nor the vessel he sailed in had been heard of at that port. Letters received by Mrs. Judson from Bengal, also brought similar intelligence.

While the missionaries left in Rangoon were in this state of fearful alarm and suspense, Mr. Hough received an order to repair instantly to the Court House with a threat, that "if he did not tell all the truth in relation to the foreigners, they would write with his heart's blood." This message spread consternation among the native teachers, domestics and adherents, some of whom heard that a royal order had arrived for the banishment of all foreign teachers. Mr. Hough was detained at the court-house from day to day on the most flimsy pretences, ignorant of the language, and with no one to intercede with the government in his behalf, for it was contrary to etiquette for a woman to appear before the Viceroy, his family being absent. Mrs.

Judson being at length convinced that the petty officers of government were acting in this matter without authority, and for the purpose of extorting money from Mr. Hough, with the intrepidity that always marked her character, "taking her life in her hand", went boldly to the palace with a petition for his release. The Viceroy immediately granted it, and commanded that Mr. Hough should receive no further molestation.

To add to the distresses of the missionaries, the cholera now raged around them with fearful violence and there were rumors of war between England and Burmah. Six months had passed, and still the fate of Mr. Judson was a fearful mystery. The English vessels were hastening their departure from the harbor and soon they would have no means of leaving the country, whatever might occur. Mrs. Judson writes: "Mr. Hough has been for some time past desirous to have Mrs. Hough, his children and myself go to Bengal. But I have ever felt resolved not to make any movement till I hear from Mr. Judson. Within a few days, however, some circumstances have occurred which have induced me to make preparations for a voyage. There is but one remaining ship in the river; and if an embargo is laid on English ships it will be impossible for Mr. Judson (if he is yet alive) to return to this place. But the uncertainty of meeting him in Bengal, and the possibility of his arriving in my absence, cause me to make preparations with a heavy heart. Sometimes I feel inclined to remain here, alone, and hazard the consequences. I should certainly conclude on this step, if any probability existed of Mr. Judson's return. This mission has never appeared in so low a state as at the present time. It seems now entirely destroyed, as we all expect to embark for Bengal in a day or two. Alas! how changed are our prospects since Mr. Judson left us! How dark, how intricate the providence that now surrounds us! Yet it becomes us to be still, and know that he is God who has thus ordered our circumstances."

A fortnight later, she writes: "Alone, my dear friends, in this great house, ... I take my pen to record the strange vicissitudes through which I have passed within a few days."

On the 5th of this month, I embarked with Mr. Hough and family for Bengal, having previously disposed of what I could not take with me.... My disinclination to proceed had increased to such a degree that I was on the point of giving up the voyage; but my passage was paid, my baggage on board, and I knew not how to separate myself from the rest of the mission family. The vessel however was several days in going down the river; and "before putting out to sea was to be detained a day or two longer at its mouth." "I immediately resolved on giving up the voyage and returning to town. Accordingly the captain sent up a boat with me, and agreed to forward my baggage the next day. I reached town in the evening,--spent the night at the house of the only remaining Englishman in the place, and to-day have come out to the mission-house, to the great joy of all the Burmans left on our premises. Mr. Hough and his family will proceed, and they kindly and affectionately urge my return. I know I am surrounded by dangers on every hand, and expect to see much anxiety and distress: but at present I am tranquil, and intend to make an effort to pursue my studies as formerly, and leave the event with God."

Thus did this heroic woman, with that divine "instinct that seems to guide the noblest natures in great emergencies, decide to return alone to the mission-house, there to await the return of her husband, or the confirmation of her worst fears concerning his fate." It was a wonderful exhibition of courage and constancy; "and gave assurance of all the distinguished qualities, which at a later period, and amid dangers still more appalling, shone with such brightness around the character of this remarkable woman. The event justified her determination; and within a week after her decision was taken, Mr. Judson arrived at Rangoon, having been driven from place to place by contrary winds, and having entirely failed of the object for which he undertook the voyage.

"Mr. and Mrs. Hough, after long delays, reached Bengal, carrying with them the press and all the implements of the printing-house. Their removal was subsequently productive of many embarrassments to the Mission, and seems never to have been fully justified either by Mr. Judson or the Board of Managers in America."[3]

---

3 Gammell.

CHAPTER X.

INTOLERANCE OF THE BURMAN GOVERNMENT.--FIRST EDIFICE FOR CHRISTIAN WORSHIP ERECTED.--INSTRUCTION OF NATIVES.--CONVERSION OF A NATIVE.--HIS BAPTISM.--THAT OF TWO TIMID DISCIPLES.--MESSRS. JUDSON AND COLMAN VISIT AVA.

A few weeks after the return of Mr. Judson, the prospects of the Mission were still further brightened by the arrival of Messrs. Colman and Wheelock, who, with their wives, had been appointed by the Board in America, Missionaries to Burmah. They were young men of good talents, fervent piety, and extraordinary devotion to the object of evangelizing the heathen.

Mr. Judson, considering himself sufficiently master of the language to preach publicly, decided to build a small zayat, on a much frequented road, where he could preach the gospel, and converse with any native who might desire it, and where Mrs. Judson could meet female inquirers, and hold a school for religious and other instruction. He knew that this might draw upon them the displeasure of the higher powers, which had hitherto favored them because of the privacy of their life, and their small influence with the natives; for this government, as they afterwards discovered, though remarkably tolerant to foreigners, is highly intolerant to its own subjects in religious matters. Dr. Malcom remarks: "Foreigners of every description are allowed the fullest exercise of their religion. They may build places of worship in any place, and have their public festivals and processions without molestation. But no Burman may join any of these religions, under the severest penalties. In nothing does the government more thoroughly display its despotism, than in its measures for suppressing all religious innovation, and supporting the established system.... The whole population is thus held in chains, as iron-like as caste itself;

and to become a Christian openly, is to hazard everything, even life itself." But the Missionaries not being at this time at all aware of the rigor of this intolerance, resolved to make the attempt, and trust in the Lord for protection.

In April, 1819, Mr. Judson preached in his new zayat to a congregation of fifteen or twenty persons, most of them entirely inattentive and disorderly. But feeble as was this beginning, it was regarded by the missionaries as an event of no ordinary importance. Here was the first altar ever erected for the worship of the true God in that country over which century after century had rolled, each sweeping its millions of idolaters into eternity; and rude and lowly as were its walls, compared with the magnificent temples that surrounded it, it was perhaps the fitter emblem of that spiritual religion which delights not in temples made with hands, but in the service of the heart, 'which is in the sight of God of great price.'

The building, which they called a ***zayat*** from its similarity to the public buildings of that name in Burmah, had three apartments; the first a mere verandah thatched with bamboo, open to the road, and the place where Mr. Judson received all occasional visitors and inquirers; the second or middle one, a large airy room, occupied on Sundays for preaching and on week days as a school-room; and the last division, a mere entry opening into the garden leading to the mission-house. During the week Mrs. Judson occupied the middle room, giving instruction in reading, &c., to a class of males and females; and also in conversing with female inquirers. Here she also studied the Siamese language, much spoken in Rangoon, and translated into that language a catechism, and the Gospel of Matthew.

The 30th of April, 1819, was made memorable by the first visit of an inquirer who became a convert to the Christian faith. On the 5th of May Mr. Judson says in his journal, "It seems almost too much to believe that God has begun to manifest his grace to the Burmans, but this day I could not resist the delightful conviction that this is really the case. Praise and glory to his name for evermore. Amen."

From this time we learn from Mr. Judson's journal, that the verandah of the zayat where he sat to receive visitors, was constantly thronged with natives, who, impelled, some by curiosity and idleness, and some by better motives, came to talk about the new religion. So much however was to be dreaded, in the opinion of most of these, from the "lord of life and death," as they called the emperor, that few dared follow out their convictions. Moung Nau, however, the convert above mentioned, adhered steadfastly to his now faith, and desired baptism. Not having any doubt of the reality of his conversion, Mr. Judson administered the ordinance to him on Sunday, June 21. On the following Lord's day, the missionaries had the unspeakable satisfaction of sitting down at the Lord's table for the first time with a converted Burman; and as Mr. Judson writes, he had the privilege to which he had been looking forward many years, of administering the communion in two languages.

Many of the expressions of this young convert are very interesting. We find them in a letter from Mrs. Judson. "In our religion there is no way to escape the punishment due to sin; but according to the religion of Christ, he himself has died in order to deliver his disciples. How great are my thanks to Jesus Christ for sending teachers to this country! and how great are my thanks to the teachers for coming!" On hearing the fifth chapter of Matthew read, he said "These words take hold on my very heart, they make me tremble. Here God commands us to do everything that is good in secret, and not to be seen of men. How unlike our religion is this! When Burmans make offerings to the pagodas they make a great noise with drums and musical instruments that others may see how good they are. But this religion makes the mind fear God; it makes it of its own accord fear sin."

In the same letter she mentions a very interesting meeting with the females before mentioned, fifteen in number, who had for some time received from her religious instruction. Their love for, and confidence in their own religion seemed to be taken away; the truth seemed to have forced itself upon their understandings; but the sinfulness of their hearts, which among heathen as well as Christian nations is the great obstacle to salvation, could only be removed by the Holy Spirit, and oh how earnest and fervent were the prayers of their teacher for the presence of that heavenly agent!

Mr. Wheelock, one of the recently arrived missionaries, was obliged on account of his failing health to try a sea-voyage; but during the passage to Bengal, in a paroxysm of fever and delirium, he threw himself overboard and was drowned.

Some of the inquirers at the zayat had no inconsiderable powers of reasoning and argument; one in particular, named Moung-Shwa-gnong; who would spend whole days at the zayat, and engage Mr. Judson in endless discussions.--Not satisfied with the Buddhist faith he had become a confirmed skeptic, and disputed every Gospel truth before he received it with much subtilty and ingenuity. But after a while he found that his visits at the zayat had attracted the notice of Government, that the viceroy on being told he had renounced the religion of his country, had said, 'Inquire further about him,' and the missionaries for a time saw him no more.

The two candidates that next presented themselves for baptism, were urgent that the ordinance should be performed, not absolutely in private, but at sunset and away from public observation. The missionaries discussed their case long with them and with each other. Mr. Judson's remarks on the subject, as well as his description of the baptism, are so full of that tenderness and pathos which is eminently a 'fruit of the Spirit,' that we must give them in his own words.

"We felt satisfied that they were humble disciples of Jesus, and were desirous of receiving this ordinance purely out of regard to his command, and their own spiritual welfare; we felt that we were all equally exposed to danger, and needed a spirit of mutual candor and forbearance, and sympathy; we were convinced; that they were influenced rather by desires of avoiding unnecessary exposure, than by that sinful fear which would plunge them into apostasy in the hour of trial; and when they assured us that if actually brought before government, they could not think of denying their Saviour, we could not conscientiously refuse their request, and therefore agreed to have them baptized to-morrow at sunset." "7. Lord's day. We had worship as usual and the people dispersed. About half an hour before sunset the two candidates came to the zayat, accompanied by three or four of their friends; and after a short prayer we proceeded to the spot where Moung-Nau was formerly baptized. The sun was not allowed to look on the humble, timid profession. No wondering crowd crowned the overshadowing hill. No hymn of praise expressed the exulting feeling of joyous hearts. Stillness and solemnity pervaded the scene. We felt, on the banks of the water, as a little, feeble, solitary band. But perhaps some hovering angels took note of the event with more interest than they witnessed the late coronation; perhaps Jesus looked down on us, pitied and forgave our weaknesses, and marked us for his own; perhaps if we deny him not, he will acknowledge us another day, more publicly than we venture at present to acknowledge him."

There was a great falling off in the attendance at the zayat after Moung-shwa-gnong's defection. None dared call to inquire from religious principle, and curiosity respecting the religion had been fully gratified. It became highly desirable to take some measures to secure the favor of the emperor. If he could be made propitious, the converts and the missionaries would have nothing to fear. Messrs. Judson and Colman, therefore, leaving their families at Rangoon, set out on their visit to Ava, to lay their case--as a Burman would express it--before 'the golden feet.' They carried with them, as presents to his majesty, the Bible, in six volumes, covered with gold leaf in the Burman style, each volume enclosed in a rich wrapper; and many other articles as presents to the different members of the government.

CHAPTER XI.

RECEPTION OF MESSRS. COLMAN AND JUDSON AT AVA.--THEIR RETURN TO RANGOON.--THEIR RESOLUTION TO LEAVE RANGOON.--OPPOSITION OF DISCIPLES TO THIS MEASURE.--INCREASE OF DISCIPLES.--THEIR STEADFASTNESS.--FAILURE OF MRS. JUDSON'S HEALTH.

The passage up the Irrawaddy to Ava, or rather Amerapoora, which was then the capital, was made in safety in a little more than thirty days. They soon found the house of their old friend the former viceroy of Rangoon, who now enjoyed a high post under government. Here they were kindly received, and promised a speedy presentation to the "golden face," *i.e.* the emperor.

The next day, Moung Yo, a favorite officer of the viceroy, came to take them to the imperial palace. He first introduced them to the private minister of state, who met them very pleasantly, received their presents, and a petition they had prepared to the emperor, which latter he was examining when some one announced that the 'golden foot' was about to advance; when the minister hastily rose up, put on his state-robes, and prepared to present them to the emperor. They were conducted through various splendor and parade, up a flight of steps into a magnificent hall. Mr. Judson says "The scene to which we were now introduced, really surpassed our expectation. The spacious extent of the hall, the number and magnitude of the pillars, the height of the dome, the whole completely covered with gold, presented a most grand and imposing spectacle. Very few were present, and those evidently great officers of state. Our situation prevented us from seeing the further avenue of the hall, but the end where we sat opened into the parade which the emperor was about to inspect.

"We remained about five minutes, when every one put himself into the most respectful attitude, and Moung Yo whispered that his majesty had entered. We looked through the hall as far as the pillars would allow, and presently caught sight of this modern Ahasuerus. He came forward, unattended--in solitary grandeur-- exhibiting the proud gait and majesty of an eastern monarch. His dress was rich but not distinctive, and he carried in his hand the gold-sheathed sword, which seems to have taken the place of the sceptre of ancient times. But it was his high aspect and commanding eye, that chiefly rivetted our attention. He strided on. Every head excepting ours, was now in the dust. We remained kneeling, our hands folded, our eyes fixed on the Monarch. When he drew near, we caught his attention. He stopped, partly turned towards us--'Who are these?' 'The teachers, great King,' I replied. 'What, you speak Burman?--the priests that I heard of last night? When did you arrive? Are you teachers of religion? Are you married? Why do you dress so?' These and other similar questions we answered; when he appeared to be pleased with us, and sat down on an elevated seat--his hand resting on the hilt of his sword, and his eyes intently fixed on us."

Moung Zah now read their petition, which set forth that they were teachers of the religion of their country, and begged the royal permission to teach the same in his dominions; and also prayed that no Burman might be subjected to molestation from government for listening to or embracing that religion; and the emperor after hearing it, took it himself, read it through and handed it back without saying a word. In the meantime Mr. Judson had given Moung Zah an abridged copy of the tract called a "Summary of Christian Doctrine," which had been got up in the richest style and dress possible. The emperor took the tract "Our hearts," says Mr. J., "now rose to God for a display of his grace. Oh have mercy on Burmah! Have mercy on her king!" But alas! the time had not yet come. He held the tract long enough to read the two first sentences, which assert that there is one eternal God, who is independent of the incidents of mortality and that besides him, there is no God; and then with an air of indifference, perhaps disdain, he dashed it down to the ground! Moung Zah stooped forward, picked it up and handed it to us. Moung Yo made a slight attempt to save us by unfolding one of the volumes which composed our present and displaying its beauty, but his majesty took no notice. Our fate was decided. After a few moments Moung Zah interpreted his royal master's will in the following terms: "In regard to the objects of your petition, his majesty gives no order. In regard to your sacred books, his majesty has no use for them--take them away." ... "He then rose from his seat, strode on to the end of the hall, and there, after having dashed to the ground the first intelligence he had ever received of the eternal God, his Maker, Preserver, his Judge, he threw himself down on a cushion, and lay listening to the music, and gazing at the parade spread out before him."

They and their presents were then hurried away with little ceremony. The next day they "ascertained beyond a doubt, that the policy of the Burman government is precisely the same as the Chinese; that it is quite out of the question whether any subjects of the emperor who embrace a religion different from his own, will be exempt from punishment; and that we, in presenting a petition to that effect, had been guilty of a most egregious blunder,--an unpardonable offence."

We cannot prevail on ourselves to give the sequel of this narrative in any other than the beautiful and picturesque language of Mr. Judson which we have so often quoted.

"It was now evening. We had four miles to walk by moonlight. Two of our disciples only followed us. They had pressed as near as they ventured to the door of the hall of audience, and listened to words which sealed the extinction of their hopes and ours. For some time we spoke not.

'Some natural tears we dropped, but wiped them soon.   Tho world was all before us, where to choose   Our place of rest, and Providence our guide.'

And as our first parents took their solitary way through Eden, so we took our way through this great city.

"Arrived at the boat, we threw ourselves down, exhausted in body and mind. For three days we had walked eight miles a day, the most of the way in the heat of the sun, which in the interior of these countries is exceedingly oppressive; and the result of our toils and travels has been--the wisest and best possible--a result, which, if we could see the end from the beginning, would call forth our highest praise. O slow of heart to believe and trust in the over-ruling agency of our own Almighty Saviour!"

They returned to Rangoon by an easy and rapid passage down the river, and calling the few disciples together frankly disclosed to them the result of their mission. To their surprise and delight it only increased their zeal and attachment for the religion they had professed. They became in turn the comforters of the missionaries, vieing with each other in trying to convince them that the cause was not yet desperate. Above all were they solicitous that the missionaries should not carry out a design they had formed to leave them, and try to find a field more favorable for their labors. One assured them he would follow them to the end of the world. Another, who having an unconverted wife, could not follow them, declared that if left there alone, he would perform no other duties but those of Christ's religion.

But what had most weight with Mr. and Mrs. Judson in inducing them to remain, was the fact that inquiry seemed to be spreading in the neighborhood, and that there seemed a further prospect of usefulness, in spite of the fear of persecution. They therefore concluded to remain for the present at Rangoon; while Mr. and Mrs. Colman should proceed to Arracan and form a station there.

Thus again were Mr. and Mrs. J. alone; but not now exclusively among heathen idolaters. The affectionate zeal of the disciples rejoiced their hearts; and others, and among them the old disputant, Moung-Shwa-gnong, seemed sincere and hopeful inquirers. Three women, induced by him, also visited Mrs. Judson to learn the way of life. One of these (the one we have before alluded to) was characterized by superior discernment and mental power, but exceedingly timid through fear of persecution. In one of her conversations she expressed her surprise that the effect of the religion of Christ upon her mind was to make her love his disciples more than her dearest natural relations. This showed that she was a real disciple, though a timid one. But surely it is not for us who sit under our own vine with none to make us afraid, to be severe on these poor heathen, for not at once overcoming the dread of suffering, so natural to the human heart! Before we judge them, let us be very sure that *our* faith would endure the fires of persecution and even of martyrdom which threatened them. They knew of instances where their countrymen who had embraced the **Roman Catholic** faith, had been subjected to the punishment of the iron-mall, an instrument of torture more dreadful than any employed against the Scottish Covenanters, in the times of their bitterest persecution. Sudden execution they might have braved, though that will appal almost any heart; but lingering torture was what they might fear, to which death should succeed only when nature could bear no more.

Females in Christian countries, who think much of your self-denials and sacrifices, when

'A moment's pain, a passing shower,　　Is all the grief ye share,'

how could *your* hearts endure if called to such trials, as might at any moment befall your poor sisters in Burmah!

Mrs. Judson's health had for some time been failing, and at length after having gone through two courses of salivation for the liver-complaint, she was obliged to try a sea-voyage. Her situation was too critical for her to think of going alone, and Mr. Judson concluded to accompany her to Bengal. Two converts expressed the strongest desire to profess Christ, before the missionaries should leave them. They were accordingly baptized. The ship being detained, the speculative, hesitating, but now sincere disciple, Moung Shwa-gnong, casting aside his fears and scruples, boldly avowed his faith, and desired baptism. Of course he was joyfully received. The scene at his baptism had such an effect upon Mah Meulah, the female who has been before mentioned, that she too could no longer delay a public profession of faith in Christ. On returning to the house after receiving the rite, she said, "Now I have taken the oath of allegiance to Jesus Christ, and I have nothing to do but to commit myself, soul and body, into the hands of my Lord, assured that he will never suffer me to fall away!"

Surely if no other proof existed of the power of gospel truth to renew the heart of men, a sufficient one would be furnished here. In the face of threatened persecution not only were old converts strengthened in their faith in, and attachment to Christ, but new ones eagerly pressed forward to unite themselves with the despised and humble flock.

Nine males and one female had now been baptized at the hazard of their lives; a grammar and dictionary had been compiled and printed; a portion of the Scriptures translated and printed; tracts had been issued; and so greatly had the missionaries gained in favor with the people, that as they went down to the ship which was to carry them to Bengal, more than a hundred natives followed them, testifying sincere grief at their departure.

CHAPTER XII.

MR. AND MRS. JUDSON VISIT BENGAL AND RETURN.--MRS. JUDSON'S HEALTH AGAIN FAILS.--HER RESOLUTION TO VISIT AMERICA.-- HER VOYAGE TO ENGLAND AND VISIT THERE.

They arrived in Calcutta on the 8th of August, 1820. The voyage was of no essential benefit to Mrs. J.'s health, neither was her visit to Calcutta; but at Serampore she so far recovered as to make them desirous to return to Rangoon, where they arrived on the 5th of January, 1821. The converts received them with the utmost affection; their old friend the vicereine again occupied her former palace and welcomed Mrs. Judson with friendly familiarity, and new inquirers presented themselves at the zayat. In translating the Scriptures, the acute and fertile mind of Moung Shwa-gnong was an invaluable assistance, while another convert of cultivated intellect was equally useful in other missionary labors. Though through fear of being subjected to extortion, some of them had been obliged to flee to the woods, not one disciple had disgraced or dishonored his profession. A violent effort and been made by some of Moung Shwa-gnong's enemies, to ruin him in the opinion of the viceroy, by complaining of him that he was making every endeavor "to turn the priests' rice-pot bottom upwards." " ***What consequence?***" said the viceroy, "***let the priests turn it back again.***" All the disciples from that time felt sure of toleration under Mya-day-men, (the name of the viceroy.)

The history of the next few months presents nothing novel in the life of this little Christian community, to which there were however some accessions. But Mrs. Judson was gradually sinking under the disease which had so long troubled her, until at length it was found essential to her ***life*** even, that she should seek some more propitious climate. After much anxious deliberation it was resolved that she should sail for Bengal, and thence to America. Her feelings on leaving the 'home of her heart,' and the husband of her youth, as well as the spiritual children that God had given them in that heathen land--to try alone the perils of a long and tedious voyage, in a state of health which rendered it doubtful whether she would ever reach the land of her nativity, or return to that of her adoption--can scarcely be conceived, much less described. Her own words are:

"Those only who have been through a variety of toil and privation to obtain a darling object, can realize how entirely every fibre of the heart adheres to that object when secured. Had we encountered no difficulties, and suffered no privations in our attempts to form a Church of Christ, under the government of a heathen despot, we should have been warmly attached to the individuals composing it, but should not have felt that tender solicitude and anxious affection, as in the present case.

"Rangoon, from having been the theatre in which so much of the power, faithfulness and mercy of God have been exhibited; from having been considered for ten years past as my home for life, and from a thousand interesting associations, had become the dearest spot on earth. Hence you will readily imagine, that no ordinary consideration would have induced my departure."

She arrived in Calcutta Sept. 22d, 1821. Finding when she reached there that the American captains of vessels declined taking passengers, without an exorbitant price, she decided not to take passage to America. On mentioning her circumstances to a lady in Calcutta, the latter strongly recommended the advantages of a voyage to England, on account of the superior accommodations, medical advice, and female passengers in English ships. A pious captain offered to take her for about one third of the price demanded for a voyage to America, provided she would share a cabin with three children, who were going to England an offer which she immediately accepted. The father of the children subsequently arrived in Calcutta, and generously paid the whole price of the cabin, which enabled her to go without any expense to the Board.

She writes: "If the pain in my side is entirely removed while on my passage to Europe, I shall return to India in the same ship, and proceed immediately to Rangoon. But if not I shall go over to America, and spend one winter in my dear native country.

"Ardently as I desire to see my beloved friends in America, I cannot prevail on myself to be any longer from Rangoon than is absolutely necessary for the preservation of my life. I have had a severe struggle relative to my immediate return to Rangoon instead of going to England. But I did not venture to go contrary to the convictions of reason, to the opinion of an eminent and skilful physician, and the repeated injunctions of Mr. Judson.

"My last letter from Rangoon was dated Oct. 26. Moung Shwa-gnong had been accused before the viceroy, and had disappeared. Mr. Judson had felt much anxiety and distress on his account, fearing he had done something in the way of retraction, which prevented his visiting him. But in a fortnight he was agreeably surprised at seeing him enter. He informed Mr. J. that having been accused, he had thought it the wisest way to keep out of sight; that he had put all his family on board a boat, and was going up the country among the sect of heretics with whom he once associated, and had now come to take leave, obtain tracts, gospels, &c. Mr. Judson furnished him with what was necessary, and bid him God speed. He will no doubt do much good among that class of people, for it is impossible for him to be any time with his friends without conversing on the subject of religion. Moung Ing had returned, as steadfast and as much devoted to the cause as ever. He and Moung Shwa-ba spend every evening in reading the Scriptures, and finding the places where the apostles preached, on a map which Mr. Judson has made for them. Another Burman has been baptized, who gives decided evidence of being a true Christian. Have we not, my dear sir, every reason to trust God in future, when we see what he has done in Rangoon. Could you see at once the difficulties in the way of the conversion of the Burmans, the grace of God would appear ten times as conspicuous as it now does. When we hardly ventured to hope that we should ever see one of them truly converted, how great is our joy to see a little church rise up in the midst of that wilderness, consisting of thirteen converted Burmans."

On her passage to England, her old enemy, the liver-complaint, again attacked her; but bodily illness did not prevent her from endeavoring to benefit the souls of her fellow-passengers; and with regard to two of them, her efforts did not seem unsuccessful.

On arriving in England, she was cordially invited by the Hon. Joseph Butterworth, M.P., to make his house her home. He afterward, at a public meeting, referred to her visit as "reminding him of the apostolic admonition, 'Be not forgetful to entertain strangers, for thereby some have entertained angels unawares.'"

At his house she met many persons, distinguished for literature and piety, among whom were Sumner, Babington and Wilberforce.

After spending some time at Cheltenham, to which place she had been sent for the benefit of its waters, she accepted a pressing invitation to visit Scotland, where, as in England, she received valuable presents and innumerable acts of kindness. The piety of her English friends seemed to her of the most high-toned character, and their ardent friendship called forth her warmest affections. Though on her way to a still dearer country, the land of her birth, she could not part with them without the tenderest regret.

CHAPTER XIII.

MRS. JUDSON'S ARRIVAL IN AMERICA.--INFLUENCE OF HER VISIT.--HOSTILE OPINIONS.--HER PERSON AND MANNERS.--EXTRACTS FROM HER LETTERS.

In the meanwhile events of some interest were transpiring in Burmah. In consequence of the persecution against Moung Shwa-gnong which had obliged him to flee for his life, and the new vigilance of priests and officers in respect to converts,--the inquirers withdrew altogether from the mission-house, and Mr. Judson was obliged to close the zayat, and suspend public preaching on the Sabbath, though still the converts visited him privately, for instruction and consolation.

Mr. J.'s solitary condition was however soon relieved by the arrival of Dr. and Mrs. Price, who came to share his labors among the heathen; and also by the return of Mr. and Mrs. Hough from Serampore, bringing with them the printing press, whose absence had occasioned no small delay and inconvenience to Mr. Judson in his labors.

On the 25th of September, 1822, Mrs. J. arrived in America. Her feelings on revisiting her native land, are best learned from a letter to Mr. Judson's parents, dated Sept 27.

"With mingled sensations of joy and sorrow, I address a few lines to the parents of my beloved husband,--joy, that I once more find myself in my own native country, and with the prospect of meeting with loved relatives and friends--sorrow, that he who has been a participator in all my concerns for the last ten years, is not now at hand to partake with me in the joyful anticipations of meeting those he so much loves.

"I left Liverpool on the 16th of August, and arrived at New York harbor day before yesterday. On account of the prevalence of yellow fever, prudence forbade my landing. Accordingly I embarked on board the steamboat for this place, where I arrived a few hours ago. It was my intention to pass a week in Philadelphia and then go to Providence, and thence to you in Woburn, as it would be on my way to Bradford, where I shall spend the winter. But Dr. Stoughton wishes me to go to Washington, which will detain me in this part of the country a week longer. However I hope to be with you in a fortnight from this time. My health is much improved since I left England and I begin to hope the disorder is entirely eradicated."

Of this visit of Mrs. Judson to America, Professor Gammell remarks in general, as follows:

"Her visit to the United States forms an epoch of no inconsiderable importance in the progress of interest in missions among the churches of various denominations in this country. She visited several of the leading cities of the Union; met a large number of associations of ladies; attended the session of the Triennial Convention at Washington; and in a multitude of social circles, alike in the South and in the North, recited the thrilling narrative of what she had seen and experienced during the eventful years in which she had dwelt in a heathen land.

"But relaxation and travelling for health and interviews with religious friends, were not her only occupation. In her retirement, in addition to maintaining an extensive correspondence, she found time to prepare the history of the mission in Burmah which was published in her name, in a series of letters addressed to Mr. Butterworth, the gentleman beneath whose roof she had been a guest during her residence in England. These records, which were principally compiled from documents which had been published before, contained the first continuous account of the Burman mission ever given to the public. The work was widely read in England and America, and received the favorable notice of several of the leading organs of public criticism.

"The influence which she exerted in favor of the cause of missions during her brief residence of eight or nine months in the United States, it is hardly possible now to estimate. She enlisted more fully in the cause not a few leading minds who have since rendered it signal service both by eloquent vindications and by judicious counsels; and by the appeals which she addressed to Christians of her own sex, and her fervid conversations with persons of all classes and denominations in America, as well as by the views which she submitted to the managers of the mission, a new zeal for its prosecution was everywhere created, and the missionary enterprise, instead of being regarded with doubt and misgiving, as it had been by many, even among Christians, began to be understood in its higher relations to all the hopes of man, and to be contemplated in its true grandeur, and ennobling moral dignity."

Such is the opinion of her visit expressed by an elegant and enlightened scholar, now that more than a quarter of a century has passed, bringing triumph to the missionary cause, and honor to its first founders and advocates; but such we regret to say was not the universal sentiment of her contemporaries. Many persons well remember the unfounded stories put in circulation respecting her, by some whose motives we will not inquire into, as they would scarcely bear investigation, in regard to her actions, her intentions, and even her apparel. As her biographer remarks in introducing some of her letters at this period: "It was said that her health was not seriously impaired, and that she visited the South with a view to excite attention and applause. To persons who would put forth or circulate such calumnies, a perusal of her letters, in which she utters her feelings to her friends without reserve, will, it is hoped, minister a rebuke sufficiently severe to awaken shame and penitence; and to those who may unwarily have been led to form unfavorable opinions respecting Mrs. Judson, we cannot doubt that these letters will afford welcome evidence of her modest and amiable disposition, consistent and exemplary demeanor, ardent piety, and steady, irrepressible devotion to the interests of the mission."

* * * * *

The person and manners of Mrs. Judson at this time, were, according to the testimony of some who well recollect her, engaging and attractive in no common degree. Her sweet and ready smile, her dark expressive eye, the animation and sprightliness of her conversation, and her refined taste and manners, made her a favorite in all circles. Her dress, for which she was indebted to the liberality of British friends, was more rich and showy than she would have chosen for herself, and as has been said, excited unkind remarks from some who did not care to investigate her reasons for wearing it. Elegant as it was said to be, it was certainly far better she should wear it, even at the risk of seeming inconsistency, than to put her friends to the expense of other and plainer clothing.

As to the imputation that she preferred the eclat of life in a southern city, to the retirement of her New England home,--it is sufficient to answer, that a constitution relaxed and enfeebled by ten years' residence in a tropical climate, was ill-fitted to bear the rigors of a New England winter, and as her whole object in her visit, was the restoration of her health, she conceived it her duty to choose such a place of sojourn as should seem most favorable to it.

* * * * *

After a stay of six weeks with her parents in Bradford, Mrs. J. found it necessary to seek a milder climate, and was advised to try that of Baltimore. She had a pleasant journey to that city, stopping one day with friends in New York, and arrived there on the 5th of December. From her letters written about this time we proceed to give some extracts.

"My journey to this place was pleasant, though fatiguing. I passed one night only in New York, and spent a most pleasant evening in the society of a large party of good people who were collected for the purpose of prayer. Many fervent petitions were presented in behalf of the perishing Burmans, and the little church established in that country. It was an evening to me full of interest; but I found at the conclusion, that my strength was quite exhausted, and I began to fear whether I should be able to continue my journey." ... "How much of heaven might Christians enjoy even here on earth if they would keep in view what ought to be their great object in life. If they would but make the enjoyment of God their main pursuit how much more consistent their profession would be with their conduct, how much more useful their lives and how much more rapidly they would ripen for eternal glory."

"Christians do not sufficiently assist one another in their spiritual walk. They are not enough in the habit of conversing familiarly and affectionately on the state of each others' souls, and kindly encouraging each other to persevere and get near to heaven. One degree of grace attained in this world, is worth more than every earthly enjoyment."

"I ought to have mentioned that I found much of the true missionary spirit existing in New York.

"I began this letter some days ago, but a violent cold has prevented my finishing it. I am very thankful that I am no farther north than Baltimore, for I feel confident the cold would soon destroy me. I have not been out of the house since I arrived, and hardly out of my chamber. My health is certainly better than when I left Boston, though I have a heavy cold and some cough.

"What can be done to excite a missionary spirit in this country? I dare not engage in the subject till I am better. It would take up my whole soul, and retard my recovery. A little while, and we are in eternity; before we find ourselves there, let us do *much* for Christ."

CHAPTER XIV.

FURTHER EXTRACTS FROM HER LETTERS.--HER ILLNESS.--HER HISTORY OF THE BURMAN MISSION.--HER DEPARTURE FROM AMERICA WITH MR. AND MRS. WADE.

In a letter to a friend at Waterville, Mrs. Judson gives a full account of the reasons that determined her to pass the winter at the south. She says: "I had never *fully* counted the cost of a visit to my native country and beloved relatives. I did not expect that a scene which I had anticipated *as so joyous*, was destined to give my health and constitution a shock which would require months to repair.

"During my passage from England my health was most perfect, not the least symptom of my original disorder remained. But from the day of my arrival, the idea that I was once more on American ground banished all peace and quiet from my mind, and for the first four days and nights I never closed my eyes to sleep! This circumstance, together with dwelling on the anticipated meeting with my friends, occasioned the most alarming apprehensions.

"I reached my father's about a fortnight after my arrival in the country--and had not then been able to procure a single night's sleep. The scene which ensued brought my feelings to a crisis, nature was quite exhausted, and I began to fear would sink. To be concise, my health began to decline in a most alarming manner, and the pain in my side and cough returned. I was kept in a state of constant excitement by daily meeting my old friends and acquaintances; and during the whole six weeks of my residence at my father's, I had *not one* night's quiet rest. I felt the cold most severely, and found, as that increased, my cough increased."

She goes on to say that under these circumstances, she was strongly urged by

Dr. Judson, a brother of her husband, who was then in Baltimore, to remove to the south, and take up her residence for the winter with him at his boarding-house. She says that painful as it was to leave her dear family, yet as she knew that freedom from company and excitement, as well as a milder climate, were absolutely essential to her recovery, she was induced to go. She adds that her health is so far re-established that she is able to give five hours a day to study and to the compilation of her History of the Burman Mission, a work she had very much at heart.

The next passage in the letter is of touching interest, as showing the meekness of the Christian spirit in receiving a rebuke, whether merited or not.

"Your kind hint relative to my being injured by the lavish attention of our dear friends in this country, has much endeared you to my heart. I am well aware that human applause has a tendency to elate the soul, and render it less anxious about spiritual enjoyments, particularly if the individual is conscious of deserving it. But I must say, that since my return to this country, I have often been affected to tears, in hearing the undeserved praises of my friends, feeling that I was far, very far from being what they imagined: and that there are thousands of poor obscure Christians, whose excellences will never be known in this world, who are a thousand times more deserving of the tender regard of their fellow-Christians than I am.

"Yet I trust I am grateful to my Heavenly Father for inclining the hearts of his children to look on me with a friendly eye. The retired life I now lead is much more congenial to my feelings, and much more favorable to religious enjoyment, than when I was kept in a continual bustle of company. Yes, it is in retirement that our affections are raised to God, and our souls refreshed and quickened by the influences of the Holy Spirit. If we would live near the threshold of Heaven, and daily take a glance at our promised inheritance we must avoid not only worldly, but religious dissipation. Strange as it may seem, I do believe there is something like religious dissipation, in a Christian's being so entirely engrossed in religious company, as to prevent his spiritual enjoyments."

In Baltimore, through the influence of Dr. Judson, she had the best medical advice and attendance the city could give; and was put upon a course of mercury in order to produce salivation. She denied herself to company, and thus secured time for writing, in which employment she was assisted by "a pious excellent young lady," whom she engaged as a copyist. Her correspondence was extensive, and occupied much of her time. One interesting letter from England informed her that Mr. Butterworth had put at interest for her Burman school L100 sterling, and that a larger sum had been collected. Her English physicians insisted that she could **not live** in India, and urged her and her husband to come to England, but her determination to return to Burmah was unalterable.

On the 19th of February she writes to her friend in Waterville: "Your kind and affectionate letter found me in bed, so weak that I was obliged to read it at intervals; but it afforded heartfelt consolation. Thanks to our Heavenly Father whose guardian care and love I have *so largely* experienced. I am now much better, and once more enjoy the prospect of gaining that degree of health which will allow my return to Burmah, there to spend my remaining days, few or many, in endeavouring to guide immortal souls to that dear Redeemer, whose presence can make joyful a sick chamber, a dying bed.

"For the last month I have been *very ill*. The disease seemed to be removed from the liver to the lungs. I have raised blood twice, which the physicians thought proceeded from the lungs, though I am inclined to think it was from the throat. I was however bled so frequently and so largely that my strength was quite reduced. At present I am free from every unfavorable symptom, but am still weak.

"I am rejoiced to hear that Mr. Boardman has offered himself to supply dear Colman's place. If actuated by motives of love to God, and concern for precious souls, tell him he will never regret the sacrifice, but will find those spiritual consolations which will more than compensate him for every privation. I shall rejoice to afford him every assistance in the acquisition of the language which my health will allow, though I fear he will not be ready to sail so early as I hope to embark.

"This is the third day I have been writing this letter, on account of my weakness. But I am gaining a little every day. Yesterday I had a little female prayer-meeting in my chamber--trust the blessed Saviour was near us. Oh it is good to get near to God, and feel whether in life or death, we are His.

"Let us, my dear sister, so live, that our union to Christ may not only be satisfactory to ourselves but to all around us. On earth we serve God--in heaven enjoy him--is a motto I have long wished to adopt. When in heaven we can do nothing towards saving immortal souls."

In a subsequent letter she mentions receiving a journal kept by her husband, with the joyful intelligence of the accession of five more converts to the little church there, three of whom were females, and members of her Wednesday meeting. "They have," she says "set up of their own accord a female prayer-meeting. Is not this encouraging?" Dr. Price had been ordered to Ava on account of his medical skill, and Mr. Judson was about to accompany him to make a further effort for toleration.

In March, Mrs. Judson went to Washington to superintend the printing of her History of the Mission, and here she was detained contrary to her wishes until the last of April. However, this detention gave her an opportunity of meeting the Baptist General Convention which held its session there at that time. A committee was appointed to confer with her respecting the Burman Mission, and at her suggestion several important measures were adopted.

When the printing of her work was completed, she presented the copy-right to the convention. The work was favorably noticed in several leading journals of the day, and has circulated extensively both in Europe and this country. It was of great service not only to the cause of the particular field of which it was the history, but to the cause of missions generally, in awaking the public mind from that strange apathy in regard to our Saviour's parting command in which for seventeen centuries it had for the most part quietly slumbered. We say **_for the most part_**, for we do not forget the self-denying labors of the Roman Catholics in propagating their doctrines in various parts of the world; indeed this has always been the bright redeeming feature of that system of semi-pagan Christianity. Well would it be if protestant Christians would imitate their zeal and self-devotion! How strange that centuries passed, even after the Reformation, before Christians began to recognize as binding that solemn injunction, "Go ye into all the world, and preach the Gospel to every creature, with its encouraging promise, Lo I am with you always even unto the end of the world!"

This *apathy* in respect to the cause nearest her heart, was a great source of grief to Mrs. J. In a letter to Dr. Wayland, written in Washington, after stating that she had found that her strength was not sufficiently restored to undertake a journey to the North, she says, "This, together with the hope of exciting more attention to the subject of missions among the members of the General Convention which will soon meet here," has induced me to remain.... "Oh my brother, my heart sickens at the apathy and unconcern relative to the subject of missions which are in many places exhibited. I sometimes say to myself, Will not the missionary flame become entirely extinct, and the mission already established in Burmah, die for want of support?... Where are our young men, fired with the love of Christ and compassion for immortal souls, who are ***desirous*** to leave their comforts and their homes for a few years, to serve their Redeemer in foreign lands? Who is willing to obey this last, this most benevolent command of our Lord, Go ye into all the world, and preach the gospel to every creature? But I must stop. Loss of sleep for this night will be the consequence of indulging myself thus far."

At the above-mentioned Convention, Mr. Jonathan Wade of New York, and Mr. George D. Boardman of Maine, had offered themselves as Missionaries to the East. Mr. Wade was soon after regularly appointed by the Board, and with his wife, was directed to take passage for India with Mrs. Judson. The latter writes to her sister from Boston, upon her arrival there from the South, "We arrived in safety at six o'clock on Thursday. We were immediately informed that Mr. and Mrs. Wade would sail with me to India. This was animating intelligence, and I felt that the hand of God was in it, for he had heard my prayers.

"Yesterday we went on board the ship, chose my cabin, and agreed with the captain to take us all for twelve hundred dollars. The accommodations are excellent, clean and airy. It is a most beautiful ship, and the captain seems disposed to do all in his power for our comfort.... I am now making preparations for my passage. Monday we have a prayer-meeting, and on Tuesday we go to Plymouth. I am doubting whether I ought to go to Bradford again or not. My nerves are in such a state that I have to make every possible exertion to keep them quiet. It will only increase my agitation to take a formal leave of my friends and home."

On the 22d of June, 1823, they sailed from Boston amidst every demonstration of personal attachment and Christian sympathy. They carried with them a valuable present and a letter from the Convention to the Burman emperor, sent in the hope of conciliating his favor toward the missionaries.

CHAPTER XV.

MESSRS. JUDSON AND PRICE VISIT AVA.--THEIR RECEPTION AT COURT.--THEIR RETURN TO RANGOON.--MRS. JUDSON'S RETURN.--A LETTER TO HER PARENTS DESCRIBING THEIR REMOVAL TO AVA.--DESCRIPTION OF AVA.

It was mentioned that during Mrs. Judson's absence from Burmah, Dr. Price, the fame of whose medical skill had reached the 'golden ears,' had been ordered to Ava, and that Mr. Judson had determined to make another attempt to procure toleration for the Christians by a second visit to the capital. In a boat furnished by government, they left Rangoon, embarked for Ava, then the capital, and were immediately introduced to the king. Dr. Price was graciously received, but at the first interview Mr. Judson was scarcely noticed. Of the second interview, we will give the account in Mr. Judson's own words.

"To-day the king noticed me for the first time.... After some time he said, 'And you, in black, what are you? a medical man too?' 'Not a medical man, but a teacher of religion, your Majesty.' He proceeded to make a few inquiries about my religion, and then put the alarming inquiry whether any had embraced it. I evaded by saying 'Not here.' He persisted 'Are there any in Rangoon?' 'There are a few.' 'Are they foreigners?' I trembled for the consequence of an answer which might involve the little church in ruin; but the truth must be sacrificed or the consequences hazarded; and I therefore replied, 'There are some foreigners and some Burmans.' He remained silent a few moments, but presently showed he was not displeased, by asking a great variety of questions on religion, and geography and astronomy, some of which were answered in such a satisfactory manner, as to occasion a general expression of satisfaction in all the court present.

"After his Majesty retired, a royal secretary entered into conversation, and allowed me to expatiate on several topics of religion in my usual way. And all this took place in the presence of the very man, now an Atwenwoon, (one of the highest officers) who many years ago, caused his uncle to be tortured under the iron mall, for renouncing Buddhism and embracing the Romish religion!...

"Thanks to God for the encouragement of this day! The monarch of the empire has distinctly understood, that some of his subjects have embraced the Christian religion, and his wrath has been restrained."

He afterwards had another interview, in which the king inquired much about America, and authorized him to invite her ships to his dominions, assuring them of protection and facilities for trade.

He mentions much flattering attention paid him by a prince of the empire and his wife, who was the king's sister, both of whom urged him not to return to Rangoon, but to bring his wife and reside at Ava. In fact, several dignitaries of the empire were so far attracted by the new theories in religion and science, as to enter into animated discussions with the missionaries respecting them. The prince above mentioned was an interesting character. Mr. Judson went so far as boldly to urge upon him the duty of making personal religion his immediate care. For a moment he was moved, but soon replied, that he was young, only twenty-eight. That he was desirous of enlarging his mind by an acquaintance with all foreign science, and then he could judge whether Christianity was worthy of his adoption or not. But, said Mr. Judson, suppose you change worlds in the meantime? His countenance fell, and he said sadly, "It is true, I do not know when I shall die."

How true it is that "as in water face answereth to face, so doth the heart of man to man." Left without excuse, this poor impenitent Burman, like thousands in America, almost, but not altogether persuaded to be Christians, postponed what he could not but purpose to a more convenient season.

On another occasion, so many persons of high rank expressed themselves favorably to the Christian faith that one who had not hitherto ventured to defend the missionaries in the presence of the king was bold enough to say, "Nearly all the world, your Majesty, believe in an eternal God; all but Burmah and Siam these little spots!" His Majesty remained silent, and soon abruptly rose and retired.

Before returning to Rangoon Mr. Judson had an interesting interview with the king. "Why," asked the latter, "does the teacher return to Rangoon? let him and

Price stay together. If one goes, the other must remain alone, and will be unhappy." Some one present explained that he was going for his wife and goods, and would soon return. His Majesty said, "Will you then come again?" and expressed a wish that he should do so and remain permanently. He and Dr. Price had previously erected a house near Ava on some land granted them by the king, which house was to be occupied by Dr. P. until Mr. Judson's return.

The following letter from Mr. Judson dated Dec. 7, 1823, announces the arrival of his wife in Rangoon. "I had the inexpressible happiness of welcoming Mrs. Judson once more to the shores of Burmah, on the 5th instant. We are now on the eve of departure for Ava.

"My last letter from brother Price mentions that the king has inquired many times about my delay, and the queen has expressed a strong desire to see Mrs. Judson in her foreign dress. We sincerely hope her majesty's curiosity will not be confined to dress.

"Mr. and Mrs. Wade appear to be in fine health and spirits, and I am heartily rejoiced at their arrival just at the present time."

Rumors of a war between the British and Burmans were growing more and more prevalent, and alas, proved but too well founded. From the very last letter written by Mrs. Judson before this most unhappy and disastrous war, we shall now make some extracts.

"Ava, February, 10, 1824.

"My Dear Parents and Sisters,

After nearly two years and a half wandering, you will be pleased to hear that I have at last arrived at home, so far as this life is concerned, and am once more quietly and happily settled with Mr. Judson. When I retrace the scenes through which I have passed, the immense space I have traversed, and the various dangers, seen and unseen, from which I have been preserved, my heart is filled with gratitude and praise to that Being, who has at all times been my protector and marked out all my way before me.

We had a quick and pleasant passage from Calcutta to Rangoon, and in seven days after our arrival there we were on our way to this place. Our progress up the river was slow indeed. The season however is cool and delightful, we were preserved from dangers by day and robbers by night, and arrived in safety in six weeks. The

Irrawaddy is a noble river; we often walked through the villages on its banks, and though we never received the least insult, we always attracted universal attention. A foreign female was a sight never before beheld, and all were anxious that their friends and relations should have a view. Crowds followed us through the villages, and some less civilized than the others, would run some way before us, in order to have a *long* look as we approached them." ... After relating a conversation with the natives on the subject of religion, and a narrow escape from drowning; she comes to their arrival at Ava, where they had difficulties such as she had never before experienced. Dr. Price urged their going immediately to the house he had just erected; but it was of brick, and the walls still so damp that they did not dare occupy it. She says, "We had but one alternative, and that was to remain in the boat till they could build a small house on the piece of ground which the king gave to Mr. J. last year. And you will hardly believe it possible, for I almost doubt my senses, that in just a fortnight from our arrival, we moved into a house built in that time, which is large enough to make us comfortable. It is in a most delightful situation, out of the dust of the town and on the bank of the river.... Our house is in a healthy situation, is raised four feet from the ground, and consists of three small rooms and a verandah.

We hardly know how we shall bear the hot season which is just commencing, for our house is built of boards, and before night is heated like an oven. Nothing but brick is a shelter from the heat at Ava, where the thermometer even in the shade frequently rises to 108 degrees. We have worship every evening in Burman, when a number of the natives assemble, and every Sabbath Mr. Judson preaches the other side of the river in Dr. Price's house. We feel it an inestimable privilege that amid all our discouragements we have the language, and are able constantly to communicate truths which can save the soul."

She then mentions that she has commenced a female school with three little girls, two of them given her by their parents, fine children, who improve very rapidly, and that she has a prospect of more pupils. They did not immediately visit the palace, as the royal family were absent on a visit at Amarapoora, their old capital, where they were to remain until the new palace in Ava should be finished. She found her old friend the viceroy's wife now degraded by the death of her husband to a low rank, but a sensible woman, and more capable, Mrs. J. thought, of receiving religious truth than when in public life. She adds that in consequence of war with the Bengal government, foreigners are not in as much esteem at court as formerly--even Americans shared the same disfavor as Englishmen, for being similar in features, dress, language and religion, it is not surprising that the Burmans should have confounded them as subjects of one government. From the circumstance of money being remitted to them through English residents in Ava, they were even suspected of being paid spies of the East India Company--but this was at a somewhat later period.

* * * * *

The capital of Burmah is not fixed, but changes with the caprice of the monarch, for wherever he fixes his imperial residence, there, for the time, is the capital. Ava, the former capital, having been forsaken during the reign of the old king for Amarapoora, was again to be the royal residence, and for this purpose a magnificent palace had been there erected, of which the emperor was now to take possession. On these occasions, all the gorgeousness of oriental magnificence has its full display. Such a scene the missionaires witnessed soon after their arrival at Ava. Mrs. Judson gives an animated description of that splendid day, when majesty with all its attendant glory entered the gates of the golden city, and amid the acclamations of millions, took possession of the palace. The numerous horses, the immense variety of vehicles, the vast number and size of richly caparisoned elephants, the myriads of people in their gala dresses, the highest officers in the kingdom drawn from the most distant as well as the nearer provinces to grace the occasion, each in his robes of state, the magnificent white elephant, caparisoned with silk and velvet, and blazing with jewels, the king and queen, in simple majesty, alone unadorned amid the gaudy throng, surpassed any pageant ever exhibited in the western world. Alas! this pomp and pride were soon to receive a disastrous humiliation.

CHAPTER XVI.

WAR WITH THE BRITISH.--NARRATIVE OF THE SUFFERINGS OF THE MISSIONARIES DURING THE WAR.

In 1824 news reached America of the breaking out of war between Burmah and British India. This of course excited the most anxious interest for the fate of the Americans in that country. At length anxiety was somewhat relieved by the intelligence that Messrs. Wade and Hough with their families, who had remained at Rangoon, were, after dreadful sufferings, safe under British protection. But over the fate of Mr. and Mrs. Judson hung the silence of death, or of a suspense worse than death, for more than two years, until hope itself died in the hearts of their friends and kindred.

But although in this long period of doubt and darkness, busy fancy had pictured many scenes of terror and many forms of violent death, as the possible lot of the missionaries; yet in her wildest nights she never could have conceived of the terrible reality which they endured, not for days and weeks only, but for *eighteen* weary months. The wildest tale of fiction has never depicted more cruel anguish, more appalling suffering borne with more heroic energy, and more sublime fortitude--the wildest fiction would not dare to portray woman's love and faith and Christian hope, so long triumphant over insult and outrage, and torture and death itself. Who after reading the following narrative of an heroic female's unparalleled endurance, will ever say that woman's is a feeble nature, incapable of withstanding the rude shocks of adverse fortune? Nay, who will not rather say, that in woman, hope and faith, and fortitude and energy, make even the frail ***body*** immortal, till her labor of love is accomplished, and its cherished object is rescued from peril?

* * * * *

"The war which now broke out between the Burman government and that of the English in Bengal, forms an important era in the history of the mission.

"Its first effect was to put an end to the labors of the missionaries, and involve them in unspeakable sufferings, yet in accordance with a mysterious though beneficent law of human affairs, its ultimate issues have proved favorable not only to the interests of that particular mission, but also to the further extension of Christian civilization among the thickly peopled countries of Eastern India. The war had its origin in feuds which had long existed on the frontiers of Chittagong." Some Burman criminals had escaped to that territory, where as it was alleged they were protected by British power. The Burman monarch determined to chastise the English by making war on their government, and had raised thirty thousand troops under the command of his greatest warrior Bandula; but the East India Company anticipated his movements, and landed their forces at Rangoon so suddenly and unexpectedly, that the city fell into their hands with scarcely a show of resistance. This was the first news that reached Ava of the commencement of hostilities. It surprised the court there, but by no means alarmed them. Never having come into collision with the English, and having the most extravagant conceit of their own invincibility, they did not for a moment doubt their power to drive the invaders from their country; and even sent by one of their generals a pair of golden fetters with which to chain the governor-general, and bring him captive to Ava.

The first effect of the intelligence of the war upon the situation of the missionaries, was an order that no man wearing a hat should enter the palace. This was somewhat startling, still nothing of importance occurred for several weeks, during which Mrs. J. continued her school, while her husband went on building a house. But at length suspicion having been excited that the Englishmen who resided in Ava were spies, they were seized and put in confinement. Dr. Price and Mr. Judson were strictly examined also, but nothing being proved against them, they were left at liberty. They might probably have escaped further molestation, had it not been found in examining the accounts of one of the Englishmen, that he had paid over considerable money to the missionaries. Ignorant of money transactions as carried on by foreigners, this was an evidence to the natives, that the teachers were in the pay of the British, and probably spies. This being represented to the king, he gave an angry order for their arrest.

On the 8th of June, Mr. Judson's house was rudely entered by an officer, followed by eight or ten men, one of whom, by the hideous tattooing on his face, they knew to be the executioner, or 'son of the prison.' On seeing Mr. Judson--"You are called by the king," said the officer, the usual form of arrest. In an instant the spotted-faced man threw him on the floor, and drew forth that instrument of torture, the small cord. Mrs. Judson tried in vain to bribe him with money. "Take her too," said the officer, "she also is a foreigner." But this order Mr. Judson prevailed on them to disregard. All was now confusion and dismay, the children crying, the neighbors collecting around and in the house, while the executioner bound Mr. Judson with the cords, and took a fiendish pleasure in making them as tight as possible. Mrs. Judson gave Moung Ing money that he might follow and procure a mitigation of this torture, instead of which, Mr. Judson was again thrown down, and the cords so tightened as almost to prevent respiration. Then he was hurried on to the court-house, thence to "the death prison," into which he was hurled, and Moung Ing saw him no more.

We may imagine the intolerable agony of Mrs. Judson when the faithful disciple returned with the sad news of his master's fate. Retiring to her room, she tried to find consolation in casting her dreadful burden of fear and suspense on her covenant God. But soon her retirement was invaded by the magistrate of the place, who ordered her to come out and submit to an examination. Of course she was obliged to obey, but before doing so she destroyed every writing she possessed, letters, journals, everything, lest her correspondence with her British friends should confirm the suspicions of their persecutors. When the magistrate had satisfied himself with the examination, he placed a guard of ten ruffians about the house, with orders that no one should enter or leave it on pain of death.

Taking her four little Burman girls into an inner room she barred the door, and obstinately refused to come out, although the guard, bent on tormenting her, threatened to break the door down if she did not. She prevented this outrage by a threat to complain of their conduct in the morning to higher authorities, but in revenge they bound her two Bengalee servants fast in the stocks in a most painful posture. By bribes and promises she at length induced them to release the servants;

but their dreadful carousings, and horrid language, combined with her suspense in regard to her husband's fate, rendered that long night one of unmitigated wretchedness.

In the morning, Moung Ing, whom she had sent to the prison, returned with the intelligence that all the white foreigners were in the death-prison chained with three pairs of fetters each to a pole, to prevent their moving! "The point of anguish now was," she says, "that I was a prisoner myself, and could make no efforts for their relief." She earnestly but vainly begged the magistrate to allow her to go and state the case to some government officer; she even wrote a letter to the queen's sister, who was civil, but afraid to interfere in their behalf. "The day," she says, "wore heavily away, and another dreadful night was before me. I endeavored to soften the feelings of the guard, by giving them tea and segars for the night; so that they allowed me to remain inside my room, without threatening as they did the night before." But, haunted by the idea of her dear husband's tortures, which she was neither permitted to share nor alleviate, she of course passed another night of anguish.

The next day she sent a message to the governor of the city, to allow her to visit him with a present. This was successful, and the guards had orders to permit her to go into town. She was pleasantly received, stated the situation of the teachers, and assured the governor that being not Englishmen but Americans, they had nothing to do with the war. She was referred to a head officer with whom she might consult as to the means of making the prisoners more comfortable; **but their release was out of the question**. The first sight of this officer, whose face exhibited the working of every evil passion, inspired her with dread, but he was the only one who could assist her. "He took me aside, and endeavored to convince me that myself, as well as the prisoners, was entirely at his disposal--that our future comfort must depend on my liberality in regard to presents--and that these must be made in a private way, and unknown to any officer of government! What must I do, said I, to obtain a mitigation of the sufferings of the two teachers? 'Pay to me,' said he, 'two hundred tickals, (about a hundred dollars,) two pieces of fine cloth, and two pieces of handkerchiefs.' At length however he consented to take what money she had about her, which was a considerable sum, and promised to relieve the teachers from their most painful situation. She goes on:

"I then procured an order from the governor for my admittance into the prison, but the sensation produced by meeting my husband in that **wretched, horrid** situation, and the scene that ensued, I shall not attempt to describe. He crawled to the door of the prison--for I was never allowed to enter--gave me some directions relative to his release; but before we could make any arrangement, I was ordered to depart by those iron-hearted jailers, who could not endure to see us enjoy the poor consolation of meeting in that miserable place. In vain I pleaded the order of the governor for my admittance; they again harshly repeated, 'Depart, or we will pull you out.'" The same evening all the foreigners succeeded, by the payment of money, in being removed from the common prison to an open shed, where Mrs. Judson was allowed to send them food, and mats to sleep on, but for some days was not permitted to see them.

Nothing but her own eloquent words can do justice to the transactions that followed. We copy as before from her letter, written two years subsequent to these events, to her brother-in-law, Dr. Judson.

"My next object was to get a petition presented to the queen, but no person being admitted into the palace who was in disgrace with his majesty, I sought to present it through the medium of her brother's wife. I had visited her in better days, and received particular marks of her favor. But now, times were altered, Mr. Judson was in prison, and I in distress, which was a sufficient reason for giving me a cold reception. I took a present of considerable value. She was lolling on her carpet as I entered, with her attendants around her. I waited not for the usual question to a suppliant, 'What do you want?' but in a bold, earnest yet respectful manner, stated our distresses and our wrongs, and begged her assistance. She partly raised her head, opened the present I had brought, and coolly replied, 'Your case is not singular; all the foreigners are treated alike.' But it *is* singular, said I, the teachers are Americans; they are ministers of religion, have nothing to do with war or politics, and came to Ava in obedience to the king's command. They have never done anything to deserve such treatment; and is it right they should be treated thus? 'The king does as he pleases,' said she, 'I am not the king, what can I do?' You can state their case to the queen and obtain their release, replied I. Place yourself in my situation--were you in America, your husband, innocent of crime, thrown into prison, in irons, and you a solitary, unprotected female--what would you do? With a slight degree of feeling, she said, 'I will present your petition; come again to-morrow. I returned to the house, with considerable hope that the speedy release of the missionaries was at hand. But the next day, the property of Mr. Gouger, (one of the Englishmen,) amounting to 25,000 dollars, was seized and carried to the palace. The officers on their return, politely informed me, that they should ***visit our house*** on the morrow. I felt obliged for this information, and accordingly made preparations to receive them by secreting as many little articles as possible; together with considerable silver; as I knew if the war should be protracted, we should be in a state of starvation without it. But my mind was in a dreadful state of agitation, lest it should be discovered, and cause my being thrown into prison. And had it been possible to procure money from any other quarter, I should not have ventured on such a step.

"The following morning, the royal treasurer, the governor of the north gate of the palace, who was in future our steady friend, and another nobleman, attended by forty or fifty followers, came to take possession of all we had. I treated them civilly, gave them seats, and tea and sweetmeats for their refreshment; and justice obliges me to say, that they conducted the business of confiscation, with more regard to my feelings than I should have thought it possible for Burmese officers to exhibit. The three officers with one of the royal secretaries alone entered the house; their attendants were ordered to remain outside. They saw I was deeply affected, and apologized for what they were about to do, by saying that it was painful for them to take possession of property not their own, but they were compelled thus to do by order of the king. "Where is your silver, gold, and jewels?" said the royal treasurer. I have no gold or jewels, but here is the key of a trunk which contains the silver--do with it as you please. The trunk was produced, and the silver weighed. This money, said I, was collected in America by the disciples of Christ, and sent here for the purpose of building a kyoung, (the name of a priest's dwelling;) and for our support while teaching the religion of Christ. Is it suitable that you should take it? (The Burmans are averse to taking religious offerings, which was the cause of my making the inquiry.) "We will state this circumstance to the king," said one of them, "and perhaps he will restore it. But is this all the silver you have?" I could not tell a falsehood. The house is in your possession, I replied, search for yourselves. "Have you not deposited silver with some person of your acquaintance?" My acquaintances are all in prison, with whom should I deposit silver? They next ordered my trunk and drawers to be examined. The secretary only was allowed to accompany me in this search. Everything nice or curious which met his view, was presented to the officers for their decision whether it should be taken or retained. I begged they would not take our wearing apparel, as it would be disgraceful to take clothes partly worn into the possession of his majesty, and to us they were of unspeakable value. They assented, and took a list only; and did the same with the books, medicines, &c. My little work-table and rocking-chair, presents from my beloved brother, I rescued from their grasp, partly by artifice, and partly through their ignorance. They left also many articles which were of inestimable value during our long imprisonment."

CHAPTER XVII.

NARRATIVE CONTINUED, AND CONCLUDED.--THEIR DELIVERANCE FROM BURMAN TYRANNY, AND PROTECTION BY THE BRITISH GOVERNMENT.

As soon as the search was completed, Mrs. Judson hastened to the wife of the queen's brother, in hopes of having a favorable answer to her petition; but to her heavy disappointment she learned that the queen had refused to interfere. With a sad heart she turned her steps to the prison-gate, but here she was denied admittance, and for ten days she found the prison-door closed against her.

"The officers who had taken possession of our property," continues Mrs. Judson, "presented it to his majesty, saying, 'Judson is a true teacher; we found nothing in his house but what belongs to priests. In addition to this money, there are an immense number of books, medicines, trunks of wearing apparel, &c., of which we have only taken a list. Shall we take them or let them remain?' 'Let them remain,' said the king, 'and put this property by itself, for it shall be restored to him again, if he be found innocent.' This was in allusion to the idea of his being a spy."

While the officers were at Mr. J.'s house, they had insisted on knowing the sum that had been paid to bribe the governor to allow the prisoners more liberty. This sum they afterwards demanded of the governor, which so enraged him that he threatened to thrust them back into the inner prison. When Mrs. J. waited on him the next morning, his first words were, "You are very bad; why did you tell the royal treasurer you had given me so much money?" "The treasurer inquired, what could I say?" she replied. "Say that you had given me nothing," said he, "and I would have made the teachers comfortable in prison; but now I know not what will be their fate." "But I cannot tell a falsehood," she replied; "my religion differs from yours; it forbids prevarication, and had you stood by me with your knife raised, I could not have said what you suggest."

This answer so pleased the wife of the governor, who sat by, that she ever afterwards was a firm friend to Mrs. Judson. The latter then by the present of a beautiful opera-glass, a gift from her English friends, and by promises of future presents, induced the governor to let her husband remain where he was; but poor Dr. Price was confined as at first, and was only relieved at the end of ten days, by his promising a piece of broadcloth, and presents from Mrs. Judson.

Sometimes she was summoned before the authorities to answer the most absurd charges, and daily she was subjected to the most harassing annoyance, from the desire of each petty officer to get money through their misfortunes. Notwithstanding her repulse in her application to the queen, hardly a day passed for seven months that she did not visit some one of the members of government, or branches of the royal family, in order to gain their influence in behalf of the teachers, though the only benefit was that their encouraging promises preserved her from despair. She did however in this manner gain friends, who sometimes assisted her with food, and who tried to destroy the impression that they were concerned in the war.

The extortions and oppressions to which the prisoners were subject were also indescribable. Sometimes Mrs. Judson was forbidden to have any intercourse with them during the day; and therefore she would have two miles to walk after dark, in returning to her house. She says, "Oh how many, many times have I returned from that dreary prison at nine o'clock at night, solitary and worn out with fatigue and anxiety, and thrown myself down in that same rocking-chair you and Deacon S. provided for me in Boston, and endeavored to invent some new scheme for the release of the prisoners. Sometimes, for a moment or two, my thoughts would glance toward America and my beloved friends there, out *for nearly a year and a half, so entirely engrossed was every thought with present scenes and sufferings, that I seldom reflected on a single occurrence of my former life, or recollected that I had a friend in existence out of Ava*.

"You my dear brother, who know my strong attachment to my friends, and how much pleasure I have hitherto experienced from retrospect, can judge from the above circumstance, how intense were my sufferings. But the point, the acme of my distress, consisted in the awful uncertainty of our final fate. My prevailing opinion was, that my husband would suffer violent death; and that I should of course become a slave, and languish out a miserable though short existence, in the tyrannic hands of some unfeeling monster. But the consolations of religion in these trying circumstances, were neither few nor small. It taught me to look beyond this world, to that rest, that peaceful, happy rest, where Jesus reigns, and oppression never enters."

In the meantime, the Burmese government was sending army after army down the river to fight the English; and constantly receiving news of their defeat and destruction. One of its officers, however, named Bandoola, having been more successful, the king sent for him to Ava, and conferred on him the command of a very large army, destined against Rangoon. As he was receiving every demonstration of court favor, Mrs. Judson resolved to wait on him with a petition for the release of the prisoners. She was received in an obliging manner, and directed to call again when he should have deliberated on the subject. With the joyful news of her flattering reception, she flew to the prison, and both she and her husband thought deliverance was at hand. But on going again with a handsome present to hear his decision, she was informed by his lady--her lord being absent--that he was now very busy, making preparations for Rangoon, but that when he had retaken that city, ***and expelled the English***, he would return and release all the prisoners.

This was her last application for their enlargement, though she constantly visited the various officials with presents in order to make the situation of the prisoners more tolerable. The governor of the palace used to be so much gratified with her accounts of the manners, customs and government of America, that he required her to spend many hours of every other day at his house.

Mrs. Judson had been permitted to make for her husband a little bamboo room in the prison enclosure far more comfortable than the shed he had occupied and where she sometimes was allowed to spend a few hours in his society. But her visits both to the prison and to the governor were interrupted by the birth of a little daughter--truly

'A child of misery, baptized in tears!'

About this time the Burmese court was thrown into consternation by news of the disastrous defeat of Bandoola, the vain-glorious chief who was to expel the English from the kingdom; and the rapid advance of the British troops towards

Ava. The first consequence of such intelligence would of course be increased rigor towards the white prisoners; and accordingly, before she had regained her strength after her confinement, Mrs. Judson learned that her husband had been put into the inner prison, in five pairs of fetters, that the room she had made for him had been torn down, and all his little comforts taken away by his jailers. All the prisoners had been similarly treated.

Mrs. Judson, feeble as she was, hastened to the governor's house. But in her long absence she had lost favor; and she was told that she must not ask to have the fetters taken off, or the prisoners released, for *it could not be done*. She made a pathetic appeal to the governor, who was an old man, reminding him of all his former kindness to them, and begging to know why his conduct was so changed to them now. His hard heart melted and he even "wept like a child." He then confessed to her that he had often been ordered to assassinate the prisoners privately, but that he would not do it; and that, come what would, he would never put Mr. Judson to death. At the same time he was resolute in refusing to attempt any mitigation of his sufferings.

The situation of the prisoners was now horrible in the extreme. There were more than one hundred of them shut up in one room, with no air but what came through cracks in the boards, and this in the hot season. Mrs. Judson was sometimes permitted to spend five minutes at the door, but the sight was almost too horrible to be borne. By incessant intreaties, she obtained permission for them to eat their food outside, but even this was soon forbidden. After a month passed in this way, Mr. Judson was seized with fever, and nothing but death was before him unless he could have more air. Mrs. Judson at length succeeded in putting up another bamboo hut in the prison enclosure, and by wearing out the governor with her entreaties, she got her husband removed into it, and though too low for them to stand upright, it seemed to them a palace in comparison with the prison.

Disastrous news of the war continued to arrive, and at length the death of Bandoola seemed to be the climax of misfortune. Who could be found to take his place? A government officer, who had for some time been in disgrace with the king, now came forward with a proposal to conquer the English and put an end to the war, provided an army was raised on a new plan. His offers were accepted, and he was clothed with full powers. He was a man of talent and enterprise, and a violent enemy to foreigners. The missionaries feared everything from his malignancy; and their fears were but too well founded.

They had been in their comfortable hut but a few days, when Mrs. J. was suddenly summoned before the governor, and detained by trifling pretexts for some time, in order--as she afterwards found--to spare her the dreadful scene that was enacted at the prison in her absence. On leaving him she met a servant running to tell her that all the white prisoners were carried away he knew not whither. She ran from street to street inquiring for them, until at length she was informed they were carried to Amarapoora. She hastened to the governor, who professed his ignorance, but promised to send off a man to inquire their fate; and said significantly, "You can do nothing more for your husband; *take care of yourself*." She returned to her room, and sank down almost in despair. This was the most insupportable day she had passed. She resolved to go to Amarapoora; packed up some valuables in trunks to leave with the governor; and took leave of Ava, as she supposed, forever. She obtained a pass for herself and infant, her two Burman girls and cook, and got on board a boat, which conveyed them within two miles of Amarapoora. There she procured a cart, but the heat and dust, with the fatigue of carrying her infant, almost deprived her of reason. But on reaching the court-house, her distress was further aggravated, by finding that she must go four miles farther to a place called Oung-pen-la. There in an old shattered building, without a roof, under the burning sun, sat the poor prisoners, chained two and two, and almost in a dying condition. She prevailed on the jailer to give her a shelter in a wretched little room half filled with grain, and in that filthy place, without bed, chair, table, or any other comfort, she spent the next *six months* of wretchedness.

The account given her by Mr. Judson of his sufferings since she had seen him was almost too dreadful to repeat. Dragged from the prison, and stripped of their clothing, they were driven under a broiling sun, over the hot sand and gravel until their naked feet were all one wound, and they earnestly longed for death to put an end to their tortures. When night came on, finding that one of the prisoners had dropped dead, and that the others were utterly unable to walk, their driver had halted till the next morning, and then conveyed them the remainder of the distance in carts. On arriving and seeing the dilapidated condition of the prison, they confidently thought they had been brought here for execution, and tried to prepare themselves to meet a dreadful and perhaps lingering death. From this apprehension they were relieved by seeing preparations made to repair the prison.

Mrs. Judson had brought from Ava all the money she could command, secreted about her person. And she records her thankfulness to her Heavenly Father that she never suffered from want of money, though frequently from want of provisions. Hitherto her health and that of her children had been good. But now commenced her personal, bodily sufferings. One of the little Burman girls whom she had adopted, and whom she had named Mary Hasseltine, was attacked on the morning after her arrival with small-pox. She had been Mrs. Judson's only assistant in the care of her infant. But now she required all the time that could be spared from Mr. Judson, whose mangled feet rendered him utterly unable to move. Mrs. Judson's whole time was spent in going back and forth from the prison to the house with her little Maria in her arms. Knowing that the other children must have the disease, she inoculated both, and those of the jailer, all of whom had it lightly except her poor babe, with whom the inoculation did not take, and who had it the natural way. Before this she had been a healthy child but it was more than three months before she recovered from the dreadful disorder.

The beneficial effects of inoculation in the case of the jailer's children, caused Mrs. Judson to be called upon to perform the operation upon all the children in the village. Mr. Judson gradually recovered, and found his situation much more comfortable than at Ava. But Mrs. Judson, overcome by watchings, fatigue, miserable food, and still more miserable lodgings, was attacked by one of the disorders of the country; and though much debilitated, was obliged to set off in a cart for Ava to procure medicines and suitable food. While there, her disorder increased so fearfully in violence, that she gave up all hope of recovery, and was only anxious to return and die near the prison. By the use of laudanum she so far checked the disease, that she was able to get back to Oung-pen-la, but in such a state that the cook whom she had left to supply her place, and who came to help her out of the wretched cart in which she had made part of the journey, was so overwhelmed by her altered and emaciated appearance that he burst into tears. To this poor cook she was indebted, during the next two months for everything, and even for her life and that of those dearest to her. He would walk miles to procure and carry food for the prisoners, then return to do everything he could for Mrs. J. Though a Bengalee, he forgot his caste, and hesitated not at any office or service which was required of him. It was afterwards in their power amply to reward him for his labor of love, and they never forgot their debt of gratitude.

At this time poor little Maria was the greatest sufferer, and her mother's anguish at seeing her distress while she was unable to relieve it, was indescribable. Deprived of her natural food by her mother's illness, while not a drop of milk could be procured in the village, her cries were heart-rending. Sometimes Mr. Judson would prevail on his keepers to let him carry the emaciated little creature around in his arms, to beg nourishment from those mothers in the village who had young children. Now indeed was the cup of misery full. While in health, the active, ardent mind of Mrs. Judson bore up under trials, every new one suggesting some ingenious expedient to lighten or avert it; but now to see those cherished ones suffering, and be herself confined by sickness, was almost too much to bear.

It was about this time they learned the death of their enemy, whose elevation to power was the cause of their removal from Ava, and whose purpose in sending them to Oung-pen-la, was indeed their destruction. Suspected of high-treason, and of embezzling public money, he was executed without a moments delay. Another officer was appointed to command the army, but with far less sanguine expectations of success. After his death, the prisoners were released from the prison, and conducted to Ava. The cause of the change was soon evident. Mr. Judson was wanted to act as interpreter between the Burmese government and the advancing army of the British. For six weeks he was kept in Maloun, steadily at work in translating, and suffering as much as when in prison except that he was not in irons. Mrs. Judson, who had remained at Ava, was seized soon after he left her with spotted fever of the most malignant character. She lost her reason, and for a long time was insensible to everything around her. But she records with lively gratitude, that just before her senses left her, a Portuguese woman had unexpectedly come and offered herself as nurse to her little daughter; and about the same time, Dr. Price, being released from prison, visited her. He represents her situation to have been the most distressing he ever witnessed, and he had no idea she could survive many hours. At one time a Burmese neighbor, who had come in with others to see her die, said "She is dead; and if the King of angels were to come in, he could not recover her." Her head was shaved, blisters were applied to it and to her feet, and she gradually revived; although the fever having run seventeen days, she was of course a long time in recovering.

While in this debilitated state, she learned through her servant that his master had arrived in town, under the charge of several Burmans, and that it was reported that he was to be sent back to the Oung-pen-la prison. Being too weak to bear ill tidings, the shock had well nigh destroyed her. When she had in some measure recovered her composure, she sent Moung Ing to her old friend, the governor of the north gate, begging him to make one more effort for Mr. Judson. Moung Ing then went in search of 'the teacher,' and at length found him in an obscure prison. Her feelings while he was gone, Mrs. Judson thus describes:

"If ever I felt the value and efficacy of prayer, I did at this time. I could not rise from my couch; I could make no efforts to secure my husband; I could only plead with that great and powerful Being who has said, 'Call upon me in the day of trouble and *I will hear*, and thou shalt glorify me;' and who made me at this time feel so powerfully this promise, that I became quite composed, feeling assured that my prayers would be answered."

She afterwards learned that as soon as Mr. Judson was found of no farther use at Maloun as interpreter he was transferred without ceremony to Ava, where happening to meet no one who knew him, he was ordered to be taken whence he came, when he went to Maloun, viz: Oung-pen-la. But at the instance of, Mrs. Judson's faithful messenger, Moung Ing, the governor of the north gate presented a petition to the high court of the empire, became security for Mr. J., obtained his release, took him to his house, and removed Mrs. Judson thither also as soon as her health permitted.

The English army, which had all along offered peace on condition of the payment of a certain sum of money, offers which the Burmans had constantly rejected, had now advanced so far as to threaten the golden city itself. The Burmans were thus compelled to negotiate, and all their negotiations from beginning to end, "were conducted by Drs. Judson and Price, though they were often interrupted or entirely broken off by the caprice and jealousy of the Burman monarch and his officers." The king placing no confidence in the English, and having the most absurd ideas of his power to force them to his own terms, sent messengers at every stage of their advance to induce Sir Archibald Campbell to abate his demands and alter his conditions. No pains was spared to fortify the golden city, even while Dr. Price and other English prisoners were engaged in the business of negotiation. Mrs. Judson had the pain of seeing their house without beautiful enclosure of fruits and flowers, entirely destroyed, to make a place for the erection of cannon.

A new message now arrived from Sir Archibald. No smaller sum than the one stipulated, (about five million dollars) would be received, but it might be paid at four different times; the first payment to be made within twelve days, or the army would continue its march. In addition, the prisoners were to be given up immediately. The king, who had learned the value of Mr. Judson's services, declared that those foreigners who were not English, were his people, and should not go. The missionaries were ordered to go again to the English camp, to propose to them to take a third of the money and give up their demand for the missionaries; and threatened that if unsuccessful in their embassy, they and their families should suffer.

Their situation was now truly perilous, for the Burman arrogance was at this time heightened by the boast of one of their generals, that he would so fortify the ancient city of Pugan, which lay in the route of the British toward Ava, that they could never advance beyond it; and that in fact he would destroy or drive them from the country. The invincible English took the city, however, with perfect ease; and the king being enraged that he had listened for a moment to the braggart, and thus provoked the British officers, had him executed without ceremony, and gave out that it was to punish him for violating his command 'not to fight the English.' The same night, Dr. Price was sent with part of the money, and some of the prisoners, but returned with the alarming intelligence, that the general was angry, would not communicate with him, and was marching upon Ava.

All was now confusion in the palace; gold and silver vessels were melted up, and the money weighed out; and Mr. Judson was hurried into a boat, and sent to the British camp. He was instructed by the English general that every foreigner who *wished* to leave the country, must be permitted to go, or peace would not be made. The members of government now had recourse to solicitation, and promised to make Mr. Judson a great man if he would remain. To avoid the oduim of expressing a wish to leave his majesty's service, he told them that Sir Archibald had ordered that all who desired it, should go; that his wife had often expressed that desire, that she therefore must be given up, and that he must follow. The prisoners were then all released, and on a cool moonlight evening, with hearts overflowing with gratitude and joy, they took their passage down the Irrawady, bidding a final adieu to the scene of their sufferings, the *golden* city of Ava.

With what delight did they the next morning hail the sight of the steamboat that was to conduct them to the British camp. "With what unspeakable satisfaction did they again find themselves surrounded by the comforts and refinements of civilized life." The kindness of General Campbell was more like that of a father to his own family, than that of a stranger to persons of another country. Indeed it was to him they owed their final release from Ava, and the recovery of all their confiscated property. Mrs. Judson thinks no people on earth were ever happier than they were at that time; the very idea that they were free from Burman treachery and tyranny, and under British protection, filling them with gratitude and joy too exquisite for expression. "What shall we render to the Lord for all his benefits to us," was the constant utterance of their hearts. Peace was soon settled; they left the camp, and after an absence of two years and three months were again in Rangoon.

CHAPTER XVIII.

INFLUENCE OF THESE DISASTERS ON THE MISSIONARY ENTERPRISE.--TESTIMONIALS TO MRS. JUDSON'S HEROIC CONDUCT.--LETTER FROM MR. JUDSON--HIS ACCEPTANCE OF THE POST OF INTERPRETER TO CRAWFORD'S EMBASSY.--MRS. JUDSON'S RESIDENCE AT AMHERST.--HER ILLNESS AND DEATH--DEATH OF HER INFANT.

Mrs. Judson concludes her long, melancholy, but most interesting letter to her brother, as follows: "A review of our trip to and adventures in Ava, suggests the inquiry, Why were we permitted to go? What good has been effected? Why did I not listen to the advice of friends in Bengal and remain till the war was concluded? But all that we can say is-- ***It is not in man that walketh to direct his steps***.--So far as my going round to Rangoon at the time I did, was instrumental in bringing those heavy afflictions upon us, I can only state that if ever I acted from a sense of duty in my life, it was at that time; for my conscience would not allow me any peace, when I thought of sending for your brother to Calcutta, in prospect of the approaching war. Our society at home have lost no property on account of our difficulties; but two years of precious time have been lost to the mission unless some future advantage may be gained, in consequence of the severe discipline to which we ourselves have been subject. We are sometimes induced to think that the lesson we have found so very hard to learn will have a beneficial effect through our lives; and that the mission may in the end, be advanced rather than retarded."

In reference to this timid and hesitating hope of some benefit which ***might possibly*** accrue to the cause of missions, from her terrible experience, the remarks of Dr. Dowling in a recent work, are so appropriate, that we will introduce them here. "Previous to the commencement of these sufferings, though a few American Baptists were partially awake to the salvation of the heathen, ... yet the contributions for the mission were meagre, and the interest it had excited was comparatively small. Something of a thrilling, exciting character was needed to arouse the churches from their indifference and lethargy; something that should touch their hearts, by showing them somewhat of the nature and extent of the sacrifices made by those devoted missionaries whom they were called upon to sustain by their benefactions and their prayers.

"Such a stimulus was afforded, when after two years of painful suspense, during which it was not known whether the missionaries were dead or alive, the touching recital of their unparalleled sufferings for Christ's sake, and of their wonderful deliverance, at length burst like an electric shock upon the American churches. And that shock has not yet spent its force, as we have recently seen in the effect produced by the simple, silent presence, in the assemblies of the saints, of the venerated man of God, who can say with an Apostle--'I bear in my body the scars of the Lord Jesus!'"[4]

That worn veteran had but to arise in a Christian assembly, and a thrill of sympathy was sent through the audience, and thousands upon thousands of dollars were pledged on the spot to that cause which his silent presence so powerfully advocated.

Another consequence of the war, was to secure British toleration and protection to a large territory, hitherto almost inaccessible to the missionaries. Of this we shall speak more fully hereafter.

Mrs. Judson proceeds: "We should have had no hesitation about remaining at Ava, if no part of the Burman empire had been ceded to the British. But as it was, we felt that it would be unnecessary exposure, besides the missionary field being more limited in consequence of intoleration. We now consider our future missionary prospects as bright indeed, and our only anxiety is to be once more in that situation when our time will be exclusively devoted to the instruction of the heathen.

... "This letter, dreadful as are the scenes herein described, gives you but a faint idea of the awful reality. The anguish, the agony of mind, resulting from a thousand

---

4 Alluding to Dr. Judson's visit to America.

little circumstances impossible to delineate on paper, can be known by those only who have been in similar situations. Pray for us, my dear brother and sister, that these heavy afflictions may not be in vain, but may be blessed to our spiritual good, and the advancement of Christ's Church among the heathen."

* * * * *

The following is extracted from a tribute to Mrs. Judson which appeared in a Calcutta paper, after the war. It was written by a fellow-prisoner of Mr. J.

"Mrs. Judson was the author of those eloquent and forcible appeals to the government, which prepared them by degrees for submission to terms of peace, never expected by any who knew the haughtiness and inflexible pride of the Burman court.

"And while on this subject, the overflowings of grateful feelings on behalf of myself and fellow-prisoners, compel me to add a tribute of public thanks to that amiable and humane female, who, though living at a distance of two miles from our prison, without any means of conveyance, and very feeble in health, forgot her own comfort and infirmity, and almost every day visited us, sought out and administered to our wants, and contributed in every way to alleviate our misery.

"When we were all left by the government destitute of food, she, with unwearied perseverance by some means or other, obtained for us a constant supply.

... "When the unfeeling avarice of our keepers confined us inside, or made our feet fast in the stocks, she, like a ministering angel, never ceased her applications to the government, until she was authorized to communicate to us the grateful news of our enlargement, or of a respite from our galling oppressions.

"Besides all this, it was unquestionably owing, in a chief degree, to the repeated eloquence and forcible appeals of Mrs. Judson, that the untutored Burman was finally made willing to secure the welfare of his country by a sincere peace."

Well may Professor Gammell write of her: "History has not recorded, poetry itself has seldom portrayed a more affecting exhibition of Christian fortitude, of female heroism, and of all the noble and generous qualities which constitute the dignity and glory of woman. In the midst of sickness and danger, and every calamity which can crush the human heart, she presented a character equal to the sternest trial, and an address and a fertility of resources which gave her an ascendency over the minds of her most cruel enemies, and alone saved the missionaries and their fellow-captives from the terrible doom which constantly awaited them."

We will conclude this account of the terrible ***two years***, by an extract from a letter of Mr. Judson dated Rangoon, March 25, 1826. "Through the kind interposition of our Heavenly Father, we have been preserved in the most imminent danger, from the hand of the executioner, and in repeated instances of most alarming illness, during my protracted imprisonment of one year and seven months, nine months in three pairs of fetters, two months in five, six months in one, and two months a prisoner at large.... The disciples and inquirers have been dispersed in all directions. Several are dead; Moung-Shwa-ba has been in the mission-house through the whole, and Moung Ing with Mrs. Judson at Ava.... I long for the time when we shall enjoy once more the stated worship and ordinances of the Lord's house."

"One result of the Burman war, was the acquisition by the British of several provinces previously under the government of the King of Burmah. Thus a safe asylum was provided for the missionaries, and for the Christian natives where they might worship God in peace, under the shelter of the English government." One of these provinces was fixed upon as the seat of the mission, and the new town of Amherst was to be the residence of the missionaries. Native Christian families began to assemble there, and Mrs. Judson made vigorous preparations to open a school. Mr. Crawford of the British Embassy after long solicitation, succeeded in persuading Mr. Judson, that by accompanying him in the capacity of interpreter to the court of Ava he might secure to the mission certain advantages he had long had greatly at heart, and he reluctantly consented to go. Leaving Mrs. Judson and her infant daughter in the house of the civil superintendent at Amherst, he proceeded to the Burman capital. The journey was every way unfortunate; attended with long delays, and in its result, as far as Mr. Judson was concerned, quite unsuccessful. But it was chiefly disastrous because it detained him from the sick and dying bed of that devoted wife to whom he was bound by every tie that can attach human hearts to each other; and compelled her to end her troubled pilgrimage ***alone***. That God who "moves in a mysterious way," had ordered it that she who had lived through appalling dangers and threatening deaths until her mission of love toward those she had cherished so fondly was accomplished, was--now that her trials seemed nearly ended, and the hopes of her heart seemingly in a train of accomplishment--suddenly called from the scene of her labors to that of her "exceeding great reward." It was as if a noble ship after encountering storms and tempests, after being often nearly wrecked, and as often saved almost by miracle, should when already in port and in sight of anxious spectators, suddenly sink forever.

In a letter to the corresponding secretary, dated Ava, Dec. 7, 1826, Mr. Judson writes: "The news of the death of my beloved wife, has not only thrown a gloom over all my future prospects, but has forever embittered the recollection of the present journey, in consequence of which I have been absent from her dying bed, and prevented from affording the spiritual comfort which her lonely circumstances peculiarly required, and of contributing to avert the fatal catastrophe, which has deprived me of one of the first of women, and best of wives. I commend myself and motherless child to your sympathy and prayers."

From a letter from Mr. Judson to Mrs. Hasseltine we learn, that when he parted from his wife, she was in good health and comfortably situated, with happy prospects of a new field of missionary labor, and the expectation of seeing her husband again in three or four months at farthest. His last letter from her was dated the 14th of September. She says, "I have this day moved into the new house, and for the first time since we were broken up at Ava, feel myself at home. The house is large and convenient, and if you were here I should feel quite happy.... Poor little Maria is still feeble.... When I ask her where Papa is, she always starts up and points toward the sea. The servants behave very well, and I have no trouble about anything except you and Maria. Pray take care of yourself.... May God preserve and bless you, and restore you again to your new and old home is the prayer of your affectionate Ann." Another letter from a friend confirmed the statement with regard to his wife's health, though it spoke unfavorably of that of the child. "But," continues Mr. Judson, "my next communication was a letter with a black seal, handed me by a person, saying he was sorry to inform me of the death of the child. I know not whether this was a mistake on his part, or kindly intended to prepare my mind for the real intelligence. I went to my room, and opened the letter with a feeling of gratitude and joy, that at any rate the mother was spared. It began thus: 'My dear Sir,--To one who has suffered so much and with such exemplary fortitude, there needs but little preface to tell a tale of distress. It were cruel indeed to torture you with doubt and suspense. To sum up the unhappy tidings in a few words-- **Mrs. Judson is no more**.' At intervals," continues Mr. Judson, "I got through the dreadful letter and proceed to give you the substance, as indelibly engraven on my heart." After adding that her disease was a violent fever, which baffled the skill of the physicians and after eighteen days carried her to the grave, he continues: "You perceive I have no account whatever of the state of her mind in view of death and eternity, or of her wishes concerning her darling babe, whom she loved most intensely. I will not trouble you, my dear mother, with an account of my own private feelings--the bitter, heart-rending anguish, which for some days would not admit of mitigation, and the comfort which the Gospel subsequently afforded, the Gospel of Jesus Christ which brings life and immortality to light."

After his return to Amherst, Mr. Judson writes: "Amid the desolation that death has made, I take up my pen to address once more the mother of my beloved Ann. I am sitting in the house she built--in the room where she breathed her last--and at a window from which I see the tree that stands at the head of her grave.... Mr. and Mrs. Wade are living in the house, having arrived here about a month after Ann's death, and Mrs. W. has taken charge of my poor motherless Maria.... When I arrived Mr. Wade met me at the landing-place, and as I passed on to the house, one and another of the native Christians came out, and when they saw me they began to weep. At length we reached the house; and I almost expected to see my love coming out to meet me as usual, but no, I only saw in the arms of Mrs. Wade, a poor puny child, who could not recognize her father, and from whose infant mind had long been erased all recollection of the mother who loved her so much. She turned away from me in alarm, and I, obliged to seek comfort elsewhere, found my way to the grave, but who ever obtained comfort there? Thence I went to the house in which I left her; and looked at the spot where last we knelt in prayer, and where we exchanged the parting kiss....

"It seems that her head was much affected and she said but little. She sometimes complained thus: 'The teacher is long in coming, and the missionaries are long in coming, I must die alone and leave my little one, but as it is the will of God, I acquiesce in his will. I am not afraid of death, but I am afraid I shall not be able to bear these pains. Tell the teacher that the disease was most violent, and I could not write; tell him how I suffered and died; tell him all you see.'... When she could not notice anything else, she would still call the child to her, and charge the nurse to be kind to it, and indulge it in everything till its father should return. The last day or two she lay almost senseless and motionless, on one side, her head reclining on her arm, her eyes closed, and at eight in the evening, with one exclamation of distress in the Burman language, she ceased to breathe."

From the physician who attended her he afterwards learned that the fatal termination of her disease, was chiefly owing to the weakness of her constitution occasioned by the severe privations, and long-protracted sufferings which she endured at Ava. "And oh!" adds her husband, "With what meekness, patience magnanimity and Christian fortitude, she bore those sufferings; and can I wish they had been less? Can I sacriligiously wish to rob her crown of a single gem? Much she saw and suffered of the evils of this evil world; and eminently was she qualified to relish and enjoy the pure and holy rest into which she has entered. True she has been taken from a sphere in which she was singularly qualified, by her natural disposition, her winning manners, her devoted zeal, and her perfect acquaintance with the language, to be extensively serviceable to the cause of Christ; true she has been torn from her husband's bleeding heart and from her darling babe; but infinite wisdom and love have presided, as ever, in this most afflicting dispensation. Faith decides that all is right."

To show that Mrs. Judson was already appreciated as she deserved by the European society in Amherst, we will subjoin part of a letter from Captain F. of that place to a friend in Rangoon: "I shall not attempt to give you an account of the gloom which the death of this amiable woman has thrown over our little society, you who were so well acquainted with her, will feel her loss more deeply; but we had just known her long enough to value her acquaintance as a blessing in this remote corner. I dread the effect it will have on poor Judson. I am sure you will take every care that this mournful intelligence may be opened to him as carefully as possible."

In the ***Calcutta Review*** of 1848, we find this noble tribute to her memory: "Of Mrs. Judson little is known in the noisy world. Few comparatively are acquainted with her name, few with her actions, but if any woman since the first arrival of the white strangers on the shores of India, has on that great theatre of war, stretching between the mouth of the Irrawady and the borders of the Hindoo Kush, rightly earned for herself the title of a heroine, Mrs. Judson has, by her doings and sufferings, fairly earned the distinction--a distinction, be it said, which her true woman's nature would have very little appreciated. Still it is right that she should be honored by the world. Her sufferings were far more unendurable, her heroism far more noble, than any which in more recent times have been so much pitied and so much applauded; but she was a simple missionary's wife, an American by birth, and she told her tale with an artless modesty--writing only what it became her to write, treating only of matters that became a woman. Her captivity, if so it can be called, was voluntarily endured. She of her own free will shared the sufferings of her husband, taking to herself no credit for anything she did; putting her trust in God, and praying to him to strengthen her human weakness. She was spared to breathe once again the free air of liberty, but her troubles had done the work of death on her delicate frame, and she was soon translated to heaven. She was the real heroine. The annals in the East present us with no parallel."

On the 26th of April, Mr. Judson writes, "My sweet little Maria lies by the side of her fond mother. Her complaint proved incurable. The work of death went forward, and after the usual process, excruciating to a parent's feelings, she ceased to breathe on the 24th inst., at 3 o'clock P.M., aged 2 years and 3 months. We then closed her faded eyes, and bound up her discolored lips, and folded her little hands--the exact pattern of her mother's--on her cold breast. The next morning we made her last bed, under the hope tree, (Hopia,) in the small enclosure which surrounds her mother's lonely grave."

Many months later he wrote; "You ask many questions about our sufferings at Ava, but how can I answer them now? There would be some pleasure in reviewing those scenes if she were alive; now I can not. The only reflection that assuages the anguish of retrospection is, that she now rests far away, where no spotted-faced executioner can fill her heart with terror; where no unfeeling magistrate can extort the scanty pittance which she had preserved through every risk to sustain her fettered husband and famishing babe; no more exposed to lie on a bed of languishment, stung with the uncertainty what would become of her poor husband and child when she was gone. No, she has her little ones around her, I trust, and has taught them to praise the source whence their deliverance flowed. Her little son, his soul enlarged to angel's size, was perhaps first to meet her at heaven's portals, and welcome his mother to his own abode--and her daughter followed her in six short months." ... "And when we all meet in Heaven--when all have arrived, and we find all safe, forever safe, and our Saviour ever safe and glorious, and in him all his beloved--oh shall we not be happy, and ever praise him who has endured the cross to wear and confer such a crown!"

PART II.
THE LIFE OF SARAH B. JUDSON.
SECOND WIFE OF
REV. ADONIRAM JUDSON, D.D.

(*Extract of a Letter from Mr. Judson.*)
"I exceedingly regret that there is no portrait of the second as of the first Mrs. Judson. Her soft blue eyes, her mild aspect, her lovely face and elegant form, have never been delineated on canvass. They must soon pass away from the memory even of her children, but they will remain forever enshrined in her husband's heart."

CHAPTER I.
BIRTH AND EDUCATION.--POETICAL TALENT.

In an article in the *North American Review* of 1835, we find the following admirable sentiments: "It is impossible to peruse the written life of any man or woman who has manifested great intellectual or moral power, whether in a holy cause or an unholy one, without a strong admiration and a deep sympathy, and a powerful impulse toward imitation. The soul is awakened, the active powers are roused, the contemplation of high achievement kindles emulation; and well would it be were the character of those leading minds, which thus draw after them the mass of mankind, always virtuous and noble. But in the vast majority of instances, the leaders of mankind, are individuals whose principles and motives the Christian must condemn, as hostile to the spirit of the gospel. More precious therefore, is the example of that pious few who have devoted themselves with pure hearts fervently, to the glory of God, and the good of man, and whose energy of purpose, and firmness of principle, and magnanimity in despising difficulty and danger, and suffering and death, in the accomplishment of a noble end, rouse into active admiration all who contemplate their glorious career."

Such a 'glorious career' was that of the honored missionary whose life has been sketched in the former part of this volume; and such too was hers who forms the subject of the present memoir. Sarah B. Hall was the eldest of thirteen children. Her parents were Ralph and Abiah Hall, who removed during her infancy from Alstead, New Hampshire, the place of her birth, to Salem, in the State of Massachusetts. Her parents not being wealthy, she was early trained to those habits of industry, thoughtfulness and self-denial which distinguished her through life. Children so situated are sometimes pitied by those who consider childhood as the proper season for careless mirth and reckless glee; but they often form characters of solid excellence rarely possessed by those to whom fortune has been more indulgent. Their struggle with obstacles in the way of improvement, and final triumph over them, is an invaluable preparation for the rude conflicts of life; their ingenuity is quickened by the hourly necessity of expedients to meet emergencies, and the many trials which are unavoidable in their circumstances, and which must be met with energy and resolution, give habits of patient endurance, and noble courage.

From all the accounts which we have of her, Sarah must have been a most engaging child. Gentle and affectionate in disposition, and persuasive and winning in manners, there was yet an ardor and enthusiasm in her character, combined with a quiet firmness and perseverance, that ensured success in whatever she attempted, and gave promise of the lofty excellence to which she afterwards attained. All who have sketched her character notice one peculiarity--and it is one which commonly attends high merit--her modest unobtrusiveness.

She was very fond of little children, and easily won their affections; but showed little disposition even in childhood, to mingle in the sports of those of her own age. This arose from no want of cheerfulness in her bosom; but from a certain thoughtfulness, and fondness for intellectual exercises which were early developed in her character.

Her principle, as well as her fondness for her mother, led her never to shrink from what are termed domestic duties, but her heart was not in them as it was in study and meditation. An illustration of this trait was recently related by her brother. Sarah was repeating some lines on the death of Nancy Cornelius, which attracted the attention of her mother, who asked her where she had learned them. With some hesitation the child confessed that she had composed them the day before, while engaged in some domestic avocation, during which her unusual abstracedness had been noticed. Her early poetical attempts evince uncommon facility in versification; and talent, that if cultivated might have placed her high in the ranks of those who have trod the flowery paths of literature; but hers was a higher vocation; and poetry, which was the delightful recreation of her childhood, and never utterly neglected in her riper years, was never to her anything *more* than a recreation.

Her effusions at the age of thirteen are truly remarkable, when we consider the circumstances under which they were written. One, which is given by her biographer as it was probably amended by the 'cultivated taste of later years,' now lies before me as it was first written; and the improved copy, though greatly superior in beauty to the first, seems to me to lack the vigor and energy, which more than atone for the many blemishes of the other. Our readers shall judge. We insert the *childish* composition; the other is to be found in her graceful memoir by 'Fanny Forrester.' She calls it "a Versification of David's lament over Saul and Jonathan."

> The 'beauty of Israel' forever is fled,
>   And low lie the noble and strong;
> Ye daughters of music encircle the dead,
>   And chant the funereal song.
> O never let Gath know their sorrowful doom,
>   Nor Askelon hear of their fate;
> Their daughters would scoff while we lay in the tomb,
>   The relics of Israel's great.
> As strong as young lions were they in the field;
>   Like eagles they never knew fear;

As dark autumn clouds were the studs of their shield,
   And swifter than wind flew their spear.
My brother, my friend, must I bid *thee* adieu!
   Ah yes, I behold thy deep wound--
Thy bosom, once warm as my tears that fast flow,
  Is colder than yonder clay mound.
Ye mountains of Gilboa, never may dew
  Descend on your verdure so green;
 Loud thunder may roar, and fierce lightning may glow
  But never let showers be seen.
Your verdure may scorch in the bright blazing sun,
  The night-blast may level your wood;
For beneath it, unhallowed, were broken and thrown
  The arms of the chosen of God.
Ye daughters of Israel, snatch from your brow
  Those garlands of eglantine fair;
Let cypress and nightshade, the emblems of woe.
  Be wreathed in your beautiful hair.
Approach, and with sadness encircle the dead
  And chant the funereal song--
The 'beauty of Israel' forever is fled,
  And low lie the noble and strong.

Some other effusions, probably of a later date, we will here insert, not only for their merit, but to show what those powers were which she sacrificed, when she turned from the cultivation of her fancy to that of her higher and nobler faculties.

"Slowly and sadly, through the desert waste,
The fainting tribes their dreary pathway traced;
Far as the eye could reach th' horizon round,
Did one vast sea of sand the vision bound.
No verdant shrub, nor murmuring brook was near,
The weary eye and sinking soul to cheer;

No fanning zephyr lent its cooling breath,
But all was silent as the sleep of death;
Their very footsteps fell all noiseless there
As stifled by the moveless, burning air;
And hope expired in many a fainting breast,
And many a tongue e'en Egypt's bondage blest.
Hark! through the silent waste, what murmur breaks?
What scene of beauty 'mid the desert wakes?
Oh! 'tis a fountain! shading trees are there.
And their cool freshness steals out on the air!
With eager haste the fainting pilgrims rush,
Where Elim's cool and sacred waters gush;
Prone on the bank, where murmuring fountains flow,
Their wearied, fainting, listless forms they throw,
Deep of the vivifying waters drink,
Then rest in peace and coolness on the brink,
While the soft zephyrs, and the fountain's flow,
Breathe their sweet lullaby in cadence low.
Oh! to the way-worn pilgrim's closing eyes,
How rare the beauty that about him lies!
Each leaf that quivers on the waving trees,
Each wave that swells and murmurs in the breeze,
Brings to his grateful heart a thrill of bliss,
And wakes each nerve to life and happiness.
When day's last flush had faded from the sky,
And night's calm glories rose upon the eye,
Sweet hymns of rapture through the palm-trees broke,
And the loud timbrels deep response awoke;
Rich, full of melody the concert ran,
Of praise to God, of gratitude in man,
While, as at intervals, the music fell,
Was heard, monotonous, the fountain's swell,
That in their rocky shrines, flowed murmuring there,

And song and coolness shed along the air;
Night mantled deeper, voices died away,
The deep-toned timbrel ceased its thrilling sway;
And there, beside, no other music gushing,
Were heard the solitary fountains rushing,
In melody their song around was shed,
And lulled the sleepers on their verdant bed."

"COME OVER AND HELP US."

"Ye, on whom the glorious gospel,
  Shines with beams serenely bright,
Pity the deluded nations,
  Wrapped in shades of dismal night;
Ye, whose bosoms glow with rapture,
  At the precious hopes they bear;
Ye, who know a Saviour's mercy,
  Listen to our earnest prayer!

See that race, deluded, blinded,
  Bending at yon horrid shrine;
Madness pictured in their faces,
  Emblems of the frantic mind;
They have never heard of Jesus,
  Never to th' Eternal prayed;
Paths of death and woe they're treading,
  Christian! Christian! come and aid!

By that rending shriek of horror
  Issuing from the flaming pile,
By the bursts of mirth that follow,
  By that Brahmin's fiend-like smile

By the infant's piercing cry,
  Drowned in Ganges' rolling wave;
By the mother's tearful eye,
  Friends of Jesus, come and save!

By that pilgrim, weak and hoary,
  Wandering far from friends and home
Vainly seeking endless glory
  At the false Mahomet's tomb;
By that blind, derided nation,
  Murderers of the Son of God,
Christians, grant us our petition,
  Ere we lie beneath the sod!

By the Afric's hopes so wretched,
  Which at death's approach shall fly
By the scalding tears that trickle
  From the slave's wild sunken eye
By the terrors of that judgment,
  Which shall fix our final doom;
Listen to our cry so earnest;--
  Friends of Jesus, come, oh, come

By the martyrs' toils and sufferings,
  By their patience, zeal, and love;
By the promise of the Mighty,
  Bending from His throne above;
By the last command so precious,
  Issued by the risen God;
Christians! Christians! come and help us,
  Ere we lie beneath the sod!"

Sarah, from her earliest years took great delight in reading. At four years, says her brother, she could read readily in any common book. Her rank in her classes in school was always high, and her teachers felt a pleasure in instructing her. On one occasion, when about thirteen, she was compelled to signify to the principal of a female seminary, that her circumstances would no longer permit her to enjoy its advantages. The teacher, unwilling to lose a pupil who was an honor to the school, and who so highly appreciated its privileges, remonstrated with her upon her intention, and finally prevailed on her to remain. Soon after she commenced instructing a class of small children, and was thus enabled to keep her situation in the seminary, without sacrificing her feelings of independence.

Her earliest journals, fragmentary as they are, disclose a zeal and ardor in self-improvement exceedingly unusual. "My mother cannot spare me to attend school this winter, but I have begun to pursue my studies at home." Again: "My parents are not in a situation to send me to school this summer, so I must make every exertion in my power to improve at home." Again, in a note to a little friend, "I feel very anxious to adopt some plan for our mutual improvement." How touching are these simple expressions! How severely do they rebuke the apathy of thousands of young persons, who allow golden opportunities of improvement to slip away from then forever--opportunities which to Sarah Hall and such as she, were of priceless value! Yet it is not one of the least of the ***compensations*** with which the providence of God abounds, that the very lack of favorable circumstances is sometimes ***most*** favorable to the development of latent resources. Thus it was with Sarah. Her whole career shows that her mind had been early trained and disciplined in that noblest of all schools, the school of adverse fortune.

CHAPTER II.

CONVERSION.--BIAS TOWARD A MISSIONARY LIFE.--ACQUAINTANCE WITH MR. BOARDMAN.

Amiable as she was, and conscientious in a degree not usual, Sarah knew that "yet one thing she lacked;" and this knowledge often disquieted her. But her first deep and decided convictions of sin, seem to have been produced, about the year 1820, under the preaching of Mr. Cornelius. Her struggles of mind were fearful, and she sunk almost to the verge of despair; but hope dawned at last, and she was enabled to consecrate her whole being to the service of her Maker. She soon after united with the first Baptist church in Salem, under the care of Dr. Bolles.

The missionary spirit was early developed in her heart. Even before her conversion, her mind was often exercised with sentiments of commiseration for the situation of ignorant heathen and idolaters; and after that event it was the leading idea of her life.

The cause of this early bias is unknown, but it was shown in her conversations, her letters and notes to friends, and in her early poetical effusions. She even tremblingly investigated her own fitness to became a vessel of mercy to the far off, perishing heathen; and then, shrinking from what seemed to her the presumptuous thought, she gave herself with new zeal to the work of benefitting these immediately around her. "Shortly after her conversion," says her brother, "she observed the destitute condition of the children in the neighborhood in which she resided. With the assistance of some young friends as teachers, she organized and continued through the favorable portions of the year, a Sunday-school, of which she assumed the responsibility of superintendent; and at the usual annual celebrations, she with her teachers and scholars joined in the exercises which accompany that festival."

"It is my ardent desire," she writes to a friend, "that the glorious work of reformation may extend till ***every knee*** shall bow to the living God. For this expected, this promised era, let us pray earnestly, unceasingly, and with faith. How can I be so inactive, when I know that thousands are perishing in this land of grace; and millions in other lands are at this very moment kneeling before senseless idols!"

And in her journal--"Sinners perishing all around me, and I almost panting to tell the far ***heathen*** of Christ! Surely this is wrong. I will no longer indulge the vain foolish wish, but endeavor to be useful in the position where Providence has placed me. I can ***pray*** for deluded idolaters, and for those who labor among them, and this is a privilege indeed."

This strong bias of her mind toward a missionary life, was well known to her mother, who still remembers with a tender interest an incident connected with it. Sarah had been deeply affected by the death of Colman, who in the midst of his labors among the heathen, had suddenly been called to his reward. Some time afterward she returned from an evening meeting, and with a countenance radiant with joy, announced--what her pastor had mentioned in the meeting--that a successor to Colman had been found; ***a young man in Maine named Boardman*** had determined to raise and bear to pagan Burmah the standard which had fallen from his dying hand. With that maternal instinct which sometimes forebodes a future calamity however improbable, her mother turned away from her daughter's joyous face, for the thought flashed involuntarily through her mind, that the young missionary would seek as a companion of his toils, a kindred spirit; and where would he find one so congenial as the lovely being before her?

Her fears were realized. Some lines written by "the enthusiastic Sarah" on the death of Colman, met the eye of the "young man in Maine," who was touched and interested by the spirit which breathes in them, and did not rest till he had formed an acquaintance with their author. This acquaintance was followed by an engagement; and in about two years Sarah's ardent aspirations were gratified--she was a missionary to the heathen.

But we are anticipating events; and will close this chapter with extracts from the "Lines on the death of Colman," of which we have spoken.

"'Tis the voice of deep sorrow from India's shore   The flower of our churches is withered, is dead, The gem that shone brightly will sparkle no more, And the tears of the Christian profusely are shed Two youths of Columbia, with hearts glowing warm Embarked on the billows far distant to rove, To bear to the nations all wrapp'd in thick gloom, The lamp of the gospel--the message of love. But Wheelock now slumbers beneath the cold wave, And Colman lies low in the dark cheerless grave. Mourn, daughters of India, mourn! The rays of that star, clear and bright, That so sweetly on Arracan shone Are shrouded in black clouds of night, For Colman is gone!

* * * * *

Oh Colman! thy father weeps not o'er thy grave; Thy heart riven mother ne'er sighs o'er thy dust; But the long Indian grass o'er thy far tomb shall wave, And the drops of the evening descend on the just. Cold, silent and dark is thy narrow abode-- But not long wilt thou sleep in that dwelling of gloom, For soon shall be heard the great trump of our God To summon all nations to hear their last doom; A garland of amaranth then shall be thine, And thy name on the martyrs' bright register shine. O what glory will burst on thy view When are placed by the Judge of the earth, The flowers that in India grew By thy care, in the never-pale wreath Encircling thy brow!

CHAPTER III.

ACCOUNT OF GEORGE DANA BOARDMAN.

We need offer no apology for turning aside from the immediate subject of our narrative, in order to introduce to our readers one, who must henceforth share with her our sympathy and our affection; we mean George Dana Boardman--the successor to Colman spoken of in the last chapter.

He was the son of a Baptist clergyman in Livermore, Maine, and was born in 1801. Though feeble in body, he had an ardent thirst for knowledge, which often made him conceal illness for fear of being detained from school. At a suitable age, he was sent to an academy in North Yarmouth, where he became distinguished for ardor in the pursuit of learning, and fine mental powers. It is related, that he went through the Latin grammar with surprising rapidity, and then expected to be allowed to use the Lexicon, but was told he must go through the grammar once or twice more. Disappointed, he returned to his seat, and in an hour or two was called up to recite, when he repeated verbatim sixteen pages of the grammar. His preceptor inquired if he had got more; he answered yes; and on being asked how much, replied, "I can recite the whole book, sir, if you wish!" He afterwards manifested equal power in mathematics. At sixteen, he engaged in school-teaching, in order to obtain means for a collegiate course--the great object of his ambition--and in this employment he manifested a knowledge of human nature and of the influences which control it, truly wonderful. The most turbulent and disorderly schools, became, in his hands, models of system and regularity.

In 1819, when 18 years old, he entered Waterville College, Maine. He was at this time a youth of good principles, inflexible purpose, strong affections, and independent opinions, but had hitherto given no evidence of piety. "But in this institution his thoughts were directed by a variety of circumstances, to a consideration of the vast and important topics of evangelical religion. His room-mate was a very pious and most warm-hearted man. The officers of the college did all in their power to elevate his thoughts and affections. In short, every external influence with which a young man could be surrounded, was calculated to lead his mind heavenward. Under the operation of these causes, he was by the Spirit of God, induced to consecrate himself, soul, body, and spirit, to religion; and in 1820, he made a public profession of his belief and was baptized."[5]

From his letters and journals, we find that he soon turned his thoughts to the subject of missions. "In the winter of 1820," he says, "the thought occurred to me that I could take my Bible, and travel through new settlements where the Gospel was seldom or never heard, and ***without sustaining the name of a preacher***, could visit from hut to hut, and tell the story of Jesus' dying love. Then in imagination, I could welcome fatigue, hunger, cold, solitude, sickness and death, if I could only win a few cottagers to my beloved Saviour."

When the news of the death of Mr. Judson's fellow missionary, Colman, reached America, his soul was filled with desire to supply the place of that beloved laborer in the Burman field. Still his chief aim was to leave the ***place*** of his labors entirely to the guidance of Providence. On graduating at college, he accepted the office of tutor in it for one year, and so great was the promise of his future eminence, that the good president predicted that he would, at a future day, preside over the institution. But his heart was fixed on other labor, and as soon as his engagement was completed, he hastened to offer his services to the Board of Foreign Missions, and was at once accepted as a missionary.

The parting scene between Boardman and his religious friends in Waterville, who had assembled to bid him farewell is said by one present on that occasion, to have been exceedingly touching. "The eye of Boardman was alone undimmed by a tear. In a tender and yet unfaltering tone he addressed a few words to his brethren. We all knelt down in prayer together for the last time. On arising, Boardman passed round the room, and gave to each his hand for the last time. His countenance was serene, his mild blue eye beamed with benignity, and though there was in his man-

---

5 North American Review.

ner a tenderness which showed he had a heart to feel, yet there was no visible emotion till he came to his room-mate. As he took ***him*** by the hand, his whole frame became convulsed, his eye filled, and the tears fell fast, as if all the tender feelings of his spirit, till now imprisoned, had at this moment broken forth--'farewell!' he faltered; and then smiling through his tears, said, as he left the room, 'we shall meet again in Heaven.'"

He had expected immediately to leave America for Burmah, in the same ship which was to take Mrs. Judson back to that country, but the Board decided to detain him some time in this country for further preparation. In June, 1823, he entered on theological studies in the seminary at Andover, and employed all his leisure hours in reading those books in the library which treated of the manners, customs, and religions of heathen countries.

In the spring of 1825 he was called to bid his country farewell. Natural affection was strong, but the call of duty was stronger still. In a letter he says, "If tenderness of feeling--if ardor of affection--if attachment to friends, to Christian society and Christian privileges--if apprehension of toil and danger in a missionary life--if an overwhelming sense of responsibility could detain me in America, I should never go to Burmah." And in his journal--"Welcome separations and farewells; welcome tears; welcome last sad embraces; welcome pangs and griefs; only let me go where my Saviour calls and goes himself; welcome toils, disappointments, fatigues and sorrows; WELCOME AN EARLY GRAVE!"

* * * * *

It is easy to imagine that the sympathy and affection between two souls constituted like Miss Hall's and Mr. Boardman's, both of whom were warmed by the same zeal for the cause of Christ and the welfare of the heathen, would be unusually strong; and indeed there is every evidence, that from the time they became fully acquainted, the most tender attachment subsisted between them. "You know," she wrote long afterward to her mother, "how tenderly I loved him;" and to an intimate friend, he said in a private conversation, "It was not the superiority of her personal charms, though these were by no means small, but it was her intrinsic excellence, heightened by her modest, unobtrusive spirit, that endeared her to my heart."

CHAPTER IV.

MARRIAGE OF MISS HALL AND MR. BOARDMAN.--THEY SAIL FOR INDIA.--LETTERS FROM MR. B.--LETTERS FROM MRS. B.--ANOTHER LETTER FROM MR. B.

It was to no slight sacrifice that the parents of Sarah Hall were summoned, when called to consent to her departure for Burmah. The eldest of a large family--arrived at an age when she could not only share her mother's duties and labors, but be to her a sympathizing friend--possessed of every quality which could endear her to her parents' hearts--emphatically their joy and pride--how could they resign her--especially how could they consent to her life-long exile from her native land; to end perchance in a cruel martyrdom on a heathen shore? Can we wonder that the mother clinging to her daughter's neck, exclaimed, "I cannot, cannot part with you!" or that the moment of departure must arrive, before she could falter, "My child, *I hope* I am willing?"

Her own feelings on leaving the home of her youth with him who was henceforth to supply to her the place of all other friends, are breathed in these graceful lines.

"When far from those whose tender care
  Protected me from ills when young;
And far from those who love to hear
  Affection from a sister's tongue;

When on a distant heathen shore,
  The deep blue ocean I shall see;
And know the waves which hither bore

Our bark, have left me none but thee;
Perhaps a thought of childhood's days
  Will cause a tear to dim my eye;
And fragments of forgotten lays
  May wake the echo of a sigh.
Oh! wilt thou then forgive the tear?
  Forgive the throbbings of my heart?
And point to those blest regions, where
  Friends meet, and never, never part!

And when shall come affliction's storm,
  When some deep, unexpected grief
Shall pale my cheek, and waste my form,
  Then wilt thou point to sweet relief?

And wilt thou, then, with soothing voice,
  Of Jesus' painful conflicts tell?
And bid my aching heart rejoice,
  In these kind accents--'***All is well?***'
When blooming health and strength shall fly
  And I the prey of sickness prove,
Oh! wilt thou watch with wakeful eye,
  The dying pillow of thy love?

And when the chilling hand of death
  Shall lead me to my house in heaven
And to the damp, repulsive earth,
  In cold embrace, this form be given;
Oh, need I ask thee, wilt thou then,
  Upon each bright and pleasant eve,
Seek out the solitary glen,
  To muse beside my lonely grave?
And while fond memory back shall steal,

>   To scenes and days forever fled;
> Oh, let the veil of love conceal
>   The frailties of the sleeping dead.
>
> And thou may'st weep and thou may'st joy,
>   For 'pleasant is the joy of grief;'
> And when thou look'st with tearful eye
>   To heaven, thy God will give relief.
>
> Wilt thou, then, kneel beside the sod
>   Of her who kneels with thee no more,
> And give thy heart anew to God,
>   Who griefs unnumbered for thee bore?
> And while on earth thy feet shall rove,
>   To scenes of bliss oft raise thine eye,
> Where, all-absorbed in holy love,
>   I wait to hail thee to the sky."

On the 3d of July, 1825, the marriage took place, Miss Hall being then 21 years old, and Mr. Boardman 24. His slender figure, and transparent complexion, even then seemed to indicate that his mission on earth might soon be fulfilled, but both he and his bride were young and sanguine, and no misgivings for the future disturbed their happiness in each other. Indeed the grief of parting with all they had ever loved and cherished, though chastened by submission to what they believed the Divine call, was sufficient to merge all lighter causes of anxiety.

On the day following their marriage they left Salem for the place of embarkation. They were to sail first to Calcutta, and if on reaching there the troubles in Burmah should prevent their going at once to that country, they were to remain in Calcutta, and apply themselves to the acquisition of the Burman language.

In expectation of their speedy departure, meetings for special prayer were held at Boston, Salem, New York, and Philadelphia. The spirit which animated these meetings, and breathed in all the supplications offered, was indicative of deep interest in the mission, and of united and determined resolution, by the grace of God to support it. Mr. and Mrs. B. were everywhere received with the utmost kindness, and nothing was withheld which could contribute to animate them in their arduous undertaking, and render their future voyage pleasant and healthful. The captain and other officers of the ship Asia in which they were to sail, made the most ample provision for their comfort and accommodation, and rendered them every attention in a manner most grateful to their feelings. At a concert of prayer in Philadelphia, Mr. Boardman was called upon to give a brief account to the audience of the motives which had induced him to devote his life to the missionary service. In his reply, he took occasion in the first place to acknowledge the goodness of God to him through his whole life. When he entered Waterville College--the first student ever admitted there not hopefully pious--his fellow-students, impressed with this fact, solemnly engaged with each other, unknown to him, to remember him in their supplications, until their prayers for his conversion should be answered. Six months from that time he found peace in believing, and his first prayer was that God would make him useful. His mind was so impressed with the condition of our Indian tribes, that he felt inclined to carry to them the message of salvation. But his venerable father, whom he consulted as to his duty, advised him "to wait on God, and He would conduct him in the right way." After some time, his choice was decided in favor of the Burman mission by such indications, that he considered his call to this service distinctly and plainly marked. He adverted in a very tender manner to some peculiar indications of Providence, especially to the manner in which his parents received the knowledge of his determination. Their remark was, ***It has long been our desire to do something for the mission; and if God will accept our son, we make the surrender with cheerfulness***[6].

In reading this account, do we not feel emotions of moral sublimity in contemplating these tender and aged parents, who, "moved with love for a benevolent God, and for their fellow-creatures, surrender their son bright with talents and virtues, rich in learning and in the respect of all who knew him, but feeble and sickly in body, to the missionary labor--whose certain and speedy end is death?"[7]

Mrs. Boardman with her husband took her final leave of her beloved native land on the 16th of July, 1825. To her sister, when two weeks out at sea, she writes:

---

6 Baptist Magazine, 1825.
7 North American Review.

"We think we never enjoyed better health. That beneficent Parent, who is ever doing us good, has bestowed upon us, in the officers of the ship, obliging and affectionate friends.... Everything regarding our table, is convenient and agreeable as we could enjoy on shore. Our family consists of the captain, two mates, two supercargoes, a physician, Mrs. Fowler, and ourselves. Mr. Blaikie, the chief supercargo, is not only a gentleman, but is decidedly pious, and strictly evangelical in his sentiments.... It is a great comfort to each of us to find one who is ever ready to converse upon those subjects which relate to the extension of the Redeemer's kingdom. It is most grateful to my own feelings, but I am even more rejoiced for the sake of Mr. B. Religious society has ever been to him a source of much real gratification. You know very well the love he has ever manifested for social intercourse. When in America amidst our beloved friends, as I have seen him enter with all his heart into conversation--have seen joy beam from his eyes when engaged in this delightful employment--I would sigh, and say to myself, dear Mr. B. how sad you will be when far removed from those whose words now so often cheer your heart. What will you do when this favorite rill of pleasure ceases to flow? But God is infinitely good, he is far better to us than our fears. He bestows upon us every blessing essential to our happiness and usefulness. It is not the *want* of privileges that I need lament, but the *misimprovement* of them."

In another letter, she expresses her mature conviction that the missionary life if entered upon with right feelings may be more favorable than any other to the promotion of spiritual growth. And certain it is, that trials, and even persecution often develop the power of Christian principle, and the strength of religious faith; while ease and outward prosperity seem to lull the souls of believers into an unworthy sloth and a sinful conformity with the world around them. The soldier of Christ must maintain a warfare; and when will he be more likely to be constantly awake to his duty, than when surrounded by the open and avowed enemies of his Master?

From Chitpore four miles above Calcutta, Mr. Boardman writes: "It gives me much pleasure to write you from the shores of India. Through the goodness of God we arrived at Sand-Heads on the 23d ult., after a voyage of 127 days. We were slow in our passage up the Hoogly, and did not arrive in Calcutta until the 2d inst. We had a very agreeable voyage,--religious service at meals, evening prayers in the cabin, and when the weather allowed, public worship in the steerage on Lord's day morning ... allow me to add that we entertain a hope that one of the sailors was converted on the passage.

"The report of our being at Sand-Heads reached Calcutta several days before we did, and our friends had made kind preparations to receive us. Soon after coming in sight of the city, we had the pleasure of welcoming on board the Asia, the Rev. Mr. Hough. He informed us, that the Burmese war was renewed after an armistice of several weeks, and that no well-authenticated accounts had been received from our dear friends Judson and Price at Ava. It is generally supposed that they are imprisoned with other foreigners, and have not the means of sending round to Bengal.

"At noon, Dec. 2d, we came on shore, ... and were received very kindly by the English Missionaries. We found Mrs. Colman waiting with a carriage to bring us out to this place. The cottage we occupy was formerly the residence of Mr. and Mrs. Eustace Carey. Mr. and Mrs. Wade, Mrs. Colman, Mrs. Boardman and myself, compose a very happy American family.... But we long to be laboring in Burmah. We are not yet discouraged by the dark cloud that hangs over our prospects there. We still hope and trust, *we firmly believe*, that eventually this war will tend to advance the cause of Christ in Burmah. We hope our friends at home will not be discouraged, but will continue to pray for us."

In another letter he says, "And now, my dear parents, I wish you could make a visit at Chitpore. You would find your two fond children sitting together very happily, and engaged in writing letters to their beloved American friends. Our mansion, to be sure, is but a bamboo cottage, with a thatched roof, but is a palace compared with most of the native huts around us. But you know a large house is by no means essential to happiness. Food and clothing sufficient, with the presence of God, are all that is absolutely necessary. Could a man have in addition, one confidential friend, who sympathized in all his joys and sorrows, and with whom he could enjoy all the endearments of social life, he might be happy indeed--and such a friend, such a wife I have, in my beloved Sarah. I fear I shall never be able to discharge the obligations I feel toward you for conferring on me so great a blessing."

Mrs. B. also writes to some acquaintances, "Unite with me, my respected friends, in gratitude to God, that he has preserved us through the dangers of a long voyage, and permitted us to land upon a heathen shore. Oh may this renewed assurance of his kind care, teach me confidence in his promises, and fill me with ardent desires to be constantly employed in his service.

"Our voyage was remarkably pleasant, our suffering from sea-sickness was much lighter than we had anticipated; our accommodations, though by no means handsome, convenient and comfortable as we could desire. Our table was well furnished with the necessaries, and many of the luxuries of life. Capt. Sheed, and the other gentlemen on board, treated us with the greatest kindness, and appeared solicitous to make our situation agreeable. In the society of Mr. Blaikie, the supercargo, we took much delight. He is a gentleman of eminent piety, belonging to the Presbyterian denomination. We had evening devotions in the cabin, ... when the weather allowed we had divine service between decks on the Sabbath. A precious privilege!

"While at sea, my time was spent in a very agreeable, and I hope not unprofitable manner.... The principal books I read besides the Bible, were the life of Parsons, Lowth's lectures on Hebrew poetry, part of Fuller's works, and of Jones' Church History. Supposing the study of the word of God well calculated to prepare my mind for the missionary work, I directed my chief attention to that. We had one very interesting exercise,--during the week several of us collected as many passages of scripture as we were able, upon a subject previously named; and on Sabbath eve, we compared our separate lists, and conversed freely upon the doctrine or duty concerning which we had written. In this manner we discussed many of the most important doctrines and duties contained in Scripture.

As we drew near Calcutta, our anxiety respecting the fate of our dear missionaries at Ava, increased. We trembled when we thought of the disturbances in Burmah, and there was only one spot where we could find peace and serenity of mind. That sweet spot was the throne of grace. Thither we would often repair and lose all anxiety and fear respecting our dear friends, our own future prospects, and the Missionary cause in Burmah. It was sweet to commit all into the hands of God. If not deceived, we felt the importance of constantly pleading for a suitable frame of mind, to receive whatever intelligence was for us; and for a disposition to engage in the service of God, at any time, and in any place he might direct. We considered it our duty to supplicate for grace to support us in the hour of trial, and for direction in time of perplexity, rather than to employ our minds in anticipating the nature of future difficulties, and in fancying how we should conduct in an imagined perplexity. This is still our opinion."

Then follows an account of their arrival, which we have already given in Mr. Boardman's letter, and she adds: "Imagine, dear Mrs. B. our joy at meeting those with whom we hope to be employed in labors of love among the poor Burmans. I shall not attempt to describe the emotions of my heart when I entered the little bamboo cottage we now occupy. Were I skilled in perspective drawing, I would send you a picture of the charming landscape seen from our verandah. In a little hut near us reside two Christian converts from heathenism. Oh, how your bosom would glow with grateful rapture to hear their songs of praise, and listen to their fervent prayers. We prefer living in this retired spot with dear Mr. and Mrs. Wade and Mrs. Colman, to a situation in Calcutta; we can pursue our studies with less interruption, and also have the advantage of Mr. Wade's assistance.

"The war in Burmah still continues, and there is at present very little prospect of our going to Rangoon soon. We still look to Burmah as our earthly home, and daily pray that we may be permitted ere long to enter that field of labor. We rejoice that we can commence the study of the language here. We have not for an instant regretted that we embarked in the undertaking."

In another letter of a later date she writes from Calcutta: "In compliance with the advice of our friends, we are now residing in a pleasant little house in Calcutta. I regretted exceedingly to leave the peaceful, retired shades of Chitpore for the noise and commotion of a city, but duty appeared to require it"--(the climate at Chitpore is insalubrious in the hot months) "and we all cheerfully submitted. I feel, my dear friend, that we are wanderers. I can look to no place as my earthly home, but Burmah.... We have not yet heard from the brethren at Ava. Oh that our Father in Heaven may prepare our hearts for whatever intelligence we may receive.

"On Monday last, I attended the examination of Mrs. Colman's schools. Imagine my feelings at seeing ninety-two little Bengallee girls, (whose mothers are kept in the most degraded ignorance and superstition,) taught to read the Scriptures.... This was only one division of the schools. The whole number belonging to this Society is nearly four hundred. There are also many other interesting schools in Calcutta.

"Mr. and Mrs. Wade with Mr. B. and myself still compose our family; we are very happy in each other, are blessed with excellent health, enjoy facilities for learning the language, and in short, possess all we could desire. We feel our want of ardent piety.... Pray for us, for we are weak and sinful."

A letter to one of her own family of about the same date, shows that her zeal for the conversion of the heathen, did not at all weaken her desire that her own kindred might be true followers of Jesus. After mentioning that a Burman teacher had been procured for them, &c., she says, "I often imagine myself in the midst of that dear family, where the happy hours of childhood flew away. Sometimes I fancy myself entering the room in the morning, and seeing you all kneeling around the family altar. My brother, have you a heart to pray to God? Have you repented and turned to him? Or are you all careless and indifferent respecting your precious soul? No, I cannot believe this is the case. Indulged as you are with hearing the gospel and other means of grace, you cannot be indifferent. The time is coming when the religion of Jesus will be indispensable to your peace of mind. You must pass through the valley of death. How can you endure that gloom without the light of God's countenance? you must stand before a righteous God at the judgment day. What will be the state of your soul if Jesus is not your friend? ***Think of this.***"

A letter from Mrs. Wade written in the spring following, speaks with enthusiasm of the pleasure they have enjoyed in the society of Mr. and Mrs. B, and, like theirs, breathes ardent wishes to be able to go to Burmah. These wishes were soon to be realized. A letter from Mr. Boardman dated Calcutta, April 12th, 1826, commences: "My dear Brother,--The joyful news of peace with Ava, and of the safety of our friends Dr. and Mrs. Judson, and Dr. Price, you will doubtless receive from other sources. We can only say that the preservation of our friends both at Rangoon and at Ava, seems to us one of the most striking and gracious displays of God's special care of his people and his cause, which has been experienced in modern times.

"Brother Wade and myself, with our beloved companions, expect to leave Calcutta in six or eight weeks, to join brother Judson. As Rangoon is not retained by the British, we do not think it best to recommence the work there, but rather to settle in some of the towns which are by treaty ceded to the British.... The members of the church in Rangoon are collecting and will probably go with us. We need divine direction.

"We have great reason to be thankful for the health we enjoy. We long to proceed to Burmah and engage in the delightful work before us. May God's strength be made perfect in our weakness."

But his cherished enterprise was still longer delayed. By the solicitation of the English missionaries, and the appointment of the American Board, he was induced to remain in Calcutta a while, and preach in Circular Road Chapel, recently vacated by the death of Mr. Lawson. Mr. Wade and his wife reached Rangoon on the 9th of November, and found there the desolate and heart-stricken Mr. Judson, and his feeble babe, of whom Mrs. Wade was able for a brief period to supply the place of a mother.

The place fixed upon as the seat of government in the newly acquired British territory in Burmah, was Amherst, on the Martaban river, about 75 miles eastward of Rangoon. This place had been laid out by British engineers under Mr. Judson's direction, and in an incredibly short time, became a city numbering in thousands of houses. In southern India, houses are built almost in a day, and the population fluctuates from place to place with a facility surprising to Europeans. It is only necessary to make a clearing in the jungle, and erect barracks for a few soldiers, and--as water rushes at once into hollows scooped in the damp sea-sand--so do the natives of India swarm into the clearing, and create a city.' To this new city of Amherst Mr. and Mrs. Boardman came in the spring of 1827, and joined Mr. and Mrs. Wade and Mr. Judson. It was bitterly painful to them to learn that the wife of the latter, that noble and beloved woman whose life had been preserved as if by miracle in a thousand dangers, and from whose society and intercourse they had hoped and expected the greatest pleasure and profit, was the tenant of a lowly grave beneath the hopia-tree; and even more immediately distressing to find that her heart-broken husband was just about to consign to the same dreary bed the only relic remaining to him of his once lovely family, 'the sweet little Maria.' One of Mr. Boardman's first labors in Burmah was to make a coffin for the child with his own hands! and to assist in its burial. Poor babe! 'so closed its brief, eventful history.' An innocent sharer in the terrible sufferings of its parents, in the midst of which indeed it came into the world; like its mother, it had survived through countless threatening deaths, and reached what seemed a haven of security, only to wring its father's heart with an intenser pang, by its unexpected and untimely death. Truly the ways of God 'are past finding out,' and 'his judgments are a great deep!'

From a short poem full of sympathy and pious sentiment which was written by

Mrs. Boardman on this occasion, we select some passages.

"Ah this is death, my innocent! 'tis he   Whose chilling hand has touched thy tender frame.

* * * * *

Thou heed'st us not; not e'en the bursting sob
Of thy dear father, now can pierce thine ear.

* * * * *

Thy mother's tale replete with varied scenes,   Exceeds my powers to tell; but other harps   And other voices, sweeter far than mine,   Shall sing her matchless worth, her deeds of love,   Her zeal, her toil, her sufferings and her death.   But all is over now. She sweetly sleeps   In yonder new-made grave; and thou, sweet babe,   Shalt soon be pillowed on her quiet breast.   Yes, ere to-morrow's sun shall gild the west,   Thy father shall have said a long adieu   To the last lingering hope of earthly joy;   For thou, Maria, wilt have found thy rest.   Thy flesh shall rest in hope, till that great day   When He who once endured far greater woes   Than mortal man can know; who when on earth   Received such little children in his arms,   Graciously blessing them, shall come again;   Then like the glorious body of thy Lord   Who wakes thy dust, this fragile frame shall be.   Then shalt thou mount with him on angels' wings   Be freed from sorrow, sickness, sin and death. And in his presence find eternal bliss."

CHAPTER V.

STATIONED AT MAULMAIN.--ATTACK OF BANDITTI.--MISSIONARY OPERATIONS.--DANGER FROM FIRE.

On consultation it was determined that Mr. and Mrs. Wade should remain in Amherst, and that Mr. and Mrs. Boardman should proceed to Maulmain, a town 25 miles up the river, which had sprung into being in the same manner as Amherst, and was nearly as populous; and that Mr. Judson should divide his time between the two stations.

In pursuance of this plan Mr. Boardman removed his family, which had been increased by the addition of a lovely daughter, now about five months old, to the new city of Maulmain. On the evening of May 28th Mr. Boardman makes this entry in his journal. "After nearly two years of wanderings without any certain dwelling-place, we have to-day become inhabitants of a little spot of earth, and have entered a house which we call our earthly home. None but those who have been in similar circumstances can conceive the satisfaction we now enjoy." ... "The population of the town is supposed to be 20,000. ***One year ago it was all a thick jungle, without an inhabitant!***"

While at Amherst, Mrs. Boardman had experienced an alarming attack of a disease incident to the climate, and had to be carried to the boat which conveyed her to her new home on a litter. On her arrival there, although she shared her husband's joy that at length they had a home on the long ***promised land*** of Burmah, still her woman's nature, enfeebled by suffering, could not but have trembled at the idea of living in a lonely spot, (for the mission-house was nearly a mile from the barracks,) with the neighboring jungle swarming with "serpents that hiss, and beasts of prey that howl." In addition to this cause of alarm, there was opposite them, on the Burman side of the river, the old decayed city of Martaban; which was the refuge of a horde of banditti, who, armed with knives and swords, would often sally forth in bands of 30 or 40, urge their light and noiseless boats across the river, satiate themselves with plunder and murder in the British town, and return with their spoils to their own territory, where they were secure from British retaliation. The English general, knowing the insecurity of the mission-house, had urged Mr. B. to remove with his family to the protection of the fort; but his object was to benefit the ***Burmans***, and to do that, he must live among them.

In their little bamboo hut, therefore, so frail that it could be cut open, as Mrs. Boardman says, with a pair of scissors, they prosecuted their study of the language under a native teacher, and even ventured to talk a little with the half-wild natives around them, and for a few weeks were unmolested. Their courage and confidence had revived, and with Mrs. B., restored health brought happiness. June 20th she writes, "We are in excellent health, and as happy as it is possible for human beings to be upon earth. It is our earnest desire to live, labor and die among this people." With such feelings, they had probably retired to rest on the night of the 24th of June, but awaking towards morning, and perceiving that the lamp which they always kept burning through the night was extinguished, they suspected mischief; and on relighting it, they found to their consternation that their house had been entered by the lawless plunderers mentioned above, and robbed of nearly every valuable article it contained; but how was their horror increased, by finding two large cuts in the moscheto curtains about their bed, through which the murderers had watched their slumbers, ready to stab them to the heart had they offered the slightest resistance, or even had they waked to consciousness. But He who "giveth his beloved sleep," had kindly steeped their senses in slumbers so profound and peaceful, that not even the infant stirred, or opened its eyes which would have instantly been sealed again,--in death.--Every trunk, box and bureau was rifled, looking-glass, watch, spoons, keys, were gone; and yet as the parents gazed at those rent curtains, and thought how the death-angel had grazed them with his wing as he passed by, their hearts rose in gratitude and praise to their Heavenly deliverer. But Mrs. Boardman's feelings are best told in her own expressive words. She says, "After the first amazement had a little subsided, I raised my eyes to the curtains surrounding our bed, and to my indescribable emotion saw two large holes cut, the one at the head, and the other at the foot of the place where my dear husband had been sleeping. From that moment, I quite forgot the stolen goods, and thought only of the treasure that was spared. In imagination I saw the assassins with their horrid weapons standing by our bedside, ready to do their worst had we been permitted to wake. Oh how merciful was that watchful Providence which prolonged those powerful slumbers of that night, not allowing even the infant at my bosom to open its eyes at so critical a moment. If ever gratitude glowed in my bosom, if ever the world appeared to me worthless as vanity, and if ever I wished to dedicate myself, my husband, my babe, my ***all***, to our great Redeemer, it was at that time.

"To this day not a trace of our goods has been found; leaving no doubt that they were taken immediately over the river to Martaban. Since our loss, we have received many kind presents from our friends, so that we now find ourselves comfortable, and we are contented and happy. Yes, my beloved friend, I think I can say, that notwithstanding our alarms, never did five months of my life pass as pleasantly as the last five have done. The thought of being among this people whom we have so long desired to see, and the hope that God would enable me to do some little good to the poor heathen, has rejoiced and encouraged my heart. I confess that once or twice my natural timidity has ***for a moment*** gained ascendancy over my better feelings,--and at the hour of midnight, when the howlings of wild beasts have been silenced by the report of a musket near us, we would say to each other, perhaps the next attack will be made upon ***us***, and the next charge may be aimed at our bosoms. Then I have been almost ready to exclaim, Oh for one little, ***little*** room of such materials, that we could, as far as human means go, sleep in safety. But these fears have been transitory, and we have generally been enabled to place our confidence in the Great Shepherd of Israel who never slumbers or sleeps, assured that he would protect us.... And we have also felt a sweet composure in the reflection that God has marked out our way; and if it best accord with his designs that we fall a prey to these blood-thirsty monsters, ***all will be right***."

The English, hearing of this robbery, stationed a guard at the Mission-house of two sepoys or native soldiers. As one of these was sitting in the verandah, a wild beast from the jungle sprang furiously upon him, but he was frightened away before the man was much injured. Such occurrences however were rare, and did not make Mrs. Boardman desire, all things considered, to change her residence She was in the place of her choice, the country of her adoption, she had a faithful and loving husband, and a lovely and almost idolized babe; their house, though small and insecure, was beautifully situated with everything in the natural landscape around to charm her cultivated eye and taste,--these were her *earthly* comforts. Besides, even the insecurity of their habitation was daily diminishing; for houses were constantly springing up around them, and more and more of the jungle was cleared and cultivated. But what gave its chief zest to her life and that of her spiritually minded husband, was the fact that they found here a field of *usefulness* in the only work that seemed to them worth living for. From various motives the natives began to visit them constantly, and in increasing numbers, to inquire concerning the new religion. Mr. B. held a religious service on the Sabbath, and opened a school for boys: Mrs. Boardman, one for girls, and both conversed as well as they were able with their numerous visitors, and employed all their leisure in mastering the language. On the 22d of July they commemorated together the Saviour's dying love, in the sacrament of the Lord's supper,--a solitary pair--yet not so, for the Master of the feast was there to bless the "two" who thus "gathered together in his name."

The population at Maulmain was now increasing, and that at Amherst diminishing so rapidly, that Mr. Judson and Mr. and Mrs. Wade thought best to remove from the latter station to the former, and arrived at Maulmain in October. Two houses of public worship were erected during the year, where Messrs. Judson and Wade were daily employed in proclaiming religious truth, and such was their success, that within a few months they admitted to the church several native members. As many native converts with their families had removed with the Missionaries from Amherst to Maulmain, Mrs. Wade and Mrs. Boardman united their schools into one, which was attended with the most gratifying success. Moung Shwa-ba and Moung Ing, who have often been mentioned in the former memoir, read the Scriptures and other religious books to all who would hear, at a sort of *reading zayat*, built for the purpose.

In March, 1828, our friends were delivered from a danger not unknown in our own country. One evening, they were startled by a roaring like that of flame, and on going to the door, discovered the whole jungle to the eastward of them enveloped in sheets of flame, which was rapidly approaching their frail cottage. Seeing no hope that their house could escape, they rapidly collected a few valuables, and with their infant prepared to flee towards the river, though in much terror lest their path should be beset by leopards, tigers, and other animals, driven from their haunts by the fire. But when within a few feet of the houses, the flames were arrested by a sudden change of the wind, and the dwellings were unhurt. "Thus again are we preserved," says Mr. B. "when no human arm could have saved us!" Truly,

"The hosts of God encamp around   The dwellings of the just."

Truly "the Lord knoweth how to deliver the godly."

CHAPTER VI.

REMOVAL TO TAVOY.--IDOLATRY OF THE PEOPLE.--LETTER FROM MRS. B.--BAPTISM OF A KAREN DISCIPLE.--SOME ACCOUNT OF THE KARENS.

The permanent collection of so many Missionaries at a single station was not approved by the Board, nor was it deemed desirable by the Missionaries themselves. In accordance, therefore, with instructions received from America, it was decided that Mr. and Mrs. Boardman should remove to Tavoy. This city is situated on the river Tavoy, 150 miles south of Maulmain, and had at that time a population of 6000 Burmans and 3000 foreigners.

The city was the stronghold of the religion of Gaudama, and the residence of two hundred priests.

On every eligible point stood an emblem or image of idolatry. Tall pagodas crowned every eminence, and humbler ones clustered around them, while thickly set groves of banyan and other sacred trees, sheltered shrines and images of Gaudama, and on festival days were crowded with devotees, kneeling in the gloomy pathways, or festooning the sacred trees with the rarest flowers. The tops of some of the thousand pagodas in the city, are hung with innumerable little bells, which, moved by the wind, chime sweetly their calls to devotion, reminding one of a passage in Moore's description of an eastern city:

> "But hark! the vesper call to prayer,
> --As slow the orb of daylight sets,--
> Is rising sweetly on the air
> From Syria's thousand minarets."

This change in their place of abode could not fail to be a severe trial to our missionaries. To Maulmain they were bound by many ties,--the sweet companionship of fellow-Christians, and the love which attaches the missionary to those spiritual children which the Lord has given him;--moreover it was their first ***home***, sanctified by signal deliverances and countless mercies;--nevertheless, like Abraham who at the call of Jehovah, "went out, not knowing whither he went,"--these "followers of them who through faith inherit the promises," obeyed the voice of duty, and feeling themselves "strangers and pilgrims on the earth," went without murmuring to their new sphere of labor. "One thing is certain," says Mr. B. in a subsequent letter "we were brought here by the guidance of Providence. It was no favorite scheme of ours."

On arriving at Tavoy, they were kindly received by Mr. Burney the English resident, and within ten days from their arrival, had procured a house, and begun to teach inquirers in the way of salvation Much as there was to discourage them in this ***city of pagoda***, "the missionary looked out on the strange magnificence of shrines and temples that lay around him,--upon the monuments that had perpetuated for many ages this idolatrous worship,--upon the priests who taught it, and the countless devotees who practised it; and as he prepared to strike the first blow at the hoary superstition which they all enshrined, he felt to the full the sublimity and greatness of the undertaking. He stood alone, the herald of truth, before this mighty array of ancient error; but he trusted implicitly in the promises of revelation, and felt assured that the day was at hand when all this empty adoration of Gaudama would give place to the worship of the living God!"[8]

A new difficulty occurred here, which however was speedily surmounted by the diligence and zeal of the missionaries; the dialect of Tavoy was so different from pure Burmese as to be almost unintelligible to those who knew only the latter, but both, fortunately, employed the same written characters. Mrs. Boardman's employments at this time are enumerated in their letters. After unwearied toil, and repeated repulses and discouragements, she succeeded in establishing a girls' school, in which she employed a woman who could read, as an assistant. She describes a visit to her school thus: "I am just returned from one of the day-schools. The sun had not risen when I arrived, but the little girls were in the house ready for instruction. My

---

8 Gammell.

walk to this school is through a retired road, shaded on one side by the old wall of the city, which is overgrown with wild creepers and pole-flowers, and on the other by large fruit-trees. While going and returning, I find it sweet and profitable to think on the shortness of time, the vanity of this delusive world,--and oh I have had some precious views of that world where the weary are at rest; and where sin, that enemy of God, and now constant disturber of my peace, will no more afflict me."

In another letter of a later date, she describes herself as sitting at her table in a back porch, from which she can see her "dear husband," in a room before her, teaching nine little heathen boys; while in one of the long verandahs on each side of the house, the native Christians are holding a prayer-meeting in their own language, and in the other, a Chinese convert is urging three or four of his deluded countrymen to turn from their stupid superstitions to the service of Jehovah.

She mentions also the baptism of a *Karen*, (the name of a tribe in Burmah,) "a *poor man*, who had been converted while in the service of Mr. Judson;" little knowing the importance of the fact thus recorded. This "poor man," in fact formerly a slave, and whom the writer of an article in a former number of the *Quarterly Review* would have sneered at as he did at the "fisherman," the *wonderful trophy of divine grace*, mentioned in Mrs. Judson's history of the mission, was the famous Ko-thay-byu, whose life has been written by Mr. Mason, and who, by his zeal and success in missionary labor, obtained the name of "the Karen Apostle." He was the first to introduce to the notice of the missionaries, the tribe to which he belonged, a people so remarkable, that we are unwilling, even in our brief sketch, to pass them over without notice.

The Karens, according to a writer in the *North American Review*, are a savage and ignorant race of men, (their *name* in the Burman language signifying *wild men*,) scattered in vast numbers over the wilds of Farther India, and inhabiting almost inaccessible tracts, among the mountains and forests. Their peculiar physiognomy, strange traditions, and some of their customs have led to the opinion that they were of Hebrew origin, though some think they are of the Caucasian variety of the human species. They differ much from the Burmans, by whom they are heavily taxed and grievously oppressed, and in every way treated as inferiors.[9] "Their traditions have been preserved, like the poems of Ossian, by fond memories delighting

9 See Gammell.

to revive the recollections of former glory and prosperity; repeated by grandsires at even-tide to their listening descendants, and sung by mourners over the graves of their elders.

"They believe in a God who is denominated Yu-wah," a name certainly similar to the Hebrew Jehovah. Some of their traditional songs are curious and interesting. For instance,

> "God created us in ancient time,
> And has a perfect knowledge of all things;
> When men call his name, *he hears*!"

And again

> "The sons of heaven are holy,
> They sit by the seat of God,
> The sons of heaven are righteous,
> They dwell together with God;
> They lean against his silver seat."

The following stanza, says the writer above referred to, might be mistaken for the production of David or Isaiah.

> "Satan in days of old was holy,
> But he transgressed God's law;
> Satan of old was righteous,
> But he departed from the law of God,
> And God drove him away."

They say that God formerly loved their nation, but on account of their wickedness he punished it, and made them the degraded creatures they now are. But they say "God will again have mercy upon us, God will save us again." One verse of one of their songs is,

> "When the Karen king arrives
> Everything will be happy;
> When Karens have a king
> Wild beasts will lose their savageness."

Professor Gammell says, in substance, that they present the extraordinary phenomenon of a people without any form of religion or established priesthood, yet believing in God, and in future retribution, and cherishing and transmitting from age to age a set of traditions of unusual purity, and containing bright predictions of future prosperity and glory.

When Ko-thay-byu, the poor convert already mentioned, was baptized, he naturally carried to his countrymen "the thrilling news, that a teacher from a far distant land had come to preach a new religion, a religion answering to the religion of their fathers." Others came to listen, and to carry back to their secluded hamlets the joyful tidings; until "from distant hills and remote valleys and forests, Karen inquirers flocked to Tavoy, and thronged around *the teacher*;" listening to the new doctrines with childlike simplicity and uncommon sensibility. Among other singular stories that they related to the wondering "teacher," one was, that more than ten years before, a book in a strange tongue had been left among them by a foreigner, who commanded them to worship it; which command they had faithfully obeyed. Mr. Boardman felt the strongest curiosity to see this ***deified book***, but owing to the prevalence of the rains, he was not gratified till the following September. He was then waited on by a large deputation of Karens, bringing with them in a covered basket, the mysterious volume, wrapped in fold after fold of muslin; on removing which it proved to be an Oxford edition of the Common Prayer Book in the English language! With the greatest simplicity they asked Mr. B. if this book contained the doctrines of the new religion, and if so, requested to be taught its contents. Mr. B. assured them that the book was good, but should by no means be made an object of worship; and accepting it from them, he gave them in its stead, portions of the Scriptures, translated into a language they could understand. They entreated him to visit them in their own villages, assuring him of the readiness of their tribe to welcome him, and to receive the gospel; and, struck with their earnestness and candor, he promised at some future time to yield to their request.

The sorcerer who had preserved the book, and prescribed to the simple heathen the forms of its worship, threw away his cudgel, or wand of office, and laid aside his fantastic dress; and Mr. Boardman sent the mysterious volume to America, to be deposited in the museum of the Baptist Missionary Society.

Who the "foreigner" may have been, that thus supplied an ignorant people with a Divinity, or object of worship; or what were his motives in so doing, will probably always remain a mystery.

If we have devoted considerable space to this notice of the Karens, their subsequent history will prove that they are not unworthy of such notice.

CHAPTER VII.

LETTER FROM MRS. B.--MR. B.'S VISIT TO THE KARENS IN THEIR VILLAGES.--DEFECTION OF DISCIPLES.--ITS EFFECT ON MR. AND MRS. B.

Extract of a letter from Mrs. Boardman to a "beloved sister," dated Tavoy, 1828.--"Nothing especial has occurred since I last wrote. We are still in good health, and happy in our work. We are now destitute of all religious society, and feel that our responsibilities are great indeed.... We have to suffer many little inconveniences in this country, but have no disposition to complain. We rejoice in the kind providence that has directed our steps, and would not exchange our condition. Our desire is to labor among the poor heathen until called to our eternal home." She then, with characteristic earnestness and affection, inquires after her sister's spiritual state. "Oh if you are a child of God, how great is your happiness; you can think of death without fear. The troubles and griefs of life do not distress you as they do the poor worldling, who looks only to the enjoyments of this life for comfort. If a Christian, you have sweet foretastes of that joy which is unspeakable and inconceivable by mortals. Though a sinner still, you feel that your sins are pardoned, and that through the merits of a crucified Saviour you will at last be accepted of God. I would fondly hope, my dear sister, that this is your happy case. But if not, oh who can tell your dreadful danger? Who can paint the alarming prospect before you? Every moment exposed to death, and yet without hope. Subject to disappointments and afflictions in this world, and yet no refuge for your anguished spirit. The weight of sins daily accumulating, and every day less prospect of obtaining pardon. The awful prospect of eternal banishment from all that is holy, oh my sister, reflect.... If you have not yet turned to the Saviour, delay no longer.... Oh may you, and all my beloved brothers and sisters, be early brought to a knowledge of the truth. I cannot express the anxiety I feel for every one of you. I also feel the solicitude of a tender sister for your temporal good. Write me particulars of the health of my dear parents, grand-parents, and each of my brothers and sisters. Though separated from you, I always wish to share your joys and sorrows.

"Your little niece is in charming health. She sends many kisses to you all, and I shall teach her to love you, though she cannot see you."

We have inserted this letter, which in its spirit is a specimen of all her letters, not only for its, intrinsic excellence, but to show that even in distant Burmah, and surrounded by cares and duties which would have diminished in a less affectionate breast her interest in her distant relatives,

"Her heart untravelled fondly turned to" them, "And dragged at each remove a lengthening chain."

While laboring for the conversion of pagans, she felt more than she had ever felt before, the awful danger of those who under the full blaze of gospel light, choose to walk in darkness; and for her family, her dear brothers and sisters, her burden was almost like that of the apostle who was, as it were, willing to give up his own title to the heavenly inheritance, if by so doing he could save his "kindred according to the flesh."[10] All her letters which we have been privileged to see, bear evidence of this.

In December of the year 1828, Mrs. Boardman was called to a trial which of all others was most fitted to make her feel that every earthly dependence is at best but a broken reed, and that

"The spider's most attenuated thread   Is cord, is cable, to our strongest hold On earthly bliss; it breaks with every breeze."

Her almost idolized husband, her guide, her only human support, protector, and companion, was attacked by that insidious and incurable malady which was destined at no distant day to close his career of usefulness on earth, and send him early to his reward. A copious hemorrhage from the lungs warned him that his time for earthly labor was short, and seemed to increase his desire to work while his day lasted. As soon as his strength was sufficiently restored after his first attack, namely, in February 1829, he resolved to fulfil his long-cherished intention to visit the Karens in their native villages. He took with him two Karens, two of his scholars, and

---

10   Romans ix. 3.

a servant. Females, who in this country of order and security, tremble at the idea of being left for one night alone in their strong and guarded dwellings, may perhaps conceive the feelings of Mrs. Boardman on being thus left by her protector.--Her own health scarce re-established after a four months' illness,--her mind agitated by fears for her stricken husband, who under burning suns, and amid unknown wilds, exposed to the fury of the sudden thunder-gust, and the wild beast of the jungles, must be absent from her, perhaps, two or three dreary weeks in which time not one "cordial, endearing report" from him, would reach her;--in her frail hut, and with two little ones dearer to her than life, exposed to the same dangers as herself,--what could support her in such circumstances but her faith in that arm whose strength is shown to be "perfect, in weakness?" A poor Karen woman, seeing her distress, tried to console her: "Weep not, mama," she said; "the teacher has gone on an errand of compassion to my poor perishing countrymen. They have never heard of the true God, and the love of his Son Jesus Christ, who died upon he cross to save sinners. They know nothing of the true religion, mama; and when they die they cannot go to the golden country of the blessed. God will take care of the teacher; do not weep, mama." Blessed faith in an omnipresent Heavenly Father! It gives even the unlettered Karen disciple, an eloquence in consolation, to which worldly philosophy is a stranger.

Mr. Boardman's journey, though perilous from the causes above mentioned, and tedious from being performed on foot, was highly interesting on account of the eager welcome, and abundant hospitality of the simple-minded Karen villagers whom he visited. On entering a village, he and his little caravan were overwhelmed with presents of provisions and fruits; and the inhabitants would exclaim, while their countenances beamed with delight, "Ah, you have come *at last*; we have long wanted to see you!" He travelled more than one hundred miles, often through unfrequented and toilsome paths among the mountains, and was three times drenched with powerful rains, from which he had no sufficient shelter; but by the aid of an interpreter he preached seventeen sermons, and was cheered by finding the readiness of the people to receive his doctrines far exceed his most sanguine expectations. On his return, both he and Mrs. Boardman had to experience an affliction extremely trying to the heart of a missionary; the defection of some of the Christian converts. Their sensitive spirits led Mr. and Mrs. B. to fear that their own unfaithfulness might have been the cause of the fall of their disciples. Mrs. Boardman's self-upbraidings were bitter; her humiliation deep and sincere. "Our hearts," she says, "have bled with anguish, and mine has sunk lower than the grave, for I have felt that my unworthiness has been the cause of all our calamities."

So keen were her self-rebukes at this time, that they break out even in her letters to her friends. In one of them she writes: "Some of these poor Burmans, who are daily carried to the grave, may at last reproach me and say, you came, it is true, to the city where we dwelt, to tell of heaven and hell, but wasted much, much of your precious time in indolence while learning our language. And when you were able to speak, why were you not incessantly telling us of this day of doom, when we visited you? Why, oh why did you ever speak of any other thing, while we were ignorant of this most momentous of all truths? How could you think on anything but our salvation?... You told us you knew of a Being that heard your lowest whispers, and most secret sighs--why then, did you not, day and night, entreat him in our behalf?" Mr. Boardman in his journal says, "My dear wife became at this time so deeply impressed with divine things, and particularly with a sense of her own sinfulness, that she had no rest night or day. We both endeavored to return to the Lord from whom we had strayed; but our path, especially that of Mrs. B. led hard by the borders of despair.... We confessed our sins to the Lord and to one another. We considered ourselves worthy to be trodden under foot of men, and were astonished to think of our pride and selfishness.... We were filled with the most distressing views of our utter sinfulness in the sight of a holy God."

Thus was this affliction, though "grievous," beginning to work out in her heart its "peaceable fruit of righteousness," by deepening her humility, quickening her zeal, and leading her to a more thorough consecration of herself to the work she had undertaken.

CHAPTER VIII.

DEATH OF THEIR FIRST-BORN.--LETTERS FROM MRS. B.

In the spring of 1829 Mr. Boardman and his family made a short sea-voyage for the benefit of their health, Mrs. Boardman having experienced another attack of illness, and their little George being frail and puny. Indeed none of the family seemed to have been healthy but the "plump, rosy-cheeked" first-born, the darling Sarah, her mother's joy and pride, and--as her Heavenly Father saw--her *idol* too! Terrible was the stroke that shattered that lovely idol; but it came--so faith assured her--from a father's hand. Sometime afterward she writes, "My ever dear Sister, I think I have not written you since the death of our beloved Sarah, which is nearly eight months ago. I have never delayed writing to you so long before. For some time after her death, little George was apparently near the grave, and I was confined to my bed for a number of weeks. As soon as my health was a little improved, the rebellion at Tavoy took place, which threw us all into confusion, and this lasted until I was taken ill again about three months since. From this illness I am but just recovering. So you see, my beloved sister, my outward circumstances have been sufficient to prevent my writing. Nor is this all--for some time after little Sarah's departure, I was too much distressed to write; I felt assured that God had taken her away from us in love, and was also assured, that she is a happy angel in heaven; but oh the thought that we should see her no more on earth, filled me with ***indescribable sorrow***. By degrees my mind became calmer; not that I forgot her, but I feel, my dear Harriet, that the dearest and sweetest pleasures of this life are empty and altogether unsatisfying. I do not look for comfort from these sources as I formerly did. We have a fine, healthy boy, but I do not allow myself to idolize him as I did his dear departed sister. In her dissolution, we saw such a wreck of what was most lovely and beautiful, that it seems as if we should be kept in future from 'worshipping the creature.'"

Particulars respecting the child's illness and death are given in another letter of nearly the same date. "Our little Sarah left us July 8th of last year--aged 2 years and 8 months.... She was a singularly lovely child. Her bright blue eyes, yellow hair, and rosy cheeks, formed a striking contrast to the dark little faces around her.... From the time she began to notice anything, we were the objects of her fondest love. If she thought she had incurred our displeasure, her tender heart seemed ready to burst; and she could not rest for a moment until she had said she was 'sorry,' and obtained the kiss of forgiveness. She had learned to obey us implicitly.... If either of us were ill, she would stroke our foreheads with her little soft hand, and kiss us *so* affectionately! Her love to her little brother George was unlimited. From the day of his birth till the day but one before she died, he was her idol.... Three days before she died, she was lying uneasily in a large swing cradle, and George was in the same room crying. We thought it might soothe the little sufferer, for he also was very ill, to lay him down beside Sarah. The proposal delighted her; with smiles she threw open her little arms and for the last time held her darling brother in her fond embrace. So great was her gratification at this privilege, that she seemed to forget her own pains.

"Little Sarah spoke English remarkably well for so young a child, and Burmese like a native; she could also say some things in the Hindostanee and Karen, and what seems a little singular, she never confounded two languages, but always spoke pure English to us, and pure Burmese to Burmans. This discrimination continued as long as she had the powers of speech. She had learned the Lord's prayer and several little hymns. Dr. Judson's lines on the death of Mee Shawayee she knew by heart in Burmese, and used to chant them for half an hour at a time.... These things may seem very trivial to you, but I muse upon them by the hour together; and it is only when I call my cooler judgment into action, that I can make myself believe they are uninteresting to any person on earth. I love to think of my sweet bud of immortality expanding so beautifully in my own presence; and fancy I can judge in some small degree of the brilliancy of the perfect flower, from these little developments.

"A few hours before she died, she called us to her, kissed us, and passed her dear hand, still full and dimpled as in health, softly over our faces. The pupils of her eyes were so dilated that she could not see us distinctly, and once, for a moment or two, her mind seemed to be wandering; then looking anxiously into my face, she said: 'I frightened, mamma! I frightened!' ... Oh with what feelings did I wash and dress her lovely form for the last time, and compose her perfect little limbs; and then see her--the dear child that had so long lain in my bosom--borne away to her newly-made grave. My heart grew faint when I thought that I had performed for her my last office of love; that she would never need a mother's hand again.

My dear husband performed the funeral service with an aching, though not desponding heart. The grave is in our own enclosure, about fifteen rods from the house--a beautiful retired spot, in a grove of Gangau-trees. Near it is a little Bethel, erected for private devotion. Thither we have often repaired; and we trust that God, who in his infinite wisdom had taken our treasure to himself, often meets us there."

The biographer of Mrs. Boardman--since her successor in the mission--mentions that a single speculative error had crept into her religious faith, on the subject of God's particular providence--that while contemplating the vastness of that agency

"That ever busy wheels the silent spheres,"

she had almost thought it derogatory to the "Majesty of heaven and earth" to conceive of him as occupied with our mean affairs, numbering the hairs of our heads, and guiding the sparrow's fall. But the blow which crushed her heart, destroyed its skepticism. She saw so clearly in this dispensation, the hand of a Father chastening his erring child; she felt so keenly that she deserved the rod, for having in a measure worshipped the gift more than the giver, that she **believed**, with all the strength of an irresistible conviction, that even so lowly a thing as her own heart was indeed a theatre for the constant display of her Maker's guiding and controlling power, not less than the starry heavens; that her own sanctification, and the providential means to effect it, even in their minutest details, were ordered by sovereign grace and wisdom; and from this time forth she never doubted again.

But it is time to detail the spirit-stirring scenes that occurred a few months after the death of the child; to which scenes allusion was made in the first of her two letters.

CHAPTER IX.

REVOLT OF TAVOY.--LETTERS FROM MRS. B.

The revolt of Tavoy from the British government, and its consequences to the missionaries and other foreigners in the city, are so well described in a letter from Mr. Boardman to a friend in America, that we will give it nearly entire.

"REV. AND DEAR SIR,

"The province of Tavoy has engaged in an open revolt against the British government. On Lord's day morning, the 9th inst. at 4 o'clock, we were aroused from our quiet slumbers by the cry of 'Teacher, master, Tavoy rebels,' and ringing at all our doors and windows. We were soon awake to our extreme danger, as we heard not only a continual report of musketry within the town, but the balls were frequently passing over our heads and ***through our house***; and in a few moments, a large company of Tavoyans collected near our gate, and gave us reason to suspect they were consulting what to do with us. We lifted our hearts to God for protection, and Mrs. Boardman and little George were hurried away through a back door to a retired building in the rear. I lay down in the house, (to escape the bullets,) with a single Burman boy, to watch and communicate the first intelligence After an hour of the greatest anxiety and uncertainty I had the happiness of seeing the sepoys (troops in the British service) in possession of the city gates in front of our house. We soon ascertained that a party of about 250 men had in the first instance attacked the powder magazine and gun-shed, which were very near our house, but a guard of sepoys had repelled them. This was a great mercy, for had the insurgents obtained the arms and ammunition, our situation would have been most deplorable. A second party of 60 had attacked the house of the principal native officer of the town, while a third party had fallen upon the guard of the prison, and let loose all the prisoners, one hundred in number, who, as soon as their irons were knocked off, became the most desperate of all the insurgents." ...

The commissioner of the province was absent at Maulmain, but his lady, Mrs. Burney, urged their immediate removal to the government house. They hesitated at first, thinking the rebellion might soon be quelled; but hearing from a rebel prisoner that the whole province was engaged in the insurrection, and that large reinforcements might be hourly expected to join the rebels, and finding that the Mission premises from their situation, were likely to be the very battleground of the contending parties,--after seeking Divine direction, they concluded to abandon them. He continues his narrative, "We caught up a few light articles on which we could lay our hands, and with the native Christians, fled as if for our lives. I visited the house once or twice after this, and saved a few clothes and papers, but the firing being near, rendered it hazardous to remain, and the last time I went, I found the house had been plundered. A large part of our books, furniture and clothes, which had remained behind were either taken away or destroyed.

"We had been at the government house but a short time, when it was agreed to evacuate the town and retire to the wharf. In the hurry of our second removal, many things which we had brought from our house, were necessarily left, to fall into the hands of the plunderers. We soon found ourselves at the wharf,--a large wooden building of six rooms, into which, besides the Europeans, were huddled all the sepoys with their baggage and ours, and several hundreds of women and children belonging to Portuguese and others, who looked to the English for protection. Our greatest danger at this time arose from having in one of the rooms where many were to sleep, and all of us were continually passing, several hundred barrels of gunpowder, to which if fire should be communicated accidentally by ourselves, or mischievously by others, we should all perish at once. The next danger was from the rebels, who if they could either rush upon us, or take us by surprise or stratagem, would doubtless massacre us all on the spot. We lifted up our hearts to God, and he heard us from his holy habitation. We were preserved in safety through the night, though anxious and sleepless. All our attempts to communicate intelligence of our situation to the people in Maulmain and Mergui were defeated, and the heavy rains soon affected the health of the sepoys. We had but a small supply of rice in the granary near the wharf, and that was continually in danger of being destroyed or burnt. But through the kind care of our Heavenly Father, we were preserved alive, and nothing of great importance occurred until the morning of Thursday, a little before day-break, when a party of 500 advanced upon us from the town, and set fire to several houses and vessels near the wharf. But God interposed in our behalf, and sent a heavy shower of rain, which extinguished the fire while the sepoys repelled the assailants.

"At breakfast the same morning we had the happiness of seeing the Diana steam-vessel coming up the river, with Major Burney on board. Our hearts bounded with gratitude to God. It was soon agreed that the Diana should return immediately to Maulmain for a reinforcement of troops, and Major Burney had the kindness to offer a passage for Mrs. Boardman and our family together with his own. After looking to God for direction, I concluded to remain behind, partly in compliance with Major Burney's advice and desire, but particularly in the hope of being useful as an interpreter and negotiator, and a preventer of bloodshed. With painful pleasure I took a hasty leave of my dear family, and in the evening the Diana left us, not however without having several shots from cannon or jinjals fired at her from the people on the city wall. The English forces, small and weak and sick as they were, were now throwing up breast-works; and on Saturday the 15th inst. it was agreed to make an attack on the town, in order if possible to take from the walls the large guns that bore upon us, and to try the strength of the rebel party. I stood at the post of observation with a spy-glass to watch and give the earliest notice of the event, and soon had the pleasure of announcing that the officers and sepoys had scaled the walls, and were pitching down outside the large guns, that were mounted there, while friendly Chinese were employed in carrying them to the wharf. The success was complete, and nothing remained but to rescue the prisoners (60 in number) whom the rebels had caught and confined. After a short cessation and a little refreshment, a second attack was made, during which the prisoners escaped and the rebels evacuated the city. A second battery of guns was also taken and brought to the wharf. In the morning we walked at large through the town; but what desolation, what barbarous destruction was everywhere exhibited! everything that could not be carried away had been cut and destroyed in the most wanton manner. Our own house was cut to pieces, our books cut scattered, torn and destroyed; our furniture either carried off, or cut, or broken in pieces, and the house itself and zayat converted into cook-houses and barracks. During the last three days, we have been picking up the scattered fragments of our furniture, books, &c. and repairing our house.

"Nga-Dah, the ringleader of the rebellion, and eleven of his principal adherents, have been caught. The inhabitants are coming in with white flags and occupying their houses. The bazaar is open, and the work of repairs is going on.

"Yesterday morning the Diana arrived with a reinforcement of European soldiers; and to-day I have come on board, expecting to proceed to Maulmain immediately. My present plan is, if my brethren approve, to return with my family, and resume our missionary labors as before. The native members of our church, now scattered, will probably come into town as soon as they hear of our return. Of the boarding scholars, all are with us except three Karens.

"My letter is already protracted to so great a length, that I can only add that our preservation and deliverance from such imminent danger, should awaken in our hearts the warmest gratitude to our Heavenly Father, and the most unwavering confidence in his kind care; and that the foregoing account should revive and deepen the impression made by previous events in the history of this mission, that we stand in need of the continual and fervent prayers of Christians in America, not only for our preservation, but for divine guidance in all our affairs.

"I remain, yours,

"G.D. Boardman

"P.S. **Saturday Morning, August 22d.** --I have just arrived at Maulmain, and have the happiness to find my family and missionary friends in comfortable health. Praised be the Lord for his goodness.

"**Aug. 29th.** --After much deliberation, it is thought best that I should leave my family here, till affairs are more settled.... I expect to embark for Tavoy to-morrow morning. May the spirit of all grace go with me!"

This is a "plain unvarnished" account of the terrible scene through which the missionaries were so wonderfully preserved, but to understand more fully their imminent peril we should know, that the town, at the time of the revolt, was almost defenceless. The English civil and military chief absent; the officer in command on his death-bed; no English troops in the town, and but about a hundred sepoys, who though trained to British modes of warfare are by no means equal in skill or valor to British troops; and the chief engineer disabled by sickness;--the Tavoyans had well chosen the time of their attack, and they were sufficiently numerous to have carried all their plans into execution; but the result, like that of all conflicts between civilized and barbarous men, shows how greatly superior a few troops, well disciplined, are to the most numerous bodies of men, unacquainted with the art of war.

But what could be more appalling to the stoutest heart, than the situation of Mrs. Boardman and her helpless family! Forced to flee from her frail hut, by bullets actually whizzing through it, and to pass through the town amid the yells of an infuriated rabble, her path sometimes impeded by the dead bodies of men who had fallen in the conflict: driven from the shelter of the government house, again to fly through the streets to the wharf-house; and there, with three or four hundred fugitives crowded together, to await death which threatened them in every form,--hearing over their heads the rush of cannon balls, and seeing from burning buildings showers of sparks falling, one of which, if it reached the magazines under their roof, was sufficient to tear the building from its foundations and whelm them all in one common ruin,--or if they escaped this danger, to know that hundreds of merciless barbarians with knives and cutlasses might at any moment rush into the building and destroy them;--can the *female* heart, we are ready to ask, **endure** such fearful trial?

> "Perchance her reason stoops, or reels;
> Perchance a courage not her own
> Braces her mind to desperate tone,"

Yes, her mind was stayed by a "courage not her own," but it was "braced" to no "desperate tone;" rather its calmness was that of a child, who, in its own utter helplessness, clings to its father's arm, and feels secure. Neither must we forget that a painful diversion of her thoughts from the terrors around her, was afforded by the necessities of her suffering babe, to whom the foul air of the wharf-house, and the want of all comforts, had nearly proved fatal. It was only her sleepless, vigilant care, that, under Providence, prevented the poor child from sharing the fate of Mrs. Burney's little infant, which did not survive the dreadful scene.

And with what transports of joy did this suffering company hail the sight of the thin blue smoke that heralded the arrival of a steamer from Maulmain! Amid what distracting fears for her husband, left in the revolted city, her infant and herself, did Mrs. Boardman decide to go on board the steamer returning to Maulmain! And with what gratitude and joy did she, after several days of painful suspense, welcome to the same city, her husband, and hear the tidings of the triumph of British power, and the restoration of tranquillity! In her happiness at meeting him alive, she noticed not that his late exposure and sufferings had increased to an alarming degree the symptoms of his dreadful malady. Inspired with something of his own enthusiasm, she saw him depart, to return to his beloved labors in Tavoy, whither she hoped and expected soon to follow him.

CHAPTER X.

MISSIONARY LABORS OF MR. BOARDMAN--HIS ILL HEALTH.--LETTER FROM MRS. B.--DEATH OF A SECOND CHILD.--LETTERS FROM MRS. B.

From Mr. Boardman's journal we learn that he remained through the summer and part of the autumn at Tavoy, diligently prosecuting his labors among the Burmese, Chinese, Karens, and Europeans, among all which classes he had singular success. In the meantime Mrs. Boardman continued at Maulmain, part of the time suffering from illness, and when able, assisting the missionaries there, until October, when she returned again to Tavoy. The animated and even glowing recital, given by Mr. Boardman in his journals and letters of this year, of the spread of gospel truth among the natives; his records of preaching, travelling, teaching and baptisms, would lead one to suppose that he was in the enjoyment of the most vigorous health, and that his frame was insensible to fatigue. But careless as he was of his own bodily ease, there was an eye that watched him with the intensest solicitude; a heart that was pierced with anxiety, knowing that though "the inner man was renewed day by day," the outer man was too surely "perishing," and would soon be laid aside, forever.

On the 29th of July, 1830, Mrs. Boardman writes to her sister from Maulmain, whither they had gone for the benefit of her children's health: "We must look beyond this frail fleeting world for our true peace. Alas, I know by most bitter experience, that it is in vain to seek for true happiness here below. My fondest earthly hopes have again and again been dashed. Torn from the bosom of my dear father's family, my heart was almost broken; and when I stood by the death-bed of my sweet, my lovely Sarah, I felt indeed that earthly hopes and joys are but a dream.

But a *darker cloud* hangs over me. Oh what desolation and anguish of spirit do I feel, when I think it is possible that in a few more months, my earthly guide, supporter, and delight, may be no more!... He has a cough which has been hanging about him a year, and he is very much reduced by it.... Oh my sister, let us see to it that our affections are set on things above."

Such "desolation and anguish of spirit" as she here describes, had her husband felt for *her* in the preceding year, when for some months before and after the birth of her second son she lay struggling with a dangerous disease, which he thought would surely terminate her life. At that time he wrote: "She still grows weaker, and her case is now more alarming. Should our friends for whom I have sent to Maulmain come even immediately, I can scarcely hope for their arrival before the crisis, or probably, fatal termination of my dear partner's disorder. My comfort in my present affliction is the thought, that if to our former trials, the Lord sees fit to add that of removing my beloved companion, he does it with a perfect knowledge of all the blessedness which death will confer on *her*, and of all the sorrows and distresses which her loss will occasion her bereaved husband and orphan children, in our present peculiar condition. It affords me great relief to have been assured by her that the bitterness of death is past, and that heavenly glories have been unfolded in a wonderful and unexpected manner to her view." And again he says, seemingly losing for a moment his strong confidence, "What will become of my children, what will become of the schools--of the poor native women--what will become of *me*, if she die?" But she recovered, and "his thankfulness knew no bounds, his letters are eloquent in their utterance of joy and praise."

In a letter of Dec. 2, 1830, Mrs. Boardman records another affliction. "God has come very near to us and wounded our hearts afresh. Our youngest child, aged 8 months, went from us to meet his sainted sister, in September last. We mourn, but not without hope; for we shall soon be in that blissful world--be pure and lovely like our departed ones in glory." And Mr. Boardman says: "Our hearts have been pierced anew by the loss of our dear babe.... He was 8 months old, and though generally feeble, one of the most lovely and interesting of babes. The Lord has dealt with us severely, but not unkindly. He gave and he hath taken away."

Both these devoted missionaries knew, however, that the best defence against such trials as they endured, is found in a steady performance of duty. In trouble as well as in joy, they devoted themselves to their great object--saving souls.--How different from those who make a sort of merit of "indulging the luxury of grief;" and show their regard for the memory of the dead by neglecting their duties to the living! Christianity, while it inculcates and fosters the tenderest sensibility to the chastisements of our heavenly Parent, never allows us in any calamity, to fold our hands in inactive despair. Our pathway is filled with duties; and,

"Heart within, and God o'er head,"

we must, like our Master, "go about doing good," though we may feel "cast down, pressed out of measure," by affliction.

Speaking of a severe illness about this time, Mr. Boardman says: "Death seemed near, ... but had no alarms, no terrors.... My beloved family and the perishing heathen, were all that made me in the least degree unwilling to die. And even them I could resign to the hands of a gracious and covenant-keeping God." In one of the last letters he ever wrote, he thus records his testimony to the devotedness of his beloved wife. "During my present protracted illness, and when I was at the worst stage, she was the tenderest, most assiduous, attentive and affectionate of nurses. Without her, I think I should have finished my career in a few days. And even when our lamented, darling babe lay struggling in the very arms of death, though she was with him constantly, night and day, she did not allow me to suffer one moment, for lack of her attentions. I cannot write what I feel on this tender subject. But oh what kindness in our Heavenly Father, that when her services were so much needed, her health was preserved, and she had strength given her to perform her arduous labors."

Mr. Boardman's life was now fast ebbing away. In September, 1830, he had written a sort of farewell to his parents, brothers and sisters, from which it appears that even then he was daily looking for the summons--"Come up hither." He says of this letter that it is his last farewell. He thanks God that he has his complaint--consumption--in its mildest form. He enumerates many circumstances of mercy with which he is favored; and adds: "But most of all for outward comfort, I have my beloved wife, whose most untiring assiduity has mitigated many of my pains, and who is ever prompt to render all the services that the purest affection can dictate, or the greatest sufferings require. And it deserves to be mentioned that she has never been so free from missionary and family cares, or from attacks of illness, as during the last three months, while I have most needed her kind and soothing attentions. Bless the Lord oh my soul, and praise his name!"

"In thinking," he adds, "on the probability of dying soon, two or three things occasion considerable unwillingness to meet the solemn event. One is, the sore affliction I know it will occasion to my dear family, especially my fond, too fond wife. Her heart will be well-nigh riven. But I must leave her with Him who is anointed to heal the broken-hearted and to bind up their wounds. My dear little son is too young to remember me long, or to realize his loss. I have prayed for him many times, and can leave him in my Heavenly Father's hands.... Then there are the perishing heathens around me.... During the last ten years, I have studied with more or less reference to being useful to the heathen. And now, if just as I am beginning to be qualified to labor a little among them my days are cut short, much of my study and preparation seems to be in vain. But I chide myself for saying so or thinking so. If I had done no good whatever here in Burmah, I ought to submit and be still under the hand of God, ... but I trust He has made me of some service to a few poor benighted souls, especially among the Karens, who shall be my glory and joy in the day of the Lord Jesus." "As to my hope and my confidence of acceptance with God, if any man has reason to renounce all his own righteousness, ... and to trust entirely and solely to grace, sovereign grace, flowing through an atoning Saviour, I am that man. A perfectly right action, with perfectly right motives, I never performed, and never shall perform, till freed from this body of sin. An unprofitable servant, is the most appropriate epitaph for my tombstone."

Thus appeared a life of self-denying sacrifices for Christ, when shone upon by the pure light of eternity. Happy then that the dying man could say, "NOT by works of righteousness which we have done but by his mercy he saves us!"

CHAPTER XI.

LETTER FROM MRS. BOARDMAN.--ILLNESS AND DEATH OF GEORGE DANA BOARDMAN.

"Tavoy, March 7, 1831.

"My beloved Parents,

"With a heart glowing with joy, and at the same time rent with anguish unutterable, I take my pen to address you. You, too, will rejoice when you hear what God has wrought through the instrumentality of your beloved son. Yes, you will bless God that you were enabled to devote him to this blessed service among the heathen, when I tell you that within the last two months, fifty-seven have been baptized, all Karens, excepting one, a little boy of the school and son of the native governor. Twenty-three were baptized in this city by Moung Ing, and thirty-four in their native wilderness by Mr. Mason.

"Mr. Mason arrived Jan. 23d, and on the 31st, he, with Mr. Boardman, myself and George, set out on a long-promised tour among the Karens. Mr. Boardman was very feeble, but we hoped the change of air and scenery would be beneficial. A company of Karens had come to convey us out, Mr. Boardman on his bed and me in a chair. We reached the place on the third day, and found they had erected a bamboo chapel on a beautiful stream at the base of a range of mountains. The place was central, and nearly one hundred persons had assembled, more than half of them applicants for baptism. Oh it was a sight calculated to call forth the liveliest joy of which human nature is susceptible, and made me, for a moment, forget my bitter griefs--a sight far surpassing all I had ever anticipated, even in my most sanguine hours. The Karens cooked, ate and slept on the around, by the river-side, with no other shelter than the trees of the forest. Three years ago they were sunk in the lowest depths of ignorance and superstition. Now the glad tidings of mercy had reached them, and they were willing to live in the open air, away from their homes, for the sake of enjoying the privileges of the Gospel.

"My dear husband had borne the journey better than we had feared, though he suffered from exhaustion and pain in his side, which, however, was much relieved by a little attention. His spirits were unusually good, and we fondly hoped that a few days' residence in that delightful, airy spot, surrounded by his loved Karens, would recruit and invigorate his weakened frame. But I soon perceived he was failing, and tenderly urged his return to town, where he could enjoy the quiet of home, and the benefit of medical advice. But he repelled the thought at once, saying he confidently expected improvement from the change, and that the disappointment would be worse for him than staying. 'And even,' added he, 'should my poor, unprofitable life be somewhat shortened by staying, ought I, on that account merely, to leave this interesting field? Should I not rather stay and assist in gathering in these dear scattered lambs of the fold? You know, Sarah, that coming on a foreign mission involves the probability of a shorter life, than staying in one's native country. And yet obedience to our Lord, and compassion for the perishing heathen, induced us to make this sacrifice. And have we ever repented that we came? No; I trust we can both say that we bless God for bringing us to Burmah, for directing our footsteps to Tavoy, and even for leading us hither. You already know, my love,' he continued, with a look of tenderness never to be forgotten, 'that I cannot live long, I must sink under this disease; and should we go home now, the all-important business which brought us out, must be given up, and I might linger out a few days of suffering, stung with the reflection, that I had preferred a few idle days, to my Master's service. Do not, therefore, ask me to go, till these poor Karens have been baptized.' I saw he was right, but my feelings revolted. Nothing seemed so valuable as his life, and I felt that I could make any sacrifice to prolong it, though it were but for one hour. Still a desire to gratify him, if no higher motive made me silent, though my heart ached to see him so ill in such a wretched place, deprived of many of the comforts of life, to say nothing of the indulgences desirable in sickness.

"The chapel was large, but open on all sides, excepting a small place built up for Mr. Mason, and a room about five feet wide and ten feet long, for the accommodation of Mr. Boardman and myself with our little boy. The roof was so low, that I could not stand upright; and it was but poorly enclosed, so that he was exposed to the burning rays of the sun by day, and to the cold winds and damp fog by night. But his mind was happy, and he would often say, 'If I live to see this one ingathering, I may well exclaim, with happy Simeon, Lord, now lettest thou thy servant depart in peace, according to thy word, for mine eyes have seen thy salvation. How many ministers have wished they might die in their pulpits; and would not dying in a spot like this, be even more blessed than dying in a pulpit at home? I feel that it would.'

"Nor was it merely the pleasing state of things around him that filled his mind with comfort. He would sometimes dwell on the infinite compassion of God, and his own unworthiness, till his strength was quite exhausted; and though he told Mr. Mason that he had not the rapture which he had sometimes enjoyed, yet his mind was calm and peaceful; and it was plainly perceptible, that earthly passions had died way, and that he was enjoying sweet foretastes of that rest into which he was so soon to enter. He would often say to me, 'My meditations are very sweet, though my mind seems as much weakened as my body. I have not had that liveliness of feeling, which I have sometimes enjoyed, owing to my great weakness, but I shall soon be released from shackles, and be where I can praise God continually, without weariness. My thoughts delight to dwell on these words, *There is no night there*.'

"I felt that the time of separation was fast approaching, and said to him, 'My dear, I have one request to make; it is, that you would pray much for George, during your few remaining days. I shall soon be left alone, almost the only one on earth to pray for him, and I have great confidence in your dying prayers.' He looked earnestly at the little boy, and said, 'I will try to pray for him; but I trust very many prayers will ascend for the dear child from our friends at home, who will be induced to supplicate the more earnestly for him, when they hear that he is left fatherless in a heathen land.'

"On Wednesday, while looking in the glass, he seemed at once to see symptoms of his approaching dissolution, and said, without emotion, 'I have altered greatly--I am sinking into the grave very fast--just on the verge.' Mr. Mason said to him, 'Is there nothing we can do for you? Had we not better call the physician? Or shall we try to remove you into town immediately?' After a few moments' deliberation, it was concluded to defer the baptism of the male applicants, and set out for home early the next morning. Nearly all the female candidates had been examined, and as it is difficult for them to come to town, it was thought best that Mr. Mason should baptize them in the evening. We knelt, and Mr. Mason having prayed for a blessing on the decision, we sat down to breakfast with sorrowful hearts.

"While we were at the table, my beloved husband said, 'I shall soon be thrown away for this world; but I hope the Lord Jesus will take me up. That merciful Being, who is represented as passing by, and having compassion on the poor cast-out infant, will not suffer me to perish. O, I have no hope but in the wonderful, condescending, infinite mercy of God, through his dear Son. I cast my poor perishing soul, loaded with sin, as it is, upon his compassionate arms, assured that all will he forever safe.' On seeing my tears, he said, 'Are you not reconciled to the will of God, my love?' When I told him I hoped I did not feel unreconciled, he continued, 'I have long ago, and many times, committed you and our little one into the hands of our covenant God. He is the husband of the widow and the father of the fatherless. Leave thy fatherless children, I will preserve them alive; and let thy widows trust in me, saith the Lord. He will be your stay and support, when I am gone. The separation will be but short. O, how happy I shall be to welcome you to heaven.' He then addressed Mr. Mason, as follows:--'Brother, I am heartily rejoiced, and bless God that you have arrived, and especially am I gratified, that you are so much interested for the poor Karens. You will, I am assured, watch over them, and take care of them; and if some of them turn back, you will still care for them. As to my dear wife and child, I know you will do all in your power to make them comfortable. Mrs. B. will probably spend the ensuing rains in Tavoy. She will be happy with you and Mrs. Mason; that is, as happy as she can be in her state of loneliness. She will mourn for me, and a widow's state is desolate and sorrowful at best. But God will he infinitely better to her, than I have ever been.' On the same day, he wished me to read some hymns on affliction, sickness, death, &c. I took Wesley's Hymn Book, the only one we had with us, and read several, among others, the one beginning 'Ah, lovely appearance of death.'

"On Wednesday evening, thirty-four persons were baptized. Mr. Boardman was carried to the waterside, though so weak that he could hardly breathe without the continual use of the fan and the smelling-bottle. The joyful sight was almost too much for his feeble frame. When we reached the chapel, he said he would like to sit up and take tea with us. We placed his cot near the table, and having bolstered him up, we took tea together. He asked the blessing, and did it with his right hand upraised, and in a tone that struck me to the heart. It was the same tremulous, yet urgent, and I had almost said, unearthly voice, with which my aged grandfather used to pray. We now began to notice that brightening of the mental faculties, which I had heard spoken of, in persons near their end.

"After tea was removed, all the disciples present, about fifty in number, gathered around him, and he addressed them for a few moments in language like the following:--'I did hope to stay with you till after Lord's-day, and administer to you once more the Lord's Supper. But God is calling me away from you. I am about to die, and shall soon be inconceivably happy in heaven. When I am gone, remember what I have taught you; and O, be careful to persevere unto the end, that when you die, we may meet one another in the presence of God, never more to part. Listen to the word of the new teacher and the teacheress as you have done to mine. The teacheress will be very much distressed. Strive to lighten her burdens, and comfort her by your good conduct. Do not neglect prayer. The eternal God, to whom you pray, is unchangeable. Earthly teachers sicken and die, but God remains forever the same. Love Jesus Christ with all your hearts, and you will be forever safe.' This address I gathered from the Karens, as I was absent preparing his things for the night. Having rested a few minutes, he offered a short prayer, and then with Mr. Mason's assistance, distributed tracts and portions of Scripture to them all. Early the next morning we left for home, accompanied by nearly all the males and some of the females, the remainder returning to their homes in the wilderness. Mr. Boardman was free from pain during the day, and there was no unfavorable change, except that his mouth grew sore. But at four o'clock in the afternoon, we were overtaken by a violent shower of rain accompanied by lightning and thunder. There was no house in sight, and we were obliged to remain in the open air, exposed to the merciless storm. We covered him with mats and blankets, and held our umbrellas over him, all to no purpose. I was obliged to stand and see the storm beating upon him, till his mattress and pillows were drenched with rain. We hastened on, and soon came to a Tavoy house. The inhabitants at first refused us admittance, and we ran for shelter into the out-houses. The shed I happened to enter, proved to be the 'house of their gods,' and thus I committed an almost unpardonable offence. After some persuasion they admitted us into the house, or rather verandah, for they would not allow us to sleep inside, though I begged the privilege for my sick husband with tears. In ordinary cases, perhaps, they would have been hospitable; but they knew that Mr. Boardman was a teacher of a foreign religion, and that the Karens in our company had embraced that religion.

"At evening worship, Mr. Boardman requested Mr. Mason to read the thirty-fourth Psalm. He seemed almost spent, and said, 'This poor perishing dust will soon be laid in the grave; but God can employ other lumps of clay to perform his will, as easily as he has this poor unworthy one.' I told him, I should like to sit up and watch by him, but he objected, and said in a tender supplicating tone, 'Cannot we sleep together?' The rain still continued, and his cot was wet, so that he was obliged to lie on the bamboo floor. Having found a place where our little boy could sleep without danger of falling through openings in the floor, I threw myself down, without undressing, beside my beloved husband. I spoke to him often during the night, and he said he felt well, excepting an uncomfortable feeling in his mouth and throat. This was somewhat relieved by frequent washings with cold water. Miserably wretched as his situation was, he did not complain; on the contrary, his heart seemed overflowing with gratitude. 'O,' said he, 'how kind and good our Father in heaven is to me; how many are racked with pain, while I, though near the grave, am almost free from distress of body. I suffer nothing, ***nothing*** to what you, my dear Sarah, had to endure last year, when I thought I must lose you. And then I have you to move me so tenderly. I should have sunk into the grave ere this, but for your assiduous attention. And brother Mason is as kind to me as if he were my own brother. And then how many, in addition to pain of body, have anguish of soul, while my mind is sweetly stayed on God.' On my saying, 'I hope we shall be at home to-morrow night, where you can lie on your comfortable bed, and I can nurse you as I wish,' he said, 'I want nothing that the world can afford, but my wife and friends; earthly conveniences and comforts are of little consequence to one so near heaven. I only want them for your sake.' In the morning we thought him a little better, though I perceived, when I gave him his sago, that his breath was very short. He, however, took rather more nourishment than usual, and spoke about the manner of his conveyance home. We ascertained that by waiting until twelve o'clock, we could go the greater part of the way by water.

"At about nine o'clock, his hands and feet grew cold, and the affectionate Karens rubbed them all the forenoon, excepting a few moments when he requested to be left alone. At ten o'clock, he was much distressed for breath, and I thought the long dreaded moment had arrived. I asked him, if he felt as if he was going home--'not just yet,' he replied. On giving him a little wine and water, he revived. Shortly after, he said, 'You were alarmed without cause just now, dear--I know the reason of the distress I felt, but am too weak to explain it to you.' In a few moments he said to me, 'Since you spoke to me about George, I have prayed for him almost incessantly--more than in all my life before.'

"It drew near twelve, the time for us to go to the boat. We were distressed at the thought of removing him, when evidently so near the last struggle, though we did not think it so near as it really was. But there was no alternative. The chilling frown of the iron-faced Tavoyan was to us as if he was continually saying, 'be gone.' I wanted a little broth for my expiring husband, but on asking them for a fowl they said they had none, though at that instant, on glancing my eye through an opening in the floor, I saw three or four under the house. My heart was well nigh breaking.

"We hastened to the boat, which was only a few steps from the house. The Karens carried Mr. Boardman first, and as the shore was muddy, I was obliged to wait till they could return for me. They took me immediately to him; but O, the agony of my soul, when I saw the hand of death was on him! He was looking me full in the face, but his eyes were changed, not dimmed, but brightened, and the pupils so dilated, that I feared he could not see me. I spoke to him--kissed him--but he made no return, though I fancied that he tried to move his lips. I pressed his hand, knowing that if he could, he would return the pressure; but, alas! for the first time, he was insensible to my love, and forever. I had brought a glass of wine and water already mixed, and a smelling-bottle, but neither was of any avail to him now. Agreeably to a previous request, I called the faithful Karens, who loved him so much, and whom he had loved unto death, to come and watch his last gentle breathings, for there was no struggle.

"Never, my dear parents, did one of our poor fallen race have less to contend with, in the last enemy. Little George was brought to see his dying father, but he was too young to know there was cause for grief When Sarah died, her father said to George, 'Poor little boy, you will not know to-morrow what you have lost to-day.' A deep pang rent my bosom at the recollection of this, and a still deeper one succeeded when the thought struck me, that though my little boy may not know to-morrow what he has lost to-day, yet when years have rolled by, and he shall have felt the unkindness of a deceitful, selfish world, **he will know**.

"Mr. Mason wept, and the sorrowing Karens knelt down in prayer to God--that God, of whom their expiring teacher had taught them--that God, into whose presence the emancipated spirit was just entering--that God, with whom they hope and expect to be happy forever. My own feelings I will not attempt to describe. You may have some faint idea of them, when you recollect what he was to me, how tenderly I loved him, and, at the same time, bear in mind the precious promises to the afflicted.

"We came in silence down the river, and landed about three miles from our house. The Karens placed his precious remains on his little bed, and with feelings which you can better imagine than I describe, we proceeded homewards. The mournful intelligence had reached town before us, and we were soon met by Moung Ing, the Burman preacher. At the sight of us he burst into a flood of tears. Next, we met the two native Christian sisters, who lived with us. But the moment of most bitter anguish was yet to come on our arrival at the house. They took him into the sleeping-room, and when I uncovered his face, for a few moments, nothing was heard but reiterated sobs. He had not altered--the same sweet smile, with which he was wont to welcome me, sat on his countenance. His eyes had opened in bringing him, and all present seemed expecting to hear his voice; when the thought, that it was silent forever, rushed upon us, and filled us with anguish sudden and unutterable. There were the Burman Christians, who had listened so long, with edification and delight, to his preaching--there were the Karens, who looked to him as their guide, their earthly all--there were the scholars whom he had taught the way to heaven, and the Christian sisters, whose privilege it had been to wash, as it were, his feet.

"Early next morning, his funeral was attended, and all the Europeans in the place, with many natives, were present. It may be some consolation to you to know that everything was performed in as decent a manner, as if he had been buried in our own dear native land. By his own request, he was interred on the south side of our darling first-born. It is a pleasant circumstance to me, that they sleep *side by side*. But it is infinitely more consoling to think, that their glorified spirits have met in that blissful world, where sin and death never enter, and sorrow is unknown.

"Praying that we may be abundantly prepared to enter into our glorious rest, I remain, my dear parents, your deeply afflicted, but most affectionate child,

"Sarah H. Boardman."

* * * * *

Well might Mr. Judson say, "One of the brightest luminaries of Burmah is extinguished, dear brother Boardman is gone to his eternal rest. He fell gloriously at the head of his troops, in the arms of victory, thirty-seven wild Karens having been brought into the camp of our king since the beginning of the year, besides the thirty-two that were brought in during the two preceding years. Disabled by wounds, he was obliged through the whole of his last expedition, to be carried on a litter; but his presence was a host, and the Holy Spirit accompanied his dying whispers with almighty influence. Such a death, next to that of martyrdom, must be glorious in the eyes of Heaven. Well may we rest assured, that a triumphal crown awaits him on the great day, and 'Well done, good and faithful servant, enter thou into the joy of thy Lord!'" This is in the spirit of Montgomery's noble hymn, with an extract from which we will close the account of George Dana Boardman.

"Soldier of Christ, well done!
  Rest from thy loved employ:
The battle fought, the victory won,
  Enter thy Master's joy.
At midnight came the cry,
  To meet thy God prepare!
He woke, and caught his Captain's eye;
  Then, strong in faith and prayer

His spirit, with a bound,
  Left its encumbering clay;
His tent, at sunrise, on the ground,
  A darkened ruin lay."

CHAPTER XII.

LETTERS FROM MRS. B.--HER DECISION TO REMAIN IN BURMAH.--
HER MISSIONARY LABORS.--HER TRIALS.--SCHOOLS.

Mrs. Boardman found the society of Mr. and Mrs. Mason a sweet solace to her sad heart. They joined her at Tavoy in the spring of 1831, and assisted her in her school, besides studying the language. Her letters to her sister show a spirit chastened and saddened, but not crushed by sorrow, and still tenderly solicitous for the spiritual welfare of her dear brothers and sisters in America. She urges them by every motive, to embrace that Saviour she had found so precious. After telling them of the "glorious revival among the Karens," and of the baptism of seventy-three of them, she asks how they feel when they hear of the conversion of these poor children of the wilderness? "Some," she says, "indeed most of those who have been baptized, were impressed with the infinite importance of religion at the first time of hearing the gospel, and gave themselves no rest till they found it in the Saviour. O, I tremble and can scarcely hold my pen while I think of the awful account *you* must render to God, if after all your privileges, you fall short of Heaven at last.... How can you resist any longer? You cannot, you will not--something tells me you will give yourself immediately, unreservedly to that compassionate Saviour whose love was stronger than death."

Her confidence was justified; for some months later she says, "Dearly beloved brother and sister, a parcel of letters from America has reached us, which we eagerly opened, ... and received the delightful, heart-cheering intelligence that you have both become followers of Jesus, and have openly professed his name, and that two others of the dear children are serious.... Oh I have wept hours at the thought of God's goodness in giving me such joyful news in the midst of my sorrows. And is it indeed true that my own dear Harriet and my dearly loved brother are adopted into the family of God's chosen ones? Are your names really written in the Lamb's book of life?... And do each of you when alone in your closet before your Heavenly Father, feel that he draws near to you, and that sweeter than all the pleasures of the world is communion with him? O I know that you do; and now do I feel a union with you unknown before. How sweet to feel, that while wandering, a lonely desolate widow, some of those whom I most love, remember me every day before a throne of grace. Now when I kneel in prayer the voice of praise is on my lips. At each thought of home, my heart leaps for joy, and I feel as if relieved of a heavy burden which continually weighed down my spirits while thinking of my absent brothers and sisters.... The accounts of the glorious revivals in different parts of our dear native land have greatly refreshed our hearts, and we are ready to exclaim, surely the millennium has dawned for happy America. Perhaps you think such intelligence makes me wish to return. But no, my dear brothers and sisters, it makes me feel just the reverse. I do most ardently long to labor in this dark land till the day dawns upon us, ... rather I should say till the Sun of Righteousness reaches the ***meridian*** of Burmah, for the day has already dawned, and the eastern Karen mountains, enveloped for ages past in midnight gloom, are rejoicing in his bright beams.

"Our schools are very flourishing.... We have sixty scholars in town, and about fifty among the Karens in the jungles. I feel desolate, lonely, and sometimes deeply distressed at my great and irreparable loss,--but I bless God I am not in despair. My darling George is in good health, and is a source of much comfort, though of deep anxiety to me. He is learning to read, but is not so forward as children at home. How it comforts my heart to be able to ask you to pray for him!"

In a hurried postscript she adds: "There are more than eighty Karens at our house, upwards of twenty of them applicants for baptism."

In another letter: "Death now seems nearer to me, and Heaven dearer than before I was afflicted; ... my afflictions are precisely the kind my soul needed.... I receive from my dear friends the Masons, every possible kindness. But alas! the hours of loneliness and bitter weeping I endure, are known only to God. But still Jesus has sweetened the cup, and I would not that it should have passed my lip."

Three courses of life were now open to Mrs. Boardman. Either to devote herself to her domestic duties, manage her household, educate her darling boy, and in quiet seclusion pass the weary days of her widowhood; or--looking abroad on the spiritual wants of the people around her, knowing that if one devoted laborer was gone there was the more need of activity in those that remained,--she might continue to employ her time and faculties in instructing and elevating those in whose service her husband had worn out his life; or, thirdly, she might take her child, her "only one," and return to the land of her birth, where she still had dear parents, brothers and sisters, who would welcome her with open arms, and where she could give her son those advantages which he never could have in a heathen land. To adopt either the first or the last of these courses, she was urged by her natural disposition, which was singularly modest and retiring, her feeble health, the enervating influence of the climate, and above all by the strong tendency to self-indulgence which always accompanies a heart-rending sorrow. "But oh," she says in a letter to a friend, "these poor, inquiring and Christian Karens, and the school-boys, and the Burmese Christians" ... and the thought of *these* made her more than willing to adopt the second course; for she says, "My beloved husband wore out his life in this glorious cause; and that remembrance makes me more than ever attached to the work and the people for whose salvation he labored till death."

During her husband's life-time. Mrs. Boardman had of course little to perform of what could properly be called missionary labor; even her teaching in the schools was very often interrupted by sickness, and the schools themselves were often broken up by untoward events which the Missionaries could not control. Now, however, new circumstances called her to new and untried duties. Yet there was no sudden or violent change in her mode of life. The honored lips that had instructed, and guided, and comforted the ignorant natives, were sealed in death; yet still those natives continued to turn their eyes and their steps to the loved residence of their teacher whenever they found themselves oppressed with difficulty or distress and could the widow of that venerated teacher refuse to those poor disciples any guidance or consolation it was in her power to bestow? No; quietly and meekly she instructed the ignorant, consoled the afflicted, led inquirers to her Saviour, and warned the impenitent to flee to him; and if insensibly she thus came to fill a place from which her nature would instinctively have shrunk, there was still about her such a modest and womanly grace, combined with such a serious and dignified purpose of soul, that the most fastidious could have found nothing to censure, while lovers of the cause she had espoused, found everything to commend. "I rejoice," writes a friend in this country to her, on hearing of her self-sacrificing labors, "that your husband's mantle has fallen upon you ... and that more than ever before, it is in your heart to benefit the heathen."

That her duties were arduous, her letters fully prove. In one of them she says, "Every moment of my time is occupied ***from sunrise till ten in the evening***. It is late-bed time, and I am surrounded by five Karen women, three of whom arrived this afternoon from the jungle, after being separated from us nearly five months by the heavy rains. The Karens are beginning to come to us in companies; and with them, and our scholars in the town, and the care of my darling boy, you will scarce think I have much leisure for letter-writing."

Thus she toiled on, cheered by the consciousness that she was in the path of duty: that her husband if permitted from his home in heaven to watch over the spot he most loved on earth, would smile approvingly on her labors; and encouraged by the affection of many of the disciples, and the interest awakened among some new inquirers.

But it cannot be doubted that her trials were at least equal to her encouragements. Long before, Mr. Boardman had written, "the thoughts of this people," the Burmans, "run in channels entirely different from ours. Their whole system has a tendency to cramp their intellectual powers;--professedly divine in its origin, it demands credence without evidence; it spurns improvement, disdains the suggestions of experience, and flatly denies the testimony of the external senses. What a man sees with his own eyes he is not to believe, because his Scriptures teach otherwise.... There is no fellowship of thought between them and us on any subject. Everything appears to them in a different light, they attribute everything to a different cause, seek a remedy of evils from a different quarter, and entertain, in fine, a set of thoughts and imaginations totally different from ours." The Karens, it is true, had fewer prejudices to be eradicated, and more easily sympathized with the missionaries than the haughty, self-sufficient Burmans; but then their very docility made them liable to another danger, that of holding their new faith lightly, and parting with it easily. All these difficulties sometimes so pressed upon Mrs. Boardman, that she was ready to say, "It requires the patience of a Job and the wisdom of a Solomon to get on with this people; much as I love them, and good as I think they are." She then spoke of the *converts*; in whom was implanted that grace which, so far as it operates on the heart, makes all, in a sense, *one* in Christ Jesus; how then must she have been tried with those who would not repent and embrace the only principles that could give her the least fellowship or communion with them?

Jan. 19, 1832. --Mrs. Boardman writes of herself and her fellow-missionaries, Mr. and Mrs. Mason, "We meet with much encouragement in our schools, and our number of day-scholars is now about eighty. These, with the boarding schools, two village schools, and about fifty persons who learn during the rainy season in the Karen jungle, make upwards of one hundred and seventy under our instruction. The scholars in the jungle cannot of course visit us often but a great many have come to be examined in their lessons, and we are surprised and delighted at the progress they have made."

Of course they had to employ, as teachers of these schools, natives, who needed constant supervision and superintendence. Some of these teachers were exceedingly interesting persons. Of the death of one of them she writes, "Thah-oung continued in his school till two days before his death, although for a long time he had been very ill. He felt, then, that he *must* die, and said to his scholars, 'I can do no more--God is calling me away from you,--I go into His presence--be not dismayed.' He was then carried to the house of his father, a few miles distant, and there he continued exhorting and praying to the very last moment. His widow, who is not yet fifteen, is one of the loveliest of our desert blossoms." And afterwards in alluding to the same event, she says, "One of our best Karen teachers came to see us, and through him we heard that the disciples were well; that they were living in love, in the enjoyment of religion, and had nothing to distress them, but the death of their beloved teacher. Poor Moung Quay was obliged to turn away his face to weep several times while answering my inquiries. Oh how they feel the stroke that has fallen upon them. And well they may, for he was to them a father and a guide."

"The superintendence of the food and clothing of both the boarding schools," she afterwards writes, "together with the care of five day-schools under native teachers, devolves wholly on me. Our day-schools are growing every week more and more interesting. We cannot, it is true, expect to see among them so much progress, especially in Christianity, as our boarders make; but they are constantly gaining religious knowledge, and will grow up with comparatively correct ideas. They with their teachers attend worship regularly on Lord's-day. The day-schools are entirely supported at present by the Honorable Company's allowance, and the civil commissioner, Mr. Maingy appears much interested in their success."

CHAPTER XIII.

CORRESPONDENCE BETWEEN MRS. BOARDMAN AND THE SUPERINTENDENT.--HER TOURS AMONG THE KARENS.--HER PERSONAL APPEARANCE.--HER ACQUAINTANCE WITH THE BURMAN LANGUAGE.--DR. JUDSON'S TRANSLATION OF THE BIBLE.

An interesting letter from the gentleman mentioned at the close of the last chapter, with Mrs. Boardman's reply, we will give entire, as they exhibit at once her firmness of principle, and the high respect she commanded from the European residents in the country.

"Tavoy, Aug. 24, 1833.

"Mr. Mason has handed me for perusal, the extract from your letter to Government, which you kindly sent him. I apprehend I have hitherto had wrong impressions in reference to the ground on which the Honorable Company patronize schools in their territories; and I hope you will allow me to say, that it would not accord with my feelings and sentiments, to banish religious instruction from the schools under my care. I think it desirable for the rising generation of this Province, to become acquainted with useful science; and the male part of the population, with the English language. But it is infinitely more important that they receive into their hearts our holy religion, which is the source of so much happiness in this state, and imparts the hope of a glorious immortality in the world to come. Parents and guardians must know that there is more or less danger of their children deserting the faith of their ancestors, if placed under the care of a Foreign Missionary; and the example of some of the pupils is calculated to increase such apprehensions. Mr. Boardman baptized into the Christian religion several of his scholars. One of the number is now a devoted preacher; and notwithstanding the decease of their beloved and revered teacher, they all, with one unhappy exception, remain firm in the Christian faith.

"The success of the Hindoo College, where religious instruction was interdicted, may perhaps be urged in favor of pursuing a similar course in schools here. But it strikes me, that the case is different here, even admitting *their* course to be right. The overthrow of a system so replete with cruel and impure rites, as the Hindoo, or so degrading as the Mahometan, **might** be matter of joy, though no better religion were introduced in its stead. But the Burman system of morality is superior to that of the nations round them, and to the heathen of ancient times, and is surpassed only by the divine precepts of our blessed Saviour. Like all other merely **human** institutions, it is destitute of saving power; but its influence on the people, so far as it is felt, is salutary, and their moral character will, I should think, bear a comparison with that of any heathen nation in the world. The person who should spend his days in teaching them mere human science, (though he might undermine their false tenets,) by neglecting to set before them brighter hopes and purer principles, would, I imagine, live to very little purpose. For myself, sure I am, I should at last suffer the overwhelming conviction of having labored in vain.

"With this view of things, you will not, my dear sir, be surprised at my saying, it is impossible for me to pursue a course so utterly repugnant to my feelings, and so contrary to my judgment, as to banish religious instruction from the schools in my charge. It is what I am confident you yourself would not wish; but I infer from a remark in your letter that such are the terms on which Government affords patronage. It would be wrong to deceive the patrons of the schools and if my supposition is correct, I can do no otherwise than request, that the monthly allowance be withdrawn. It will assist in establishing schools at Maulmain on a plan more consonant with the wishes of Government than mine has ever been. Meanwhile I trust, I shall be able to represent the claims of my pupils in such a manner, as to obtain support and countenance from those, who would wish the children to be taught the principles of the Christian faith.

"Allow me, my dear sir, to subscribe myself,

"Yours, most respectfully,

"Sarah H. Boardman."

"My dear Madam,

"I cannot do otherwise than honor and respect the sentiments conveyed in your letter, now received. You will, I hope, give me credit for sincerity, when I assure you, that in alluding to the system of instruction pursued by you, it has ever been a source of pride to me, to point out the quiet way, in which your scholars have been made acquainted with the Christian religion. My own Government in no way proscribes the teaching of Christianity. The observations in my official letter are intended to support what I have before brought to the notice of Government, that ***all*** are received, who present themselves for instruction at your schools, without any stipulation as to their becoming members of the Christian faith.

I cannot express to you how much your letter has distressed me. It has been a subject of consideration with me, for some months past, how I could best succeed in establishing a college here, the scholars of which were to have been instructed in the same system which you have so successfully pursued. Believe me,

"Yours very faithfully,

"A.D. Maingy

"*Saturday.*"

Appropriations were afterward made by the British government for schools throughout the Provinces "to be conducted on the plan of Mrs. Boardman's schools at Tavoy;" and although the propagation of Christianity in the *other* schools was subsequently prohibited, yet in *her own*, she always taught as her conscience dictated.

It had been one of Mr. Boardman's practices to make frequent tours among the Karen villages, to preach the gospel, and strengthen the disciples and the feeble churches. Even from this duty, as far as the visitation was concerned, his widow did not shrink, although she *did* shrink from writing or speaking much on the subject; doubtless always regarding it as a cross, which although she might bear with patience, she would willingly lay down as soon as duty should permit. Attended by her faithful Karens, and her little boy borne in their arms,--leaving Mr. Mason to his indispensable task of acquiring the language, she would thread the wild passes of the mountains, and the obscure paths of the jungle, fording the smaller streams and carried over the larger in a chair borne on bamboo poles by her followers,--carrying joy and gladness to the hearts of the simple-minded villagers, and cheering her own by witnessing their constancy and fidelity.

In her own inimitable style "Fanny Forrester" gives an account of an adventure of Mrs. Boardman during one of these excursions; in which the impression she made upon an English officer who encountered her far from civilized habitations, so unexpectedly that he almost mistook her for an angel visitant from a better sphere, was sufficiently pleasant to form the basis of a lasting friendship between them. Indeed there are many testimonials to Mrs. Boardman's personal loveliness and grace of manner. In Calcutta, where she resided nearly two years, she was regarded as a "finished lady;" and in a well-written tribute to her memory, published in the Mother's Journal, she is described as "of about middle stature, agreeable in personal appearance, and winning in manners. The first impression of an observer respecting her in her youth, would be of a gentle, confiding, persuasive being, who would sweeten the cup of life to those who drank it with her. But further acquaintance would develop strength as well as loveliness of character. It would be seen that she could do and endure, as well as love and please. Sweetness and strength, gentleness and firmness, were in her character most happily blended. Her mind was both poetical and practical. She had a refined taste, and a love for the beautiful as well as the excellent." But all these fine gifts and endowments were consecrated; the offering she had made on her Saviour's altar was unreserved; nor do we find that she ever cast back to the world where she might have shone so brilliantly, "one longing, lingering look."

She is said by her fellow Missionaries to have made wonderful proficiency in the Burman language, and indeed she translated into it Bunyan's Pilgrim's Progress. She loved the language much; and used to read the Scriptures in it in preference to reading them in English. She once said to Mrs. Mason, "I should be willing to learn Burmese, for the sake of reading the Scriptures in that language."

The translation of the Scriptures into Burmese is a work for which Burmah is indebted to Dr. Judson For many years this devoted servant of Christ employed on this great work every moment he could spare from pastoral labor; and there is something truly sublime in the record he has left of the completion of it, in his Journal under date of Jan. 31, 1834: "Thanks be to god, I can now say, I have attained! I have knelt down before him, with the last leaf in my hand, and imploring his forgiveness for all the sins which have polluted my labors in this department, and his aid in future efforts to remove the errors and imperfections which necessarily cleave to the work, I have commended it to his mercy and grace; I have dedicated it to his glory. May he make his own inspired word, now complete in the Burman tongue, the grand instrument of filling all Burmah with songs and praises to our great God and Saviour, Jesus Christ Amen."

CHAPTER XIV.

MRS. BOARDMAN'S SECOND MARRIAGE.--REMOVAL TO MAULMAIN.--LETTER FROM MRS. JUDSON.--HER SON SENT TO AMERICA.--HER HUSBAND'S ILLNESS.

On the tenth of April, 1834, Mrs. Boardman was married to one whose character she afterwards declared to be "a complete assemblage of all that woman could wish to love and honor," the Rev. Dr. Judson With him she removed to her new home in Maulmain, which had undergone wonderful changes since she left it in 1828. Then, the only church there had *three* native members; now she found there three churches numbering two hundred members! Her duties now were different from what they had been, but not less important; and in a letter written to a very intimate friend one year after her marriage, we find her thus expressing herself: "I can truly say that the mission cause, and missionary labor is increasingly dear to me, every month of my life. I am now united with one whose heavenly spirit and example is deeply calculated to make me more devoted to the cause than I ever have been before. O that I may profit by such precious advantages."

Many Missionaries had arrived from America and established themselves in different places; several resided at Maulmain; so that Mrs. Judson, as we must now call her, could enjoy much Christian society besides that of the natives. But neither she nor her fellow-laborers had much time to devote exclusively to social intercourse. Beside schools to superintend, and Bible-classes to conduct, and prayer-meetings to attend, societies were to be formed among the half-educated native females in which they could be instructed in maternal and social duties. In addition to these cares, Mrs. Judson took upon herself the task of acquiring a new language, in order to instruct the Peguans, a people who had put themselves under the protection of the British, after revolting against the Burmans. This people were so numerous in Maulmain that the missionaries felt constrained to furnish them with instruction.

Under these labors, Mrs. Judson's health again failed but after some weeks of suffering, she began to recover, and for many subsequent years her health was uninterrupted. In a letter written some time after, she accounts for her enjoyment of health, in the following manner:--

"When I first came up from Tavoy, I was thin and pale; and though I called myself pretty well, I had no appetite for food, and was scarce able to walk half a mile. Soon after, I was called to endure a long and severe attack of illness, which brought me to the brink of the grave. I was never so low in any former illness, and the doctor who attended me, has since told me, that he had no hope of my recovery; and that when he came to prescribe medicine for me, it was more out of regard to the feelings of my husband, than from any prospect of its affording me relief. I lay confined to my bed, week after week, unable to move, except as Mr. Judson sometimes carried me in his arms from the bed to the couch for a change; and even this once brought on a return of the disease, which very nearly cost me my life. * * I never shall forget the precious seasons enjoyed on that sick bed. Little George will tell you about it, if you should ever see him. I think he will always remember some sweet conversations I had with him, on the state of his soul, at that time. Dear child! his mind was very tender, and he would weep on account of his sins, and would kneel down and pray with all the fervor and simplicity of childhood. He used to read the Bible to me every day, and commit little hymns to memory by my bedside. * * It pleased my Heavenly Father to raise me up again, although I was for a long time very weak. As soon as I was able, I commenced riding on horseback, and used to take a long ride every morning before sunrise. After a patient trial, I found that riding improved my health; though many times I should have become discouraged and given it up, but for the perseverance of my husband. After riding almost every day, for four or five months, I found my health so much improved, and gained strength so fast, that I began to think walking might be substituted. About this time, my nice little pony died, and we commenced a regular system of exercise on foot, walking at a rapid pace, far over the hills beyond the town, before the sun was up, every morning. We have continued this perseveringly up to the present time; and, during these years, my health has been better than at any time previous, since my arrival in India; and my constitution seems to have undergone an entire renovation."

In "Burmah proper," that is, that part of Burmah not under British government, the native Christians enjoyed no toleration from the Government, and often suffered bitterly; but in Maulmain, and other places in British Burmah, religion flourished, and converts were multiplied. Mr. Vinton, (a new missionary,) preached with great power in the Karen churches, and that people, says Mrs. Judson, "flocked into the kingdom by scores." Mr. Judson was revising his translation of the Bible--a task of five years' duration,--and preaching to the Burmese church; while Mrs. J. instructed in the schools and translated into Peguan such tracts as were thought most calculated to acquaint that people with Christian doctrine. She afterwards translated into that language the New Testament and the Life of Christ; but on the arrival of Mr. Haswell, she gave up to him all her books and papers in this language, and only attended to it in future so far as to assist him in his studies.

Of the severest trial to which Mrs. Judson was called during the remainder of her life she gives an account in the following eloquent words: "After deliberation, accompanied with tears, and agony and prayers, I came to the conviction that it was my duty to send away my only child, my darling George, and yesterday he bade me a long farewell.... Oh I shall never forget his looks, as he stood by the door, and gazed at me for the last time. His eyes were filling with tears, and his little face red with suppressed emotion. But he subdued his feelings, and it was not till he had turned away, and was going down the steps that he burst into a flood of tears. I hurried to my room; and on my knees, with my whole heart gave him up to God; and my bursting heart was comforted from above.... My reason and judgment tell me that the good of my child requires that he should be sent to America; and this of itself would support me in some little degree; but when I view it as a ***sacrifice***, made for the sake of Jesus, it becomes a delightful privilege.... I cannot but hope he will one day return to Burmah, a missionary of the cross, as his dear father was.... This is in some respects the severest trial I ever met with."

It would be delightful to accompany the dear boy in his perilous journey to the Father-land, and to transcribe the yearning and affectionate letters of his mother, both to him, and to those to whose charge he was entrusted--they could not but heighten our opinion of her excellence in the maternal relation, as well as of the great sensibility of her heart; but we are warned that our pages are swelling to too great a number. Ours is but a sketch, an outline; those who would see the full length portrait of our heroine, must consult the glowing canvass of her biographer and successor, "Fanny Forrester."

Her next trial was, to see her beloved husband suffering with a severe cough, which she feared would end in pulmonary consumption. To avert this dreaded result, he was obliged to leave her and try a long sea-voyage. The account of their parting, and her touching letters during his absence would greatly enrich our little sketch, had we room to copy them. We *must* find a place for one short extract from the letters.

"Your little daughter and I have been praying for you this evening.... At times the sweet hope that you will soon return, restored to perfect health, buoys up my spirit, but perhaps you will find it necessary to go farther, a necessity from which I cannot but shrink with doubt and dread; or you may come back only to die with me. This last agonizing thought crushes me down in overwhelming sorrow. I hope I do not feel unwilling that our Heavenly Father should do as he thinks best with us; but my heart shrinks from the prospect of living in this dark, sinful, friendless world, without you.... But the most satisfactory view is to look away to that blissful world, where separations are unknown. There, my beloved Judson, we shall *surely* meet each other; and we shall also meet many loved ones who have gone before us to that haven of rest."

Her fears were not realized; in a few months Mr. Judson was restored to her and the suffering mission cause in greatly improved health.

CHAPTER XV.

ILLNESS OF HER CHILDREN.--DEATH OF ONE OF THEM.--HER MISSIONARY LABORS, AND FAMILY CARES.--HER DECLINING HEALTH.--POEM.--HER LAST ILLNESS AND DEATH.

The seventh year of her marriage with Mr. Judson, was a year of peculiar trial to Mrs. J. All her four children were attacked by whooping-cough followed by one of the diseases of the climate, with which she also was so violently afflicted that her life was for a time despaired of. She felt sure, as she afterwards said, that her hour of release was come, that her master was calling her; and she blessed God that she was entirely willing to leave all, and go to him. The only hope of recovery for any of them was a sea-voyage, and they embarked for Bengal, but their passage was stormy, and they derived little benefit from their stay at Serampore, where they had taken up their residence. A voyage to the Mauritius was recommended, and the alarming situation of three of the children, as well as Mrs. Judson's feeble state, determined them to try it. But before they embarked, it was her melancholy lot to lay one of her darlings in the grave, and he, the very one about whose health she had felt the least uneasiness. He sleeps, says his mother, in the mission burial-ground, where moulders the dust of Carey, Marshman and Ward. Her tears at his burial flowed not only for him that was dead, but for another who she expected would soon follow him. To avert this calamity she hastened her voyage, which though fearfully tempestuous, proved beneficial to the sufferers, and after a short sojourn in the soft climate of the Isle of France, the family returned to their home in Maulmain, restored, with the exception of one son, to sound health. This son, who bore the name of his father, was called by the natives Pwen, which signifies "a flower," a name adopted by his parents. After a long illness he too was restored to health.

Mrs. Judson's labors during the latter part of her life, are recorded by her husband; and it may well excite the wonder of those women who consider the care of their own families a sufficient task, that she could find time and strength for such an amount of labor. It has been said that her translation of Bunyan's Pilgrim's Progress is a work worth living for. Her husband says, "It is one of the best pieces of composition we have published." She also translated a tract written by her husband; edited a "Chapel hymn book," and furnished for it twenty of its best hymns; and published four volumes of Scripture Questions for use in the Sabbath Schools. When we consider that she was the mother of a rapidly increasing family; and the head of an establishment, which like all in the East require constant and vigilant superintendence; and that she was exemplary in the discharge of her maternal and domestic duties, we are led to fancy she must have possessed some secret charm by which she could stay the hurrying feet of time; and "hold the fleet angel fast until he blessed her." Such a secret was her untiring zeal, which prompted an incessant industry. The sands of time are indeed numerous, and when each is valued as a sparkling treasure, they form a rich hoard, laid up where neither moth nor rust corrupt; but if we let them escape unheeded, or sit and idly watch their flow, and even shake the glass to hasten it, they will gather into a millstone weight to sink us in endless, unavailing regret. Though she is dead, Mrs. Judson's works still live; and generation after generation of Burmans will associate her name with that of her honored husband, as benefactors to their race.

In December, 1844, the health of Mrs. Judson began to decline. Her anxious husband, determined to leave no means untried, to save a life so precious to the mission and so invaluable to himself and his family, decided to quit for a while his loved labors in Burmah and accompany his wife to America. They in May 1845 sailed, and on reaching the Isle of France, she found herself so far restored that she could no longer conscientiously detain her husband from his duties in India, and she resolved to let him go back to their home there, while she with her children, should complete the journey that still seemed necessary for her entire restoration. One of the sweetest of her poems was occasioned by this resolution.

"We part on this green islet, Love,
 Thou for the Eastern main,

I, for the setting sun, Love--
  Oh, when to meet again?

My heart is sad for thee, Love,
  For lone thy way will be;
And oft thy tears will fall, Love,
  For thy children and for me.

The music of thy daughter's voice
  Thou'lt miss for many a year;
And the merry shout of thine elder boys
  Thou'lt list in vain to hear.

When we knelt to see our Henry die,
  And heard his last faint moan,
Each wiped the tear from other's eye--
  Now, each must weep alone.

My tears fall fast for thee, Love,--
  How can I say farewell!
But go;--thy God be with thee, Love,
  Thy heart's deep grief to quell!

Yet my spirit clings to thine, Love,
  Thy soul remains with me,
And oft we'll hold communion sweet,
  O'er the dark and distant sea.

And who can paint our mutual joy,
  When, all our wanderings o'er,
We both shall clasp our infants three,
  At home, on Burmah's shore.

> But higher shall our raptures glow,
>   On yon celestial plain,
> When the loved and parted here below
>   Meet, ne'er to part again.
>
> Then gird thine armor on, Love,
>   Nor faint thou by the way,
> Till Boodh shall fall, and Burmah's sons
>   Shall own Messiah's sway."

But her health still sinking, her husband could not leave her, and she was borne back to the ship. Her life ebbed away so rapidly, that he feared he must consign her to an ocean grave. But a kind Providence ordered it, that her death did not occur till the ship anchored at St. Helena. Her end was as peaceful as her life had been consistent and exemplary.

"No shade of doubt or fear, or anxiety crossed her mind." So writes her husband: "She had a prevailing preference to depart and be with Christ. I am longing to depart! she would say; and then the thought of her dear native land, to which she was approaching after an absence of twenty years, and a longing desire to see her son George, her parents, and the friends of her youth, would draw down her ascending soul, and constrain her to say, 'I am in a strait betwixt two; the will of the Lord be done.'

"In regard to her children she ever manifested the most surprising composure and resignation, so much so that I was once constrained to say, you seem to have forgotten the dear little ones we have left behind. 'Can a mother forget'--she replied, and was unable to proceed. During her last days she spent much time in praying for the early conversion of her children.

"On the evening of the 31st of August, ... I sat alone by the side of her bed, endeavoring to administer relief to the distressed body, and consolation to the departing soul. At two o'clock in the morning, wishing to obtain one more token of recognition, I roused her attention and said, 'Do you still love the Saviour?' 'O yes,' she replied, 'I ever love the Lord Jesus Christ.' I said again, 'Do you still love me?' She replied in the affirmative, by a peculiar expression of her own. 'Then give me one more kiss;' and we exchanged that token of love for the last time. Another hour passed,--and she ceased to breathe."

"So fades the summer cloud away;   So sinks the gale when storms are o'er; So gently shuts the eye of day;   So dies the wave along the shore."

Arrangements were made to carry the body on shore. The Rev. Mr. Bertram from the Island came on board, and was led into the state-room where lay all that was mortal of Mrs. Judson. "Pleasant," he says, "she was even in death. A sweet smile of love beamed on her countenance, as if heavenly grace had stamped it there. The bereaved husband and three weeping children fastened their eyes upon the loved remains, as if they could have looked forever."

The coffin was borne to the shore; the boats forming a kind of procession, their oars beating the waves at measured intervals, as a sort of funeral knell--The earth received her dust, and her bereaved husband continued his sad voyage towards his native land, again a widowed mourner.

PART III.
BIOGRAPHICAL SKETCH
OF MRS. EMILY C. JUDSON.

THIRD WIFE OF REV. ADONIRAM JUDSON, D.D.

CHAPTER I

REMARKS ON HER GENIUS.--HER EARLY LIFE.--CONVERSION.--EMPLOYMENTS.--TALES AND POEMS.--ACQUAINTANCE WITH DR. JUDSON.--MARRIAGE.--VOYAGE TO INDIA.--BIOGRAPHY OF MRS. S.B. JUDSON.--POEM WRITTEN OFF ST. HELENA.--POEM ON THE BIRTH OF AN INFANT.--LINES ADDRESSED TO A BEREAVED FRIEND.--LETTER TO HER CHILDREN.--"PRAYER FOR DEAR PAPA."--POEM ADDRESSED TO HER MOTHER.--HER ACCOUNT OF DR. JUDSON'S LAST ILLNESS AND DEATH.

Our labor of sketching the lives of the *three* distinguished women who were permitted to share the happiness and lighten the cares of one of the most worthy and venerated of missionaries, now brings us on delicate ground. The last wife of Dr. Judson, happily for her numerous friends and for his and her children, survives him. Long may she be spared to train those children in the ways of lofty piety, to gladden the wide circle of friends and relatives now anxiously expecting her return to her native land, and to gratify the admirers of her genius with the graceful and eloquent effusions of her pen. Graceful and eloquent they have always been, but of late--touched by a coal from that altar on which she has laid her best sacrifice, *herself*--they have gained a higher and purer flow, awakened by a holier inspiration. The world admired the brilliancy of "Fanny Forrester." Christians *love* the exalted tenderness, the sanctified enthusiasm of Emily C. Judson.

Much as it would gratify us, and her friends to give an extended account of her life, delicacy forbids us to do more than merely to sketch those features in it, which are already the property of much of the reading public. Our outline will necessarily be meagre, but we will enrich it by several of her poems written in India, hitherto scarce published except in perishable newspapers and periodicals. We might indeed make it more interesting by incidents and anecdotes, drawn from those of her early associates who love to dwell on the rich promise of her childhood and youth; but by doing so, we should incur the risk of intruding on the sacredness of the family circle; and we forbear.

She was born in Eaton, a town near the centre of the state of New York. In her childhood, she exhibited an exuberance of imagination that enabled her to delight her young associates with tales, which, according to one of them, she would sit up in bed in the morning to write, and then read aloud to them. She would, even then, write verses also, but in this gift she was perhaps inferior to a sister, who died in early life, and whose numerous poems were unfortunately, and to the grief of her family, accidentally lost. At an early period she embraced religion and was baptized by the Rev. Mr. Dean, a missionary to China, then in this country. Her interest was awakened in the heathen, even at that time, and she indulged in many ardent longings to go as a missionary to them. The late Dr. Kendrick judiciously advised her to pursue the path of duty at home, and quietly wait the leadings and openings of Providence. This advice she followed, and as a means of improving the straitened circumstances of her family, she left home and engaged as a teacher in a seminary in Utica.

Desirous to increase still farther her mother's limited resources, she determined to employ her pen; and published some short religious tales, which, however, brought her little fame, and small pecuniary emolument. But in 1844, by a skilful and happy letter to the conductor of the ***New York Mirror***, she so attracted the attention of the fastidious and brilliant editor of that magazine, that he engaged her as a constant contributor. This arrangement, though of great pecuniary advantage, was, in a religious view, a snare to her. As a writer of light, graceful stories of a purely worldly character, she had in this country, few rivals, and her name, attached to a tale or a poem, became a passport to popular favor. In a letter to her aged pastor, written a year after her marriage, she laments her extreme worldliness at that period, which she says, even led her to be ashamed of her former desire to be a missionary. Yet her writings are marked by purity, and generally inculcated nothing unfriendly either to virtue or religion. But it was the religion of sentiment, and the virtue of the natural heart; of which it must be confessed we find far more in fictitious tales, than in real life. When we consider the nobleness of the motive that led her to seek a popular path to favor and emolument--to increase the comforts of her excellent and honored mother--our censure, were we disposed to indulge any, is disarmed and almost changed to admiration.

During Dr. Judson's visit to America, in 1845, while riding in a public conveyance with Mr. G., who was escorting him to his home in Philadelphia, a story written by "Fanny Forrester," fell into the hands of Dr. J. He read it with satisfaction, remarking that he should like to know its author. "You will soon have that pleasure," said Mr. G., "for she is now visiting at my house." An acquaintance then commenced between them, which, notwithstanding the disparity in their years, soon ripened into a warm attachment, and after a severe struggle, she broke, as she says, the innumerable ties that bound her to the fascinating worldly life she had adopted, and consented to become, what in her early religious zeal she had so longed to be--a missionary.

And now the spell of worldliness was indeed broken. With mingled shame and penitence she reviewed her spiritual declensions, and with an humbled, self-distrusting spirit renewed her neglected covenant with the God and guide of her youth. In Dr. Judson, to whom she was married on the 2d of June, 1846, she found a wise and faithful friend and counsellor, as well as a devoted husband. In his tried and experienced piety, she gained the support and encouragement she needed in her Christian life. Conscious that she had given to the world's service too many of her noble gifts, she commenced a work of an exclusively religious character and tendency, the biography of her predecessor, the second Mrs. Judson. In one year it was completed, and in speaking of it in a letter from India, whither she had accompanied Dr. J. immediately after their marriage, she playfully remarked that her husband was pleased with it, and she cared little whether any one else liked it or not.

On her passage to India, Mrs. Judson passed in sight of that island which must ever attract the gaze of men of every clime and nation,--the rocky prison and tomb of the conqueror of nations, Napoleon Bonaparte. But to her the island had more tender associations; awakened more touching recollections. It was as the grave of Sarah Judson, that her successor gazed long and tearfully on the Isle of St. Helena; and she thus embodied her feelings in song.

LINES WRITTEN OFF ST. HELENA.

Blow softly, gales! a tender sigh
  Is flung upon your wing;
Lose not the treasure as ye fly,
Bear it where love and beauty lie,
  Silent and withering.

Flow gently, waves! a tear is laid
  Upon your heaving breast;
Leave it within yon dark rock's shade
Or weave it in an iris braid,
  To crown the Christian's rest

Bloom, ocean isle, lone ocean isle!
  Thou keep'st a jewel rare;
Let rugged rock, and dark defile,
Above the slumbering stranger smile
  And deck her couch with care.

Weep, ye bereaved! a dearer head,
  Ne'er left the pillowing breast;
The good, the pure, the lovely fled,
When mingling with the shadowy dead,
  She meekly went to rest.

Mourn, Burmah, mourn! a bow which spanned
  Thy cloud has passed away;
A flower has withered on thy sand,
A pitying spirit left thy strand,
  A saint has ceased to pray.

Angels rejoice, another string
  Has caught the strains above.
Rejoice, rejoice! a new-fledged wing
Around the Throne is hovering,
  In sweet, glad, wondering love.

Blow, blow, ye gales! wild billows roll!
  Unfurl the canvas wide!
O! where she labored lies our goal:
Weak, timid, frail, yet would my soul
  Fain be to hers allied.

Ship Faneuil Hall, Sept. 1846.

On the birth of an infant, she expressed her first maternal feelings, in verses of such exquisite beauty, that they can never be omitted in any collection of the gems of poetry--least of all in any collection of ***her*** poems.

The following are the verses alluded to:

MY BIRD.

Ere last year's moon had left the sky,
  A birdling sought my Indian nest
And folded, oh so lovingly!
  Her tiny wings upon my breast.

From morn till evening's purple tinge,
  In winsome helplessness she lies;
Two rose leaves, with a silken fringe,
  Shut softly on her starry eyes.

There's not in Ind a lovelier bird;
  Broad earth owns not a happier nest
O God, thou hast a fountain stirred,
  Whose waters never more shall rest!

This beautiful, mysterious thing,
  This seeming visitant from heaven,
This bird with the immortal wing,
  To me--to me, thy hand has given.

The pulse first caught its tiny stroke,
  The blood its crimson hue, from mine--
This life, which I have dared invoke,
  Henceforth is parallel with thine.

A silent awe is in my room--
  I tremble with delicious fear;
The future with its light and gloom,
  Time and Eternity are here.

Doubts--hopes, in eager tumult rise;
  Hear, O my God! one earnest prayer:--
Room for my bird in Paradise,
  And give her angel plumage there!

Maulmain, January, 1848.

The following touching lines show that she could skilfully employ her ready pen in consoling those on whom had fallen the stroke of bereavement:

LINES

Addressed to a missionary friend in Burmah on the death of her little boy, thirteen months old, in which allusion is made to the previous death of his little brother.

> A mound is in the graveyard,
>   A short and narrow bed;
> No grass is growing on it,
>   And no marble at its head:
> Ye may sit and weep beside it
>   Ye may kneel and kiss the sod,
> But ye'll find no balm for sorrow,
>   In the cold and silent clod.
>
> There is anguish in the household,
>   It is desolate and lone,
> For a fondly cherished nursling
>   From the parent nest has flown;
> A little form is missing;
>   A heart has ceased to beat;
> And the chain of love lies shattered
>   At the desolator's feet.
>
> Remove the empty cradle,
>   His clothing put away,
> And all his little playthings
>   With your choicest treasures lay;
> Strive not to check the tear drops,

That fall like summer rain,
For the sun of hope shines thro' them--
   Ye shall see his face again.

Oh! think where rests your darling,--
   Not in his cradle bed;
Not in the distant graveyard,
   With the still and mouldering dead
But in a heavenly mansion,
   Upon the Saviour's breast,
With his brother's arms about him,
   He takes his sainted rest.

He has put on robes of glory
   For the little robes ye wrought;
And he fingers golden harp strings
   For the toys his sisters brought.
Oh, weep! but with rejoicing;
   A heart gem have ye given,
And behold its glorious setting
   In the diadem of Heaven.

The following letter and beautiful poems need little explanation. The letter is addressed to some of Dr. Judson's children, who resided in Worcester, Massachusetts, having been sent home from India to be educated in America. His health having failed, Dr. J. had sailed for the Isle of Bourbon for its restoration, and it was during his absence that these effusions were penned.

Maulmain, April 11, 1850.

My very dear Children,

I have painful news to tell you--news that I am sure will make your hearts ache; but I hope our heavenly Father will help you to bear it. Your dear papa is very, very ill indeed; so much so that the best judges fear that he will never be any better. He began to fail about five months ago, and has declined so gradually that we were not fully aware of his danger until lately; but within a few weeks those who love him have become very much alarmed.

In January we went down to Mergui by the steamer, and when we returned, thought he was a little better, but he soon failed again. We spent a month at Amherst, but he received little if any benefit. Next, the doctors pronounced our house (the one you used to live in) unhealthy, and we moved to another. But all was of no use. Your dear papa continued to fail, till suddenly, one evening, his muscular strength gave way and he was prostrated on the bed, unable to help himself. This occurred about two weeks ago. The doctor now became alarmed, and said the only hope for him was in a long voyage. It was very hard to think of such a thing in his reduced state, particularly as I could not go with him; but after we had wept and prayed over it one day and night, we concluded that it was our duty to use the only means which God had left us, however painful.

We immediately engaged his passage on board a French barque, bound for the Isle of Bourbon; but before it sailed he had become so very low that no one thought it right for him to go alone. They therefore called a meeting of the mission and appointed Mr. Ranney. It was a great relief to me, for he is a very kind man, and loves your dear papa very much; and he will do everything that can be done for his comfort. The officers of the vessel too, seemed greatly interested for him, as did every one else. He was carried on board a week ago yesterday, in a litter, and placed on a nice easy cot made purposely for him. I stayed with him all day, and at dark came home to stay with the children.

The next day found that the vessel had only dropped down a little distance, and so I took a boat and followed. I expected this would certainly be the last day with him, but it was not. On Friday I went again, and though he did not appear as well as on the previous days, I was forced to take, as I then supposed, a final leave of him. But when morning came, I felt as though I could not live through the day without knowing how he was. So I took a boat again, and reached the vessel about 2 o'clock P.M. He could only speak in whispers, but seemed very glad that I came. The natives I had sent to fan him till he should get out of the river, came to me and begged to have him taken on shore again: and so small was my hope of his recovery, that my heart pleaded on their side, though I still thought it a duty to do as the doctor had ordered. I came away at dark, and though his lips moved to say some word of farewell, they made no sound.

I hope that you, my dear boys, will never have cause to know what a heavy heart I bore back to my desolate home that night. The vessel got out to sea about 4 o'clock on Monday, and last night the natives returned, bringing a letter from Mr. Ranney. Your precious papa has revived again--spoke aloud--took a little tea and toast--said there was something animating in the touch of the sea breeze, and directed Mr. Ranney to write to me that he had a strong belief it was the will of God to restore him again to health. I feel somewhat encouraged, but dare not hope too much.

And now, my dear boys, it will be three, perhaps four long months before we can hear from our beloved one again, and we shall all be very anxious. All we can do is to commit him to the care of our heavenly Father, and, if we never see him again in this world, pray that we may be prepared to meet him in heaven

* * * * *

Your most affectionate mother,

Emily C. Judson

PRAYER FOR DEAR PAPA.

Poor and needy little children,
  Saviour, God, we come to Thee,
For our hearts are full of sorrow,
  And no other hope have we.
Out, upon the restless ocean,
  There is one we dearly love,--
Fold him in thine arms of pity,
  Spread thy guardian wings above.

When the winds are howling round him,
  When the angry waves are high,
When black, heavy, midnight shadows,
  On his trackless pathway lie,
Guide and guard him, blessed Saviour,
  Bid the hurrying tempests stay;
Plant thy foot upon the waters.
  Send thy smile to light his way.

When he lies, all pale, and suffering,
  Stretched upon his narrow bed,
With no loving face bent o'er him,
  No soft hand about his head,
O, let kind and pitying angels,
  Their bright forms around him bow;

Let them kiss his heavy eyelids,
  Let them fan his fevered brow.

Poor and needy little children,
  Still we raise our cry to Thee
We have nestled in his bosom,
  We have sported on his knee;
Dearly, dearly do we love him,
  --We, who on his breast have lain--
Pity now our desolation!
  Bring him back to us again!

If it please thee, Heavenly Father,
  We would see him come once more,
With his olden step of vigor,
  With the love-lit smile he wore;
But if we must tread Life's valley,
  Orphaned, guideless, and alone,
Let us lose not, 'mid the shadows,
  His dear footprints to thy Throne.

Maulmain, April, 1850.

SWEET MOTHER.

The wild, south-west Monsoon has risen,
  With broad, gray wings of gloom,
While here, from out my dreary prison,
  I look, as from a tomb--Alas!
  My heart another tomb.

Upon the low-thatched roof, the rain,
  With ceaseless patter, falls;

My choicest treasures bear its stain--
  Mould gathers on the walls--Would Heaven
  'Twere only on the walls!

Sweet Mother! I am here alone,
  In sorrow and in pain;
The sunshine from my heart has flown,
  It feels the driving rain--Ah, me!
  The chill, and mould, and rain.

Four laggard months have wheeled their round
  Since love upon it smiled;
And everything of earth has frowned
  On thy poor, stricken child--sweet friend,
  Thy weary, suffering child.

I'd watched my loved one, night and day.
  Scarce breathing when he slept;
And as my hopes were swept away,
  I'd on his bosom wept--O God!
  How had I prayed and wept!

They bore him from me to the ship,
  As bearers bear the dead;
I kissed his speechless, quivering lip,
  And left him on his bed--Alas!
  It seemed a coffin-bed!

When from my gentle sister's tomb,
  In all our grief, we came,
Rememberest thou her vacant room!
  Well, his was just the same, that day.
  The very, very same.

Then, mother, little Charley came--
  Our beautiful fair boy,
With my own father's cherished name--
  But oh, he brought no joy!--My child
  Brought mourning, and no joy.

His little grave I cannot see,
  Though weary months have sped
Since pitying lips bent over me,
  And whispered, "He is dead!"--Alas
  'Tis dreadful to be dead!

I do not mean for one like me,
  --So weary, worn, and weak,--
Death's shadowy paleness seems to be
  Even now, upon my cheek--his seal
  On form, and brow and cheek.

But for a bright-winged bird like him,
  To hush his joyous song,
And, prisoned in a coffin dim,
  Join Death's pale, phantom throng--*My boy*
  To join that grisly throng!

Oh, Mother, I can scarcely bear
  To think of this to-day!
It was so exquisitely fair,
  --That little form of clay--my heart
  Still lingers by his clay.

And when for one loved far, far more,
  Come thickly gathering tears;

My star of faith is clouded o'er,
  I sink beneath my fears--sweet friend,
  My heavy weight of fears.

Oh, should he not return to me,
  Drear, drear must be life's night!
And, mother, I can almost see
  Even now the gathering blight--my soul
  Faints, stricken by the blight.

Oh, but to feel thy fond arms twine
  Around me, once again!
It almost seems those lips of thine
  Might kiss away the pain--might soothe
  This dull, cold, heavy pain.

But, gentle Mother, through life's storms,
  I may not lean on thee,
For helpless, cowering little forms
  Cling trustingly to me--Poor babes!
  To have no guide but me!

With weary foot, and broken wing,
  With bleeding heart, and sore,
Thy Dove looks backward, sorrowing,
  But seeks the ark no more--thy breast
  Seeks never, never more.

Sweet Mother, for this wanderer pray,
  That loftier faith be given;
Her broken reeds all swept away,
  That she may lean on Heaven--her soul
  Grow strong on Christ and Heaven.

All fearfully, all tearfully,
  Alone and sorrowing.
My dim eye lifted to the sky,
  Fast to the cross I cling--O Christ!
To thy dear cross I cling.

Maulmain, August 8th, 1850

From the sad voyage which drew forth this most touching poem Dr. Judson never returned. He died on board the ship which was bearing him to more healthful climes; and his body was committed to the ocean. One of the most excellent of Mrs. Judson's productions is her account of the closing scenes in her husband's life, contained in a letter to his sister. Long as it is, we cannot bring ourselves to abridge it. It will convince our readers that if the three whose lives we have sketched, have been among the first of women, they were united to one who knew and appreciated their excellence, and who was ***worthy*** to share their affection.

CLOSING SCENES IN THE LIFE OF DR. JUDSON. BY HIS WIDOW.

Last month I could do no more than announce to you our painful bereavement, which though not altogether unexpected, will, I very well know, fall upon your heart with overwhelming weight. You will find the account of your brother's last days on board the Aristide Marie, in a letter written by Mr. Ranney from Mauritius, to the Secretary of the Board; and I can add nothing to it, with the exception of a few unimportant particulars, gleaned in conversation with Mr. R. and the Coringa servant. I grieve that it should be so--that I was not permitted to watch beside him during those days of terrible suffering; but the pain, which I at first felt, is gradually yielding to gratitude for the inestimable privileges which had previously been granted me.

There was something exceedingly beautiful in the decline of your brother's life--more beautiful than I can describe, though the impression will remain with me as a sacred legacy, until I go to meet him where suns shall never set, and life shall never end. He had been, from my first acquaintance with him, an uncommonly spiritual Christian, exhibiting his richest graces in the unguarded intercourse of private life; but during his last year, it seemed as though the light of the world on which he was entering, had been sent to brighten his upward pathway. Every subject on which we conversed, every book we read, every incident that occurred, whether trivial or important, had a tendency to suggest some peculiarly spiritual train of thought, till it seemed to me that more than ever before, "Christ was all his theme." Something of the same nature was also noted in his preaching, to which I then had not the privilege of listening. He was in the habit, however, of studying his subject for the Sabbath, audibly, and in my presence, at which time he was frequently so much affected as to weep, and some times so overwhelmed with the vastness of his conceptions, as to be obliged to abandon his theme and choose another. My own illness at the commencement of the year had brought eternity very near to us, and rendered death, the grave, and the bright heaven beyond it, familiar subjects of conversation. Gladly would I give you, my dear sister, some idea of the share borne by him in those memorable conversations; but it would be impossible to convey, even to those who knew him best, the most distant conception. I believe he has sometimes been thought eloquent, both in conversation and in the sacred desk; but the fervid, burning eloquence, the deep pathos, the touching tenderness, the elevation of thought, and intense beauty of expression, which characterized those private teachings, were not only beyond what I had ever heard before, but such as I felt sure arrested his own attention, and surprised even himself. About this time he began to find unusual satisfaction and enjoyment in his private devotions; and seemed to have few objects of interest continually rising in his mind each of which in turn became special subjects of prayer. Among these, one of the most prominent was the conversion of his posterity. He remarked, that he had always prayed for his children, but that of late he had felt impressed with the duty of praying for their children and their children's children down to the latest generation. He also prayed most fervently, that his impressions on this particular subject might be transferred to his sons and daughters, and thence to their offspring, so that he should ultimately meet a long unbroken line of descendants before the throne of God, where all might join together in ascribing everlasting praises to their Redeemer.

Another subject, which occupied a large share of his attention, was that of brotherly love. You are, perhaps, aware, that like all persons of his ardent temperament, he was subject to strong attachments and aversions, which he sometimes had difficulty in bringing under the controlling influence of divine grace. He remarked that he had always felt more or less of an affectionate interest in his brethren, as brethren--and some of them he had loved very dearly for their personal qualities; but that he was now aware he had never placed his standard of love high enough. He spoke of them as children of God, redeemed by the Saviour's blood, watched over and guarded by his love, dear to his heart, honored by him in the election, and to be honored hereafter before the assembled universe; and he said it was not sufficient to be kind and obliging to such, to abstain from evil speaking, and make a general mention of them in our prayers; but our attachment to them should be of the race, ardent and exalted character--it would be so in heaven, and we lost immeasurably by not beginning now. "As I have loved you, so ought ye also to love one another," was a precept continually in his mind, and he would often murmur, as though unconsciously, "'As I have loved you'--'as I have loved you'"--then burst out with the exclamation, "Oh, the love of Christ! the love of Christ!"

His prayers for the mission were marked by an earnest, grateful enthusiasm, and in speaking of missionary operations in general, his tone was one of elevated triumph, almost of exultation--for he not only felt an unshaken confidence in their final success but would often exclaim, "What wonders--oh, what wonders God has already wrought!"

I remarked, that during this year his literary labor, which he had never liked, and upon which he had entered unwillingly and from a feeling of necessity, was growing daily more irksome to him; and he always spoke of it as his "heavy work," his "tedious work," "that wearisome dictionary," &c., though this feeling led to no relaxation of effort. He longed, however, to find some more spiritual employment, to be engaged in what he considered more legitimate missionary labor, and drew delightful pictures of the future, when his whole business would be but to preach and to pray.

During all this time I had not observed any failure in physical strength; and though his mental exercises occupied a large share of my thoughts when alone, it never once occurred to me that this might be the brightening of the setting sun; my only feeling was that of pleasure, that one so near to me was becoming so pure and elevated in his sentiments, and so lovely and Christ-like in his character. In person he had grown somewhat stouter than when in America, his complexion had a healthful hue compared with that of his associates generally; and though by no means a person of uniformly firm health, he seemed to possess such vigor and strength of constitution, that I thought his life as likely to be extended twenty years longer, as that of any member of the mission. He continued his system of morning exercise, commenced when a student at Andover, and was not satisfied with a common walk on level ground, but always chose an up-hill path, and then frequently went bounding on his way, with all the exuberant activity of boyhood.

He was of a singularly happy temperament, although not of that even cast, which never rises above a certain level, and is never depressed. Possessing acute sensibilities, suffering with those who suffered and entering as readily into the joys of the prosperous and happy, he was variable in his moods; but religion formed such an essential element in his character, and his trust in Providence was so implicit and habitual, that he was never gloomy, and seldom more than momentarily disheartened. On the other hand, being accustomed to regard all the events of this life, however minute or painful, as ordered in wisdom and tending to one great and glorious end, he lived in almost constant obedience to the apostolic injunction, "Rejoice evermore!" He often told me that although he had endured much personal suffering, and passed through many fearful trials in the course of his eventful life, a kind Providence had also hedged him round with precious, peculiar blessings, so that his joys had far outnumbered his sorrows.

Toward the close of September of last year, he said to me one evening, "What deep cause have we for gratitude to God!--do you believe there are any other two persons in the wide world so happy as we are?" enumerating, in his own earnest manner, several sources of happiness, in which our work as missionaries, and our eternal prospects, occupied a prominent position. When he had finished his glowing picture, I remarked (I scarcely know why, but there was a heavy cloud upon my spirits that evening), "We are certainly very happy now, but it cannot be so always--I am thinking of the time when one of us must stand beside the bed, and see the other die."

"Yes," he said, "that will be a sad moment; I felt it most deeply a little while ago, but now it would not be strange if your life were prolonged beyond mine--though

I should wish if it were possible to spare you that pain. It is the one left alone who suffers, not the one who goes to be with Christ. If it should only be the will of God that we might go together, like young James and his wife. But he will order all things well, and we can safely trust our future to his hands."

That same night we were roused from sleep by the sudden illness of one of the children. There was an unpleasant, chilling dampness in the air, as it came to us through the openings in the sloats above the windows, which affected your brother very sensibly, and he soon began to shiver so violently, that he was obliged to return to his couch, where he remained under a warm covering until morning. In the morning he awoke with a severe cold, accompanied by some degree of fever; but as it did not seem very serious, and our three children were all suffering from a similar cause, we failed to give it any especial attention. From that time he was never well, though in writing to you before, I think I dated the commencement of his illness, from the month of November, when he laid aside his studies. I know that he regarded this attack as trifling, and yet one evening he spent a long time in advising me with regard to my future course, if I should be deprived of his guidance; saying that it is always wise to be prepared for exigences of this nature. After the month of November, he failed gradually, occasionally rallying in such a manner as to deceive us all, but at each relapse sinking lower than at the previous one, though still full of hope and courage, and yielding ground only, inch by inch, as compelled by the triumphant progress of disease. During some hours of every day he suffered intense pain; but his naturally buoyant spirits and uncomplaining disposition led him to speak so lightly of it, that I used sometimes to fear the doctor, though a very skilful man, would be fatally deceived.

As his health declined, his mental exercises at first seemed deepened; and he gave still larger portions of his time to prayer, conversing with the utmost freedom on his daily progress, and the extent of his self-conquest. Just before our trip to Mergui, which took place in January, he looked up from his pillow one day with sudden animation, and said to me earnestly, "I have gained the victory at last. I love every one of Christ's redeemed, as I believe he would have me love them--in the same manner, though not probably to the same degree as we shall love one another in heaven; and gladly would I prefer the meanest of his creatures, who bears his name, before myself." This he said in allusion to the text, "In honor preferring one another," on which he had frequently dwelt with great emphasis. After farther similar conversation he concluded, "And now here I lie at peace with all the world, and what is better still, at peace with my own conscience. I know that I am a miserable sinner in the sight of God, with no hope but in the blessed Saviour's merits; but I cannot think of any particular fault, any peculiarly besetting sin, which it is now my duty to correct. Can you tell me of any?"

And truly, from this time no other word would so well express his state of feeling, as that one of his own choosing--*peace*. He had no particular exercises afterwards, but remained calm and serene, speaking of himself daily as a great sinner, who had been overwhelmed with benefits, and declaring, that he had never in all his life before, had such delightful views of the unfathomable love and infinite condescension of the Saviour, as were now daily opening before him. "Oh, the love of Christ! the love of Christ!" he would suddenly exclaim, while his eye kindled, and the tears chased each other down his cheeks, "we cannot understand it now--but what a beautiful study for eternity!"

After our return from Mergui, the doctor advised a still farther trial of the effects of sea air and sea-bathing, and we accordingly proceeded to Amherst, where we remained nearly a month. This to me was the darkest period of his illness--no medical adviser, no friend at hand, and he daily growing weaker and weaker. He began to totter in walking, clinging to the furniture and walls, when he thought he was unobserved (for he was not willing to acknowledge the extent of his debility), and his wan face was of a ghastly paleness. His sufferings too were sometimes fearfully intense, so that in spite of his habitual self-control, his groans would fill the house. At other times a kind of lethargy seemed to steal over him, and he would sleep almost incessantly for twenty-four hours, seeming annoyed if he were aroused or disturbed. Yet there were portions of the time, when he was comparatively comfortable, and conversed intelligently; but his mind seemed to revert to former scenes, and he tried to amuse me with stories of his boyhood--his college days--his imprisonment in France, and his early missionary life. He had a great deal also to say on his favorite theme. "The love of Christ:" but his strength was too much impaired for any continuous mental effort. Even a short prayer made audibly, exhausted him to such a degree that he was obliged to discontinue the practice.

At length I wrote to Maulmain, giving some expression of my anxieties and misgivings, and our kind missionary friends, who had from the first evinced all the tender interest and watchful sympathy of the nearest kindred immediately sent for us--the doctor advising a sea-voyage. But as there was no vessel in the harbor bound for a port sufficiently distant, we thought it best, in the meantime, to remove from our old dwelling, which had long been condemned as unhealthy, to another mission-house, fortunately empty. This change was at first attended with the most beneficial results, and our hopes revived so much, that we looked forward to the approaching rainy season for entire restoration. But it lasted only a little while, and then both of us became convinced, that though a voyage at sea involved much that was exceedingly painful, it yet presented the only prospect of recovery, and could not, therefore, without a breach of duty, be neglected.

"Oh, if it were only the will of God to take me now--to let me die here!" he repeated over and over again, in a tone of anguish, while we where considering the subject. "I cannot, cannot go!--this is almost more than I can bear! was there ever suffering like our suffering!" and the like broken expressions, were continually falling from his lips. But he soon gathered more strength of purpose; and after the decision was fairly made, he never hesitated for a moment, rather regarding the prospect with pleasure. I think the struggle which this resolution cost, injured him very materially; though probably it had no share in bringing about the final result. God, who saw the end from the beginning had counted out his days, and they were hastening to a close. Until this time he had been able to stand, and to walk slowly from room to room; but as he one evening attempted to rise from his chair, he was suddenly deprived of his small remnant of muscular strength, and would have fallen to the floor, but for timely support.

From that moment his decline was rapid. As he lay helplessly upon his couch, and watched the swelling of his feet, and other alarming symptoms, he became very anxious to commence his voyage, and I felt equally anxious to have his wishes gratified. I still hoped he might recover--the doctor said the chances of life and death were in his opinion equally balanced--and then he always loved the sea so dearly! There was something exhilarating to him in the motion of a vessel, and he spoke with animation of getting free from the almost suffocating atmosphere incident to the hot season, and drinking in the fresh sea breezes He talked but little more, however, than was necessary to indicate his wants, his bodily sufferings being too great to allow of conversation; but several times he looked up to me with a bright smile, and exclaimed as heretofore, "Oh, the love of Christ! the love of Christ!"

I found it difficult to ascertain, from expressions casually dropped, from time to time, his real opinion with regard to his recovery; but I thought there was some reason to doubt whether he was fully aware of his critical situation. I did not suppose he had any preparation to make at this late hour, and I felt sure that if he should be called ever so unexpectedly, he would not enter the presence of his Maker with a ruffled spirit; but I could not bear to have him go away, without knowing how doubtful it was whether our next meeting would not be in eternity; and perhaps too, in my own distress, I might still have looked for words of encouragement and sympathy, to a source which had never before failed.

It was late in the night, and I had been performing some little sick-room offices, when suddenly he looked up to me, and exclaimed, "This will never do! You are killing yourself for me, and I will not permit it You must have some one to relieve you. If I had not been made selfish by suffering, I should have insisted upon it long ago."

He spoke so like himself--with the earnestness of health, and in a tone to which my ear had of late been a stranger, that for a moment I felt almost bewildered with sudden hope. He received my reply to what he had said, with a half-pitying, half-gratified smile, but in the meantime his expression had changed--the marks of excessive debility were again apparent, and I could not forbear adding, "It is only a little while, you know."

"Only a little while," he repeated mournfully; "this separation is a bitter thing, but it does not distress me now as it did--I am too weak." "You have no reason to be distressed," I answered, "with such glorious prospects before you. You have often told me it is the one left alone who suffers, not the one who goes to be with Christ." He gave me a rapid, questioning glance, then assumed for several moments an attitude of deep thought. Finally, he slowly unclosed his eyes, and fixing them on me, said in a calm, earnest tone, "I do not believe I am going to die. I think I know why this illness has been sent upon me--I needed it--I feel that it has done me good--and it is my impression, that I shall now recover, and be a better and more useful man."

"Then it is your wish to recover?" I inquired. "If it should be the will of God, yes. I should like to complete the dictionary, on which I have bestowed so much labor, now that it is so nearly done; for though it has not been a work that pleased my taste, or quite satisfied my feelings, I have never underrated its importance. Then after that come all the plans we have formed. Oh, I feel as though only just beginning to be prepared for usefulness."

"It is the opinion of most of the mission," I remarked, "that you will not recover." "I know it is," he replied; "and I suppose they think me an old man, and imagine that it is nothing for one like me to resign a life so full of trials. But I am not old--at least in that sense--you know I am not. Oh! no man ever left this world with more inviting prospects, with brighter hopes or warmer feelings--warmer feelings"--he repeated, and burst into tears. His face was perfectly placid, even while the tears broke away from the closed lids, and rolled, one after another, down to the pillow. There was no trace of agitation or pain in his manner of weeping, but it was evidently the result of acute sensibilities, combined with great physical weakness. To some suggestions which I ventured to make, he replied, "It is not that--I know all that, and feel it in my inmost heart. Lying here on my bed, when I could not talk, I have had such views of the loving condescension of Christ, and the glories of heaven, as I believe are seldom granted to mortal man. It is not because I shrink from death, that I wish to live; neither is it because the ties that bind me here though some of them are very sweet, bear any comparison with the drawings I at times feel towards heaven; but a few years would not be missed from my eternity of bliss, and I can well afford to spare them, both for your sake and for the sake of the poor Burmans. I am not tired of my work, neither am I tired of the world; yet when Christ calls me home. I shall go with the gladness of a boy bounding away from his school. Perhaps I feel something like the young bride, when she contemplates resigning the pleasant associations of her childhood, for a yet dearer home--though only a very little like her--for *there is no doubt resting on my future*." "Then death would not take you by surprise," I remarked, "if it should come even before you could get on board ship." "Oh, no," he said, "death will never take me by surprise--do not be afraid of that--I feel *so strong in Christ*. He has not led me so tenderly thus far, to forsake me at the very gate of heaven. No, no; I am willing to live a few years longer, if it should be so ordered; and if otherwise, I am willing and glad to die now. I leave myself entirely in the hands of God, to be disposed of according to his holy will."

The next day some one mentioned in his presence, that the native Christians were greatly opposed to the voyage, and that many other persons had a similar feeling with regard to it I thought he seemed troubled; and after the visitor had withdrawn, I inquired if he still felt as when he conversed with me the night previous. He replied, "Oh yes; that was no evanescent feeling. It has been with me, to a greater or less extent, for years, and will be with me, I trust, to the end. I am ready to go ***to-day***--if it should be the will of God, this very hour; but I am not ***anxious*** to die--at least when I am not beside myself with pain."

"Then why are you so desirous to go to sea? I should think it would be a matter of indifference to you." "No," he answered quietly, "my judgment tells me it would be wrong not to go--the doctor says ***criminal***. I shall certainly die here--if I go away, I may possibly recover. There is no question with regard to duty in such a case; and I do not like to see any hesitation, even though it springs from affection."

He several times spoke of a burial at sea, and always as though the prospect were agreeable. It brought, he said, a sense of freedom and expansion and seemed far pleasanter than the confined, dark, narrow grave, to which he had committed so many that he loved. And he added, that although his burial-place was a matter of no real importance, yet he believed it was not in human nature to be altogether without a choice.

I have already given you an account of the embarkation, of my visits to him while the vessel remained in the river, and of our last sad, silent parting; and Mr. Ranney has finished the picture. You will find in this closing part, some dark shadows, that will give you pain; but you must remember that his present felicity is enhanced by those very sufferings, and we should regret nothing that serves to brighten his crown in glory. I ought also to add, that I have gained pleasanter impressions in conversation with Mr. R. than from his written account; but it would be difficult to convey them to you; and, as he whom they concern was accustomed to say of similar things, "you will learn it all in heaven."

During the last hour of your sainted brother's life, Mr. Ranney bent over him and held his hand; while poor Pinapah stood at a little distance weeping bitterly. The table had been spread in the cuddy, as usual, and the officers did not know what was passing in the cabin, till summoned to dinner. Then they gathered about the door, and watched the closing scene with solemn reverence. Now--thanks to a merciful God! his pains had left him, not a momentary spasm disturbed his placid face, nor did the contraction of a muscle denote the least degree of suffering; the agony of death was passed, and his wearied spirit was turning to its rest in the bosom of his Saviour. From time to time, he pressed the hand in which his own was resting, his clasp losing in force at each successive pressure; while his shortened breath (though there was no struggle, no gasping, as if it came and went with difficulty) gradually grew softer and fainter, until it died upon the air--and he was gone. Mr. Ranney closed the eyes, and composed the passive limbs,--the ship's officers stole softly from the door, and the neglected meal was left upon the board untasted.

They lowered him to his ocean-grave without a prayer; for his freed spirit had soared above the reach of earthly intercession, and to the foreigners who stood around, it would have been a senseless form. And there they left him in his unquiet sepulchre; but it matters little, for we know that while the unconscious clay is "drifting on the shifting currents of the restless main," nothing can disturb the hallowed rest of the immortal spirit. Neither could he have a more fitting monument, than the blue waves which visit every coast; for his warm sympathies went forth to the ends of the earth, and included the whole family of man. It is all as God would have it, and our duty is but to bend meekly to his will, and wait, in faith and patience, till we also shall be summoned home.

CHAPTER II.

CONCLUSION.

* * * * "Last scene of all
To close this sad, eventful history."

Scarcely four years ago,--in sickness and loneliness, and sad suspense,--in her Burman home, from which had departed (alas, forever!) its light and head--Emily C. Judson penned the foregoing beautiful letter. Read again its closing sentence, and note how short a time she has "waited in faith and patience;" how ***soon*** she has been "summoned home." For ***her***, it would be wrong for us to mourn. She has rejoined that circle, which she loved so well on earth, in a land where

"Sickness and sorrow, pain and death
Are felt and ***feared*** no more."

But to her aged parents--to the little flock to whom she was as the tenderest mother--to the literary world, which enjoyed the ripe fruits of her genius--to the Christian world, of which she was a shining ornament and glory, her loss is irreparable. In her own inimitable words, we may exclaim:

"Weep, ye bereaved! a dearer head
Ne'er left the pillowing breast;
The good, the pure, the lovely fled,

When mingling with the shadowy dead
  She meekly went to rest.

"Angels, rejoice! another string
  Has caught the strains above,
Rejoice, rejoice! a new-fledged wing
Around the throne is hovering,
  In sweet, glad, wondering love."

But though one of the sweet fountains that well up here and there in our desert world, and surround themselves with greenness, and beauty, and life, has been exhaled to heaven, still it is refreshing to know that its streams, which made glad so many hearts, have not perished, for they were of "living water, springing up" into immortality. The writer is lost to us; her writings remain. By them "she being dead yet speaketh," and through them, whensoever we will, she may talk with us.

Mrs. Judson's final malady was consumption, but for several years her health had been feeble. One who saw her just before she left America says: "Looking upon her, we saw at once that it was a spirit which had already outworn its frame--a slight, pale, delicate, and transparent creature, every thought and feeling shining through, and every word and movement tremulous with fragility. * * * We said farewell with no thought that she would ever return."

From her voyage across the ocean she suffered less than was apprehended, and for a time she found the climate of India rather congenial than otherwise to her constitution. Her short residence at Rangoon, whither her husband removed with his family soon after reaching Burma, was indeed a period of great suffering, and would have given a shock to a much hardier constitution. Her narrative of their sufferings there, contained in the life of her husband, by Dr. Wayland, excites our wonder that she survived them. But after their removal to Maulmain, she was restored to comparative health.

A letter from her husband, written in the latter part of 1848, when her little Emily Frances, her "bird," was one year old, gives a glowing picture of their happiness and their labors. He playfully says: "Even 'the young romance writer' had made a little book, (Scripture questions,) and she manages to conduct a Bible class, and native female prayer-meetings, so that I hope she will yet come to some good."

But a letter written to Miss Anable, Philadelphia, in the spring of 1849, is in a different strain: "A dark cloud is gathering round me. A crushing weight is upon me. I cannot resist the dreadful conviction that dear Emily is in a settled and rapid decline." After speaking of the many means he had unsuccessfully employed for her restoration, he says "The symptoms are such that I have scarcely any hope left. * * * If a change to any place promised the least relief, I would go anywhere. But we are here in the healthiest part of India, in the dry, warm season, and she suffers so much at sea that a voyage could hardly be recommended for itself. My only hope is, the doctor declares her lungs are not seriously affected. * * * When at Tavoy, she made up her mind that she must die soon, and that is now her prevailing expectation; but she contemplates the event with composure and resignation. * * * Though she feels that in her circumstances, prolonged life is exceedingly desirable, she is quite willing to leave all at the Savior's call. Praise be to God for his love to her." Some days later he adds: "Emily is better. * * * But though the deadly-pressure is removed from my heart, I do not venture to indulge any sanguine hopes after what I have seen. * * * Do remember us in your prayers."

The doctor's predictions proved correct; Mrs. Judson partially recovered from this attack, although in August her husband writes: "Emily's health is very delicate--her hold on life very precarious."

Alas! his own hold on life was more precarious still. In the following spring, the heart that had beat for her so fondly and truly was consigned to its "unquiet sepulchre;" "the blue waves which visit every coast" his only and "fitting monument;" while the object of his tender solicitude was compelled to endure four months the agony of suspense as to *his* fate, terminated by the sad certainty of his death.

After the death of her husband, Mrs. Judson expressed a strong desire to remain in Burmah and devote herself to the cause which was so dear to her husband's and her own heart. But her health, always delicate, was so unfavorably affected by that climate that her physicians were of opinion another rainy season would terminate her life. A numerous family of children, several of whom were in this country, needed her maternal care and guidance; and for their sakes, as well as for her own, she left Burmah in the winter following her husband's death, and arrived in this country in October, 1851, after an absence of five years and three months. She found in the beautiful village of Hamilton a sequestered and lovely home for herself and her family, which consisted of her aged parents, the five children of Sarah B. Judson, and her own "bird," Emily Frances. The cares of her family, and literary labors, here divided her time until the prostration of her health by her last sickness, since which period she has "set her house in order," and calmly awaited the summons of death. Peacefully and sweetly did the summons come, and on the first of June she fell asleep in Jesus. With a sister poet she might have said--

"I'm passing through the eternal gates,
  Ere June's sweet roses blow."

She had often spoken of this rich and glorious month as her "time to die," and repeated Bryant's hymn,--

"'Twere pleasant that in flowery June,
When brooks send up a cheerful tune,
  And groves a joyous sound,
The sexton's hand my grave to make,
The rich, green mountain-turf should break."

Nature had no more ardent lover than she; and it is pleasant to think that her dust is returning to dust in a lovely village church-yard, under the "pure air of heaven, and amid the luxuriance of flowers." Pleasant also is it to read that a vast concourse of sincere admirers and loving friends, and among them all her children, eagerly testified their respect to her, by attending her remains to their burial. To her glorified spirit such manifestations may indeed be of little moment. Yet even her glorified spirit may feel a new thrill of pleasure in beholding, from its serene sphere, the love that prompted them, and sought in the choice of her last resting-place to give even to the unconscious dead one more proof of affection.

In so imperfect a sketch as ours, a delineation of the character of Mrs. Judson will not be attempted. We would not, if we could, anticipate her memoir, which, it is said, will soon be published. From documents open to the public, we shall merely glean such notices of her life and character as shall induce in our readers a desire to know those details of her personal history which will doubtless be found in her biography.

From what we can learn, we infer that the prominent traits in her character were strong affections, energy, and disinterestedness. Of a slight and delicate frame and constitution, and a sensibility almost amounting to sensitiveness, she at an early age engaged in duties and made sacrifices scarcely expected from the robust and vigorous. And her exertions had for their end mainly to benefit those she loved. Whether she taught in the district school, or in the higher seminary, or wrote Sunday-school books, or contributed to literary periodicals, her affection for her mother, and desire to lighten her burdens, seem to have stimulated her exertions and called forth her powers. In her early religious experience, the same disinterestedness manifested itself; for no sooner did she feel the renewing power of faith in her own heart, than she longed to impart even to the distant heathen the same precious blessing. Unselfish affection is also, we think, a strongly marked trait in her married life. Not long after their arrival in Burmah, Mr. Judson writes: "Emily loves the children as if they were her own." And again, nearly two years later: "We are a deliciously happy family;" and again, "Emily has taken to my two boys as if they were her own; so that we are a very happy family; not a happier, I am sure, on the broad earth."

Another proof of the same trait, was her loving and sympathetic appreciation of a peculiar trait in her husband, which, had her disposition been less noble, might have caused her some annoyance. Of this trait Dr. Wayland thus speaks: "There was a feature in Dr. Judson's affection as a husband, which was, I think, peculiar. He was, as it is well known, married three times, and no man was ever more tenderly attached to each of his wives. The present affection, however, seemed in no respect to lessen his affection for those for whom he mourned. He ever spoke of those who had gone before, with undiminished interest. In one of his letters to his daughter, after saying he did not believe there existed on earth so happy a family as his, he soon after adds: 'My tears fall frequently for her who lies in her lone bed at St. Helena.' It was at his suggestion that Mrs. Emily Judson wrote the life of her predecessor. He frequently refers with delight to the time when he, and all those whom he so much loved, shall meet in Paradise, no more to part, but to spend an eternity together in the presence of Christ. Those that were once loved were loved to the end; but this did not prevent the bestowment of an equal amount of affection on a successor." To quote the words of another, speaking of Mrs. Mary Ware, who, placed in similar circumstances to Mrs. Judson, showed the same noble superiority to a common weakness of her sex: "She had no sympathy and little respect for that narrow view which insists that the departed and the living cannot share the same pure love of the same true heart. With regard to a former wife--'she was the nearest and dearest to him'--she would say, 'how then can I do otherwise than love and cherish her memory?' And **her** children she received as a precious legacy; they were to her from the first moment like her own; neither she nor they knew any distinction."

Since writing the above, we have seen a poem, entitled "Love's Last Wish," addressed to her husband, by Mrs. Judson when she thought herself near death, which expresses so beautifully the sentiment we have here attributed to her, that, did our limits permit, we would copy the whole. We can only give an extract.

> "Thou say'st I'm fading day by day,
>   And in thy face I read thy fears;
> It would be hard to pass away
>   So soon, and leave thee to thy tears.
> I hoped to linger by thy side,
>   Until thy homeward call was given,
> Then silent to my pillow glide,
>   And wake upon thy breast in heaven.

* * * * *

> "I do not ask to be forgot;
> I've read thy heart in every line,
> And know that there one sacred spot,
>   Whate'er betide, will still be mine,
> For death but lays its mystic spell

Upon affection's earthliness,--
I know that, though thou lov'st me well,
Thou lov'st thy sainted none the less.

* * * * *

And when at last we meet above,
  Where marriage vows are never spoken,
We all shall form one chain of love,
  Whose spirit-links can ne'er be broken."

    Of Mrs. Judson's happiness in her married and missionary life, we feel bound to say a few words, because the tone of some articles, written since her death, would lead to the impression that, so far from having had any enjoyment as a wife, a mother, and a missionary, she had sacrificed not only all her literary aspirations, but her whole earthly happiness to her desire to benefit the heathen. Thus one widely circulated article speaks of her mission-life as a "slow martyrdom of sacrifices and sorrows;" * * * as "filled with bitterness,"--speaks, too, of the agony wrung out of her heart by suspense in regard to her husband's fate, expressed in that exquisite piece to her mother, (page 334,) as "one hour of the ***years she suffered*** in Burmah." That the life of any faithful missionary is one of exile, toil, and privation, we are not disposed to deny. The world knows it too well; and seeing that such toils are uncheered by the acquisition of fame or wealth--the only reward it can appreciate--the world considers the life of the missionary a living death, endured like martyrdom, only for the sake of its crown in the life to come. But not in this light was their life considered by the noble three whose history we have sketched in this volume, nor by Dr. Judson. The elevated sources of happiness opened even in this world to those who literally obey the command to forsake all for Christ, cast far into the shade all merely selfish enjoyment; while the pure domestic affections, and the bliss resulting from them, are as much the portion of the missionary, as of his favored brethren at home. Who can read the letters of Dr. Judson, in Dr. Wayland's memoir of him, or the exquisite letters of his widow found in this volume, without the conviction that the latter years of her life, privileged as they were with the high companionship of one so gifted and so dear as was her husband, and in the midst of social and domestic duties that brought their own exceeding great reward, were, of all her years, the richest and the happiest!

But her own idea of the comparative happiness of her *two lives*, may be best gathered from her poetry, for it is a characteristic and charm of her verse that it is the pouring forth of her deepest feelings at the moment when they swayed her soul with strongest influence. We extract a few verses from a poem written at Rangoon, during that period of great physical suffering to which we have alluded, but of which Dr. Judson writes: "My sojourn in Rangoon, though tedious and trying in some respects, I regard as one of the greenest spots, one of the brightest oases, in the diversified wilderness of my life. If this world is so happy, what must heaven be?"

TO MY HUSBAND.

"Tis May, but no sweet violet springs
  In these strange woods and dells;
The dear home-lily never swings
  Her little pearly bells;
But search my heart and thou wilt see
What wealth of flowers it owes to thee.

The robin's voice is never heard
  From palm and banyan trees;
And strange to me each gorgeous bird,
  Whose pinion fans the breeze;
But love's white wing bends softly here,
Love's thrilling music fills my ear.

*   *   *   *   *

The pure, the beautiful, the good,

Ne'er gather in this place;
None but the vicious and the rude,
  The dark of mind and face;
But ***all the wealth of thy vast soul***
Is pressed into my brimming bowl.

*   *   *   *   *

Here closely nestled by thy side,
  Thy arm around me thrown,
I ask no more. ***In mirth and pride***
  I've stood--oh so alone!
Now, what is all this world to me,
Since I have found my world in thee?

Oh if we are so happy here,
  Amid our toils and pains,
With thronging cares and dangers near
  And marr'd by earthly stains,
How great must be the compass given
Our souls, to ***bear*** the bliss of heaven!"

    As to the sacrifice of her literary taste and reputation, this is so far from the fact, that we may assert without fear of contradiction, that the world never knew her best excellence as a writer, till it was startled, as it were, by her deathless utterances, wafted by east winds from her Indian home. Her memoir of her predecessor, and her appeals for Burmah, have thrilled thousands of hearts that knew nothing of her "Alderbrook;" and her "Bird," has, perhaps, awakened in many a mother's heart its first deep appreciation of the holy responsibilities of maternity. The Christian world gained much, the literary world lost nothing, when Fanny Forester became a missionary.
    But her harp is idle now, and its loosened strings will wait long for a hand to tune and draw from them such soul-moving cadences as we have been wont to

hear. In purer air she sweeps a nobler lyre; and methinks her song may well be, "Blessed are the dead that die in the Lord; even so, saith the Spirit, for they rest from their labors, and their works do follow them."

www.bookjungle.com *email: sales@bookjungle.com fax: 630-214-0564 mail: Book Jungle PO Box 2226 Champaign, IL 61825*

The Codes Of Hammurabi And Moses
W. W. Davies

QTY

The discovery of the Hammurabi Code is one of the greatest achievements of archaeology, and is of paramount interest, not only to the student of the Bible, but also to all those interested in ancient history...

Religion   ISBN: *1-59462-338-4*   Pages:132
MSRP $12.95

The Theory of Moral Sentiments
Adam Smith

QTY

This work from 1749. contains original theories of conscience amd moral judgment and it is the foundation for systemof morals.

Philosophy   ISBN: *1-59462-777-0*   Pages:536
MSRP $19.95

Jessica's First Prayer
Hesba Stretton

QTY

In a screened and secluded corner of one of the many railway-bridges which span the streets of London there could be seen a few years ago, from five o'clock every morning until half past eight, a tidily set-out coffee-stall, consisting of a trestle and board, upon which stood two large tin cans, with a small fire of charcoal burning under each so as to keep the coffee boiling during the early hours of the morning when the work-people were thronging into the city on their way to their daily toil...

Childrens   ISBN: *1-59462-373-2*   Pages:84
MSRP $9.95

My Life and Work
Henry Ford

QTY

Henry Ford revolutionized the world with his implementation of mass production for the Model T automobile. Gain valuable business insight into his life and work with his own auto-biography... "We have only started on our development of our country we have not as yet, with all our talk of wonderful progress, done more than scratch the surface. The progress has been wonderful enough but..."

Biographies/   ISBN: *1-59462-198-5*   Pages:300
MSRP $21.95

The Art of Cross-Examination
Francis Wellman

I presume it is the experience of every author, after his first book is published upon an important subject, to be almost overwhelmed with a wealth of ideas and illustrations which could readily have been included in his book, and which to his own mind, at least, seem to make a second edition inevitable. Such certainly was the case with me; and when the first edition had reached its sixth impression in five months, I rejoiced to learn that it seemed to my publishers that the book had met with a sufficiently favorable reception to justify a second and considerably enlarged edition. ...

QTY

Reference   ISBN: *1-59462-647-2*   Pages:412   MSRP *$19.95*

On the Duty of Civil Disobedience
Henry David Thoreau

Thoreau wrote his famous essay, On the Duty of Civil Disobedience, as a protest against an unjust but popular war and the immoral but popular institution of slave-owning. He did more than write—he declined to pay his taxes, and was hauled off to gaol in consequence. Who can say how much this refusal of his hastened the end of the war and of slavery?

QTY

Law   ISBN: *1-59462-747-9*   Pages:48   MSRP *$7.45*

Dream Psychology Psychoanalysis for Beginners
Sigmund Freud

Sigmund Freud, born Sigismund Schlomo Freud (May 6, 1856 - September 23, 1939), was a Jewish-Austrian neurologist and psychiatrist who co-founded the psychoanalytic school of psychology. Freud is best known for his theories of the unconscious mind, especially involving the mechanism of repression; his redefinition of sexual desire as mobile and directed towards a wide variety of objects; and his therapeutic techniques, especially his understanding of transference in the therapeutic relationship and the presumed value of dreams as sources of insight into unconscious desires.

QTY

Psychology   ISBN: *1-59462-905-6*   Pages:196   MSRP *$15.45*

The Miracle of Right Thought
Orison Swett Marden

Believe with all of your heart that you will do what you were made to do. When the mind has once formed the habit of holding cheerful, happy, prosperous pictures, it will not be easy to form the opposite habit. It does not matter how improbable or how far away this realization may see, or how dark the prospects may be, if we visualize them as best we can, as vividly as possible, hold tenaciously to them and vigorously struggle to attain them, they will gradually become actualized, realized in the life. But a desire, a longing without endeavor, a yearning abandoned or held indifferently will vanish without realization.

QTY

Self Help   ISBN: *1-59462-644-8*   Pages:360   MSRP *$25.45*

www.bookjungle.com *email: sales@bookjungle.com fax: 630-214-0564 mail: Book Jungle PO Box 2226 Champaign, IL 61825*

QTY

☐ **The Rosicrucian Cosmo-Conception Mystic Christianity** by *Max Heindel*   ISBN: *1-59462-188-8*   **$38.95**
The Rosicrucian Cosmo-conception is not dogmatic, neither does it appeal to any other authority than the reason of the student. It is; not controversial, but is: sent forth in the, hope that it may help to clear...   New Age/Religion Pages 646

☐ **Abandonment To Divine Providence** by *Jean-Pierre de Caussade*   ISBN: *1-59462-228-0*   **$25.95**
"The Rev. Jean Pierre de Caussade was one of the most remarkable spiritual writers of the Society of Jesus in France in the 18th Century. His death took place at Toulouse in 1751. His works have gone through many editions and have been republished..."   Inspirational/Religion Pages 400

☐ **Mental Chemistry** by *Charles Haanel*   ISBN: *1-59462-192-6*   **$23.95**
Mental Chemistry allows the change of material conditions by combining and appropriately utilizing the power of the mind. Much like applied chemistry creates something new and unique out of careful combinations of chemicals the mastery of mental chemistry...   New Age Pages 354

☐ **The Letters of Robert Browning and Elizabeth Barret Barrett 1845-1846 vol II**   ISBN: *1-59462-193-4*   **$35.95**
by *Robert Browning* and *Elizabeth Barrett*   Biographies Pages 596

☐ **Gleanings In Genesis (volume I)** by *Arthur W. Pink*   ISBN: *1-59462-130-6*   **$27.45**
Appropriately has Genesis been termed "the seed plot of the Bible" for in it we have, in germ form, almost all of the great doctrines which are afterwards fully developed in the books of Scripture which follow...   Religion/Inspirational Pages 420

☐ **The Master Key** by *L. W. de Laurence*   ISBN: *1-59462-001-6*   **$30.95**
In no branch of human knowledge has there been a more lively increase of the spirit of research during the past few years than in the study of Psychology, Concentration and Mental Discipline. The requests for authentic lessons in Thought Control, Mental Discipline and...   New Age/Business Pages 422

☐ **The Lesser Key Of Solomon Goetia** by *L. W. de Laurence*   ISBN: *1-59462-092-X*   **$9.95**
This translation of the first book of the "Lernegton" which is now for the first time made accessible to students of Talismanic Magic was done, after careful collation and edition, from numerous Ancient Manuscripts in Hebrew, Latin, and French...   New Age/Occult Pages 92

☐ **Rubaiyat Of Omar Khayyam** by *Edward Fitzgerald*   ISBN:*1-59462-332-5*   **$13.95**
Edward Fitzgerald, whom the world has already learned, in spite of his own efforts to remain within the shadow of anonymity, to look upon as one of the rarest poets of the century, was born at Bredfield, in Suffolk, on the 31st of March, 1809. He was the third son of John Purcell...   Music Pages 172

☐ **Ancient Law** by *Henry Maine*   ISBN: *1-59462-128-4*   **$29.95**
The chief object of the following pages is to indicate some of the earliest ideas of mankind, as they are reflected in Ancient Law, and to point out the relation of those ideas to modern thought.   Religion/History Pages 452

☐ **Far-Away Stories** by *William J. Locke*   ISBN: *1-59462-129-2*   **$19.45**
"Good wine needs no bush,' but a collection of mixed vintages does. And this book is just such a collection. Some of the stories I do not want to remain buried for ever in the museum files of dead magazine-numbers an author's not unpardonable vanity..."   Fiction Pages 272

☐ **Life of David Crockett** by *David Crockett*   ISBN: *1-59462-250-7*   **$27.45**
"Colonel David Crockett was one of the most remarkable men of the times in which he lived. Born in humble life, but gifted with a strong will, an indomitable courage, and unremitting perseverance...   Biographies/New Age Pages 424

☐ **Lip-Reading** by *Edward Nitchie*   ISBN: *1-59462-206-X*   **$25.95**
Edward B. Nitchie, founder of the New York School for the Hard of Hearing, now the Nitchie School of Lip-Reading, Inc, wrote "LIP-READING Principles and Practice". The development and perfecting of this meritorious work on lip-reading was an undertaking...   How-to Pages 400

☐ **A Handbook of Suggestive Therapeutics, Applied Hypnotism, Psychic Science**   ISBN: *1-59462-214-0*   **$24.95**
by *Henry Munro*   Health/New Age/Health/Self-help Pages 376

☐ **A Doll's House: and Two Other Plays** by *Henrik Ibsen*   ISBN: *1-59462-112-8*   **$19.95**
Henrik Ibsen created this classic when in revolutionary 1848 Rome. Introducing some striking concepts in playwriting for the realist genre, this play has been studied the world over.   Fiction/Classics/Plays 308

☐ **The Light of Asia** by *sir Edwin Arnold*   ISBN: *1-59462-204-3*   **$13.95**
In this poetic masterpiece, Edwin Arnold describes the life and teachings of Buddha. The man who was to become known as Buddha to the world was born as Prince Gautama of India but he rejected the worldly riches and abandoned the reigns of power when...   Religion/History/Biographies Pages 170

☐ **The Complete Works of Guy de Maupassant** by *Guy de Maupassant*   ISBN: *1-59462-157-8*   **$16.95**
"For days and days, nights and nights, I had dreamed of that first kiss which was to consecrate our engagement, and I knew not on what spot I should put my lips..."   Fiction/Classics Pages 240

☐ **The Art of Cross-Examination** by *Francis L. Wellman*   ISBN: *1-59462-309-0*   **$26.95**
Written by a renowned trial lawyer, Wellman imparts his experience and uses case studies to explain how to use psychology to extract desired information through questioning.   How-to/Science/Reference Pages 408

☐ **Answered or Unanswered?** by *Louisa Vaughan*   ISBN: *1-59462-248-5*   **$10.95**
Miracles of Faith in China   Religion Pages 112

☐ **The Edinburgh Lectures on Mental Science (1909)** by *Thomas*   ISBN: *1-59462-008-3*   **$11.95**
This book contains the substance of a course of lectures recently given by the writer in the Queen Street Hall, Edinburgh. Its purpose is to indicate the Natural Principles governing the relation between Mental Action and Material Conditions...   New Age/Psychology Pages 148

☐ **Ayesha** by *H. Rider Haggard*   ISBN: *1-59462-301-5*   **$24.95**
Verily and indeed it is the unexpected that happens! Probably if there was one person upon the earth from whom the Editor of this, and of a certain previous history, did not expect to hear again...   Classics Pages 380

☐ **Ayala's Angel** by *Anthony Trollope*   ISBN: *1-59462-352-X*   **$29.95**
The two girls were both pretty, but Lucy who was twenty-one who supposed to be simple and comparatively unattractive, whereas Ayala was credited, as her Bombwhat romantic name might show, with poetic charm and a taste for romance. Ayala when her father died was nineteen...   Fiction Pages 484

☐ **The American Commonwealth** by *James Bryce*   ISBN: *1-59462-286-8*   **$34.45**
An interpretation of American democratic political theory. It examines political mechanics and society from the perspective of Scotsman James Bryce   Politics Pages 572

☐ **Stories of the Pilgrims** by *Margaret P. Pumphrey*   ISBN: *1-59462-116-0*   **$17.95**
This book explores pilgrims religious oppression in England as well as their escape to Holland and eventual crossing to America on the Mayflower, and their early days in New England...   History Pages 268

www.bookjungle.com *email: sales@bookjungle.com fax: 630-214-0564 mail: Book Jungle PO Box 2226 Champaign, IL 61825*

QTY

The Fasting Cure by *Sinclair Upton* ISBN: *1-59462-222-1* **$13.95**
In the Cosmopolitan Magazine for May, 1910, and in the Contemporary Review (London) for April, 1910, I published an article dealing with my experiences in fasting. I have written a great many magazine articles, but never one which attracted so much attention... *New Age/Self Help/Health Pages 164*

Hebrew Astrology by *Sepharial* ISBN: *1-59462-308-2* **$13.45**
In these days of advanced thinking it is a matter of common observation that we have left many of the old landmarks behind and that we are now pressing forward to greater heights and to a wider horizon than that which represented the mind-content of our progenitors... *Astrology Pages 144*

Thought Vibration or The Law of Attraction in the Thought World ISBN: *1-59462-127-6* **$12.95**
by *William Walker Atkinson* *Psychology/Religion Pages 144*

Optimism by *Helen Keller* ISBN: *1-59462-108-X* **$15.95**
Helen Keller was blind, deaf, and mute since 19 months old, yet famously learned how to overcome these handicaps, communicate with the world, and spread her lectures promoting optimism. An inspiring read for everyone... *Biographies/Inspirational Pages 84*

Sara Crewe by *Frances Burnett* ISBN: *1-59462-360-0* **$9.45**
In the first place, Miss Minchin lived in London. Her home was a large, dull, tall one, in a large, dull square, where all the houses were alike, and all the sparrows were alike, and where all the door-knockers made the same heavy sound... *Childrens/Classic Pages 88*

The Autobiography of Benjamin Franklin by *Benjamin Franklin* ISBN: *1-59462-135-7* **$24.95**
The Autobiography of Benjamin Franklin has probably been more extensively read than any other American historical work, and no other book of its kind has had such ups and downs of fortune. Franklin lived for many years in England, where he was agent... *Biographies/History Pages 332*

Name	
Email	
Telephone	
Address	
City, State ZIP	

☐ Credit Card   ☐ Check / Money Order

Credit Card Number	
Expiration Date	
Signature	

Please Mail to: Book Jungle
PO Box 2226
Champaign, IL 61825
or Fax to: 630-214-0564

ORDERING INFORMATION

web: *www.bookjungle.com*
email: *sales@bookjungle.com*
fax: *630-214-0564*
mail: *Book Jungle PO Box 2226 Champaign, IL 61825*
or PayPal *to sales@bookjungle.com*

Please contact us for bulk discounts

DIRECT-ORDER TERMS

20% Discount if You Order Two or More Books
Free Domestic Shipping!
Accepted: Master Card, Visa, Discover, American Express

www.ingramcontent.com/pod-product-compliance
Lightning Source LLC
Chambersburg PA
CBHW080448170426
43196CB00016B/2723